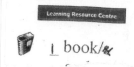

FCE
Testbuilder

Mark Harrison

Macmillan Education
Between Towns Road, Oxford OX4 3PP
A division of Macmillan Publishers Limited
Companies and representatives throughout the world
ISBN 9780230727861 (+key)
ISBN 9780230727878 (- key)

Text © Mark Harrison 2010
Design and illustration © Macmillan Publishers Limited 2010
First published 2010

Original design by eMC Design Ltd.
Page make-up by xen.
Illustrated by Ben Swift and xen
Cover design by Jim Evoy

The publishers would like to thank Karen Harris, Director of Studies, East Finchley School of English and the following students for writing Sample Answers: Test 1, Part 1 letter, Caroline Marie Häfele; Test 2, Part 2 letter, Luciane Lupeti Neves; Part 2 essay, Erdem Kiliç; Part 2 review, Zuzana Svitelova; Test 3, Part 2 report, Mitsuko Oda; Part 2 story, Vlatka Cesnik; Part 2 article, Chris Cook.
We would also like to thank Louise Tester and Sarah Dymond.

The author and publishers would like to thank the following for permission to reproduce their photographic material:

Alamy/ Gianni Muratore p121(tl), Alamy/ Stockshot p127(tr); Corbis/ David Bergman p122(br), Corbis/ Fabio Cardoso p121(tr), Corbis/ Robert Harding World Imagery p127(br), Corbis/ Ariel Skelley p123(bl), Corbis/ Hein van den Heuvel p122(tc), Corbis/ Yang Liu p122(tr); Getty/ Getty Images pp123(tl), 123(br), Getty/ Bongarts p125(tl), Getty/ Daly & Newton p125(tr), Getty/ FilmMagic p125(br), Getty/ Joos Mind p122(tl), Getty/ Ed Pritchard p123(tr), Getty/ Redferns p127(tl), Getty/ Ken Wramton p122(bl); Jupiter Images/ p122(cl); Photoalto/ p127(bl); Photolibrary/ Image Source p121(tr), Photolibrary/ Imagestate RM p122(cr); Punchstock/ Digital Vision p121(bl); Rex Features/ Ken McKay p125(bl).

The author and publishers are grateful for permission to reprint the following copyright material:

Adapted material from article: 'Grace Darling' by Sue Wilkes, copyright © Sue Wilkes 2008, first published in Aquila Magazine July/August 2008, www.aquila.co.uk, reprinted with permission; Adapted material from article: 'Meet the Curator' by Lisette Petrie, copyright © Lisette Petrie 2008, first published in Aquila Magazine 12/05/08, www.aquila.co.uk, reprinted with permission; Adapted material from article: 'Life on a Reservation' by Godfrey Hall, copyright © Godfrey Hall 2008, first published in Aquila Magazine 09/02/08, www.aquila.co.uk, reprinted with permission; Adapted material from 'Backache generation' by Jenny Hope, copyright © Jenny Hope, first appeared in The Daily Mail 05/06/08, reprinted by permission of the publisher; Adapted material from 'Wales has the hardest accent' – The Big Interview – The Piers Morgan Interview ….. Emma Roberts, first appeared in First News, copyright © First News, Issue 118, 15-21Aug 2008, reprinted by permission of the publisher; Adapted material from publication 'Love me Tender: The stories behind the world's best-loved songs' by Max Cryer, copyright © Max Cryer, first appeared in The Telegraph Review article Story Behind the Song, reprinted by permission of Exisle Publishing; Adapted material from publication 'Doctored Evidence' by Donna Leon, copyright © Donna Leon 2004, published by William Heinemann Ltd. Reprinted by permission of The Random House Group Ltd., for territories of UK, Europe & Commonwealth; Excerpt from 'Doctored Evidence' by Donna Leon, copyright © 2004 by Donna Leon and Diogenes Verlag AG Zurich. Used by permission of Grove/Atlantic, Inc., for territories World excluding UK, Europe & Commonwealth; Adapted material from Interview with Sébastien Foucan 'Born to

Run Free' by Lawrence Barretto, copyright © Lawrence Barretto 2008, first appeared in Sport Magazine, Issue 96, 24/10/08, reprinted by permission of the publisher; Material from 'Hooked up to nature's sat nav' by Max Davidson, copyright © Max Davidson, first appeared in Telegraph Travel 11/10/08, reprinted by permission of the publisher; Material from 'Too indecorous for Darwin' by Stephen Moss, copyright © Stephen Moss, first appeared in Telegraph Review 01/11/08, reprinted by permission of the publisher; Material from 'Making the Leap' by Thea Jourdan, copyright © Thea Jourdan, first appeared in Telegraph Careers Supplement 09/10/08, reprinted by permission of the publisher; Material from 'Scientists explain excitement of children' by Roger Highfield, copyright © Roger Highfield, first appeared in The Daily Telegraph 16/09/08, reprinted by permission of the publisher; Material from 'Why a Disney ice-cream can outlive the Coliseum' by Tamsin Kelly, copyright © Tamsin Kelly, first appeared in Telegraph Weekend 27/09/08, reprinted by permission of the publisher; Material from 'The hard sell behind a stroll on the Catwalk' by James Hall, copyright © James Hall, first appeared in Telegraph Business Supplement 15/10/08, reprinted by permission of the publisher; Material from 'New riders on the storm making waves' by Tarquin Cooper, copyright © Tarquin Cooper, first appeared in Telegraph Weekend 26/04.08, reprinted by permission of the publisher; Material from 'Get the picture – go back to the drawing board' by Emily Baker, copyright © Emily Baker, first appeared in Telegraph Weekend 11/10/08, reprinted by permission of the publisher; Material from 'It's cool to camp' by Michael Cowton, copyright © Michael Cowton, first appeared in The Sunday Telegraph 18/05.08, reprinted by permission of the publisher; Material from 'A detour that gave us the Danube blues' by Johnny Morris, copyright Johnny Morris, first appeared in Telegraph Travel 07/06/08, reprinted by permission of the publisher; Material from 'Taking tele-sales to a new level' by Andrew Cave, copyright © Andrew Cave, first appeared in The Daily Telegraph 30/10/08, reprinted by permission of the publisher; Material from 'Give it some stick' by Lucy Atkins, copyright © Lucy Atkins, first appeared in Telegraph Weekend 27/09/08, reprinted by permission of the publisher; Material from 'Meet the dodo's playmates' by Richard Gray, copyright © Richard Gray, first appeared in The Sunday Telegraph 11/05/08, reprinted by permission of the publisher; Material from 'Have blog, will travel' by Suzy Bennett, copyright © Suzy Bennett, first appeared in Telegraph Travel, reprinted by permission of the publisher; Material from 'A nose for what makes good sense' by Andrew Cave, copyright © Andrew Cave, first appeared in Telegraph Jobs Supplement, reprinted by permission of the publisher; Material from 'Brain training games can boost IQ' by Roger Highfield, copyright © Roger Highfield, first appeared in The Daily Telegraph 29/04/08, reprinted by permission of the publisher; Adapted material 'Promiscuous' job hunting is ongoing' from Hendon & Finchley Times Recruitment article, copyright © 07/12/06, reprinted by permission of Times News; Material 'A Whale of a Time' and 'Laughter is the Best Medicine' from DK Find Out! Magazine, Issues 49 & 52 respectively, both copyright © Dorling Kindersley 2006, reprinted by permission of Titan Publishing Group Limited, www.titancomicsuk.co.uk.

The author and publishers would like to thank Cambridge ESOL for the material from the FCE Handbook (on page 117) and the sample answer sheets (on pages 118 and 119). Reproduced with the permission of Cambridge ESOL.

Printed and bound in Thailand

2014   2013   2012
10   9   8   7

CONTENTS

INTRODUCTION

FCE Testbuilder is much more than a book of practice tests. It not only enables students to practise doing tests of exactly the kind they will find in the exam, it also provides them with valuable details on what is tested in each part of the exam, exercises to help them answer the questions in the tests and explanations of the answers to all the questions in the tests. The book gives students extensive preparation for the exam and helps them to increase their ability to perform well when they take the exam.

FCE Testbuilder contains:

Four complete practice tests

These tests reflect exactly the level and types of question to be found in the exam.

A summary of the content of the exam and guidance on marking and grades is on pages 5 to 6.

Further Practice and Guidance pages

These pages are included for each part of each paper and give information and help for every task that candidates have to do in the exam. They are divided into these sections:

What's tested: full details of what is tested in each part of the exam.

Tips: advice on how to do each task and what to remember when doing the tasks.

Exercises: a step-by-step approach to answering the questions in the test, encouraging students to think about the questions and arrive at the correct answers by using appropriate processes.

Authentic samples for the Writing Paper

There are sample answers for each kind of writing required in the Writing Paper in the Further Practice and Guidance pages. Candidates are asked to assess these sample answers and there are detailed assessments of them in the Key.

Key and Explanation

This section contains detailed explanations of every answer to every question in the tests. Explanations for Reading, Use of English and Listening include useful information on vocabulary and grammar. This section also contains task-specific mark schemes for all Writing Paper tasks and answers for the exercises in the Further Practice and Guidance pages.

This book also contains:

- **General Assessment Guide for the Writing and Speaking Papers**
- **Sample answer sheets (as used by candidates when taking the exam)**
- **Listening scripts**
- **CD track listing**

How to use *FCE Testbuilder*

Simply follow the instructions page by page. Clear instructions are given throughout the book about the order in which you should do things. By following the instructions, you:

- complete one part of an exam paper, perhaps under exam conditions, and then check the answers and go through the explanations of the answers in the Key.

or

- look at one part of an exam paper and do the Further Practice and Guidance page(s) relating to it before answering the questions in the test. After doing the exercises in the Further Practice and Guidance section for that part of the paper, you answer the questions in the test. Then you check your answers and go through the explanations in the Key.

Note to teachers

You may wish to do the Further Practice and Guidance exercises as class discussion or pairwork, or ask students to prepare them before class.

First Certificate in English

The following is a summary of what the exam consists of and the marks for each task. Full details of what is tested in each part of each paper are given in the Further Practice and Guidance pages.

Paper 1 Reading (1 hour)

Part	Task	Marks
1	Text: eight multiple-choice questions (four options per question). 2 marks per question.	16
2	Gapped text; seven missing sentences: fill the seven gaps from a choice of eight sentences. 2 marks per question	14
3	Text in sections or series of short texts; 15 matching questions: match statement with section of text or short text. 1 mark per question.	15
TOTAL	30 questions	45

Paper 2 Writing (1 hour 20 minutes)

Part	Task	Marks
1	Letter or email, using given input and notes (candidates must do this task).	20
2	Questions 2–4: choose one from article, essay, report, review, story, letter *or* questions 5a and 5b: write about one of the set books.	20
TOTAL	2 questions	40

Marks for each answer are based on the Task-specific Mark Scheme for each question, which results in a score out of 20 (see Key) and the General Assessment Criteria, which give a Band Score from 0–5 (see page 117).

Paper 3 Use of English (45 minutes)

Part	Task	Marks
1	Short text with 12 gaps: 12 multiple-choice questions (four options per question), choose the correct word(s) to fill each gap. 1 mark per question.	12
2	Short text with 12 gaps: fill each gap with one word. 1 mark per question.	12
3	Short text with 10 gaps: fill each gap by forming the correct word from words given next to the text. 1 mark per question.	10
4	Eight single sentences: use a word given to complete a gapped sentence so that it means the same as the given sentence. 2 marks per question.	16
TOTAL	42 questions	50

Paper 4 Listening (40 minutes)

Part	Task	Marks
1	Eight short recordings: one multiple-choice question (three options per question) for each recording. 1 mark per question.	8
2	Monologue or conversation: complete 10 gapped sentences with information from the recording. 1 mark per question.	10
3	Five short monologues: matching (match options to speakers, choose from six options for each speaker). 1 mark per question.	5
4	Interview, discussion or monologue: seven multiple-choice questions (three options per question). 1 mark per question.	7
TOTAL	30 questions	30

Paper 5 Speaking (14 minutes)

Part	Task	Marks
1	Social and personal conversation (candidates and examiner) (3 minutes).	
2	Talking about pictures: two pairs of pictures, each candidate talks for 1 minute about one pair of related pictures and answers a question about the other pair of related pictures (4 minutes).	
3	Discussion between candidates based on a situation presented in pictures and words; candidates make a decision (3 minutes).	
4	Discussion between candidates and examiner on topics related to Part 3 task (4 minutes).	
TOTAL		20

A mark out of 20 is given, based on various categories of assessment (see page 117).

Marking

Marks are calculated so that each paper is worth 40 marks.

Calculate as follows:

    Paper 1: candidate score multiplied by 9 and then divided by 10 = score out of 40   *0.9 /each*
    Example: 36 marks out of 45 = 36 x 9 = 324
                324 ÷ 10 = 32 marks out of 40 approximately.

    Paper 2: candidate score is out of 40   *1 /each*

    Paper 3: candidate score x 8 ÷ 10 = score out of 40   *0.8 /each*
    Example: 38 marks out of 50 = 30 marks out of 40 approximately

    Paper 4: candidate score ÷ 3 x 4 = score out of 40   *0.75*
    Example: 24 marks out of 30 = 32 marks out of 40

    Paper 5: candidate score x 2

This gives a total of 200 marks. Divide by 2 to get a percentage.

Approximate percentages for each grade:

Pass		**Fail**	
A	80% and above	D	55–59%
B	75–79%	E	54% and below
C	60–74%		

FCE TEST 1

PAPER 1 READING 1 hour

Part 1

Read the text and the test questions. Before you answer the test questions, go on to the Further Practice and Guidance pages which follow.

You are going to read an article about a method for finding your way called 'natural navigation'. For questions 1–8, choose the answer (**A**, **B**, **C** or **D**) which you think fits best according to the text.

Mark your answers **on the separate answer sheet**.

Natural navigation

Max Davidson learns how to find his way using only stars, sun, trees and wind

'Take the Circle, District or Piccadilly Line to South Kensington, then walk up Exhibition Road. It will take you between 10 and 15 minutes. The Royal Geographical Society is on the junction between Exhibition Road and Kensington Gore.' The instructions are so idiot-proof that at 9 am precisely all seven of us are in our places, like expectant schoolchildren.

A man in a check suit, with a neatly trimmed beard, enters and introduces himself. 'Tristan Gooley. Welcome.' He flashes a shy smile. 'Just to put this all into context, I think I can safely say that you are the only people in the world studying this particular topic today.' It is quite an intro. There are a few oohs and ahs from the audience. Tristan Gooley, navigator extraordinary, has his audience in the palm of his hand. We are here because we are curious about how you get from A to B. And if you are curious about how to get from A to B, who better to ask than Tristan Gooley? He is the only man alive who has both flown and sailed solo across the Atlantic. You can't argue with that sort of CV.

'Natural navigation', his new baby, is exactly what that phrase suggests: route-finding that depends on interpreting natural signs – the sun, the stars, the direction of the wind, the alignment of the trees – rather than using maps, compasses or the ubiquitous satnav. 'Of course, 99.9 per cent of the time, you will have other ways of finding wherever it is you want to get to. But if you don't …' Gooley pauses theatrically, 'there is a lot to be said for understanding the science of navigation and direction-finding. If people become too dependent on technology, they can lose connection with nature, which is a pity.'

The natural navigator's best friend, inevitably, is the sun. We all know that it rises in the east, sets in the west and, at its zenith, is due south. But if it is, say, three in the afternoon and you are lost in the desert, how do you get your bearings? The

answer, says Gooley, is to find a stick. By noting the different places where its shadow falls over a short period of time, you will quickly locate the east-west axis. 'The sun influences things even if you can't see it,' he explains. You might not be in the desert, but walking along a forest track in Britain. One side of the track is darker in colour than the other. 'Ah-ha!' thinks the natural navigator. 'It is darker because it is damper, which means it is getting less sun, because it is shaded by the trees, which means that south is that way.' You can now stride confidently southwards – or in whichever direction you wish to head – without fiddling with a map.

As the day wears on, the detective work forces us to look at the world in new and unexpected ways. Just when we think we are getting the hang of it, Cooley sets us a particularly difficult task. A photograph of a house comes up on the screen. An orange sun is peeping over the horizon behind the house. There is a tree in the foreground. 'Just study the picture for a few minutes,' Gooley says, 'and tell me in which direction the photographer is pointing the camera.' Tricky. Very tricky. Is the sun rising or setting? Is the tree growing straight up or leaning to the right? Is that a star twinkling over the chimney? Are we in the northern or southern hemisphere? 'South-east,' I say firmly, having analysed the data in minute detail. 'Not quite.' 'Am I close?' 'Not really. The answer is north-west.' Ah well. Only 180 degrees out.

Still, if I am bottom of the class, I have caught the natural navigation bug. What a fascinating science, both mysterious and universal. It is hardly what you would call a practical skill: there are too many man-made aids to navigation at our disposal. But it connects us, thrillingly, to the world around us – and to those long-dead ancestors who circled the globe with nothing but stars to guide them. It reminds us what it means to be human.

1   What is the writer's main point in the first paragraph?
    A   that the Royal Geographical Society was easy for all of them to find
    B   that the route to the Royal Geographical Society might sound complicated
    C   that all of them wanted to arrive at the Royal Geographical Society on time
    D   that they did not need instructions to find the Royal Geographical Society

2   What does the writer say about Tristan Gooley in the second paragraph?
    A   He was different from what he had expected.
    B   He began in an impressive way.
    C   He had always wanted to meet him.
    D   He seldom gave talks to the public.

3   What does Tristan Gooley say about 'natural navigation'?
    A   It can be more accurate than using technology.
    B   It is quite a complicated skill to master.
    C   It should only be used in emergency situations.
    D   It is not required most of the time.

4   According to Gooley, the use of a stick which he explains
    A   only works in the desert.
    B   involves more than one piece of information.
    C   works best at particular times of the day.
    D   may surprise some people.

5   The example of walking along a forest track illustrates
    A   the fact that the sun may not be important to finding your way.
    B   the difference between the desert and other locations.
    C   the advantage of learning natural navigation.
    D   the relationship between natural navigation and other skills.

6   What does 'it' in the phrase 'getting the hang of it' (line 58) refer to?
    A   something unexpected
    B   the day
    C   a particular problem
    D   natural navigation

7   What does the writer say about the task involving a photograph?
    A   It was not as simple as it first appeared.
    B   He needed more information in order to do it successfully.
    C   He became more confused the longer he spent on it.
    D   He was not surprised to hear that his answer was wrong.

8   The writer's attitude towards natural navigation is that
    A   it would take a long time to be good at it.
    B   it is a valuable skill in the modern world.
    C   it is only likely to appeal to a certain kind of person.
    D   it is exciting but not very useful.

WHAT'S TESTED

The questions in Part 1 of the Reading Paper test you on your ability to understand a wide variety of aspects of a text. Questions may focus on any of the following:

- **details and specific information** given in the text
- **the main idea** in part of the text or in the whole text
- **an opinion/attitude** expressed or described in the text
- **the meaning in the context** of a word or phrase in the text
- **implication:** something suggested but not directly stated in the text
- **exemplification:** the use of examples in the text and what they are examples of
- **reference:** understanding what a word or phrase in the text refers to or relates to
- **a comparison** made in the text
- **the writer's purpose** in part of the text or in the whole text.

TIPS

- The questions follow the same order as the text.
- If there is a question on the whole text, it will always be the last question.
- Begin by reading the whole text and looking at each question as you read through the text. Don't try to answer any questions while you are doing this. In this way, you will get a general idea of what the text is about and what it contains and you will also find out what the questions require you to do. Then read each part of the text and answer the question that relates to it. If you don't follow this system, you may become confused and answer questions incorrectly because you are not clear about the text in general and how the questions relate to it.
- Read each question very carefully to make sure that you are clear about exactly what is asked for each one. A choice may be true according to the text but not the answer to the question you have been asked.

The following exercises will help you to choose the correct answer to each question in the test. When you have completed each exercise, check your answer(s) and then choose your answer for the question in the test.

Question 1
1 Does the writer say that anyone got lost?
2 Does the writer say that anyone arrived late?
3 Does the writer mention the instructions they were given?
4 Does the writer mention the people's intentions about arriving there?
5 Does the writer say that the people had been there before?
6 What does 'idiot-proof' mean?
   A hard to understand
   B impossible for anyone to get wrong
   C totally unnecessary

Question 2
1 Does the writer mention his opinion of Tristan Gooley before that day?
2 Did the writer know anything about Tristan Gooley before that day?
3 Does the writer mention Tristan Gooley's first words?
4 Does the writer describe reactions to what Tristan Gooley says?
5 Does Tristan Gooley say that the event is unusual?
6 Does the writer mention the number of talks Tristan Gooley gives?

Question 3

Which of these does Tristan Gooley mention in the third paragraph?

   A   people relying on technology

   B   the process of learning natural navigation

   C   when natural navigation is useful

   D   errors made by technology

   E   when natural navigation should not be used

   F   how often people might need to use natural navigation

Question 4

   1   What does 'say' in the third sentence of the fourth paragraph mean in this context?

       A   only

       B   for example

       C   exactly

   2   Do you note something more than once?

   3   Does Gooley mention people's reactions to the idea of using a stick?

Question 5

Which of these are mentioned in connection with the forest track?

   A   the influence of the sun on the appearance of the track

   B   a way in which the track contrasts with the desert

   C   what natural navigation enables you to do when you look at the track

   D   using both map-reading skills and natural navigation when walking along the track

Question 6

If you 'get the hang of something', you

   A   become tired by it.

   B   learn how to do it.

   C   are surprised by it.

   D   fail to do it correctly.

Question 7

Which of these does the writer mention in connection with the photograph task?

   A   how difficult it was

   B   changing his opinion of it

   C   things they weren't told

   D   questions he wanted to ask

   E   how long it took him to do it

   F   his feelings while doing it

   G   believing that his answer was correct

   H   asking whether his answer was nearly correct

Question 8

   1   When the writer says that he has 'caught the natural navigation bug', he means that

       A   he has become very interested in it.

       B   he thinks it is very hard to learn how to do it.

       C   he has understood how important it is.

   2   What does 'hardly' in the third sentence of the sixth paragraph mean?

       A   definitely

       B   not really

       C   occasionally

   3   Does the writer compare his attitude with the attitudes of the other people that day?

Now check your answers to the questions in the test.

Part 2

You are going to read a review of a book about ornithology – the study of birds. Seven sentences have been removed from the article. Choose from the sentences **A–H** the one which fits each gap (**9–15**). There is one extra sentence which you do not need to use.

Mark your answers **on the separate answer sheet**.

The Wisdom of Birds by Tim Birkhead

Review by Stephen Moss

You wait for one history of ornithology to come along and a whole flock appears over the horizon. **9** .... However, in the past few years a clutch of scientists, journalists, taxonomists and birders (including myself) have turned their attentions to this fascinating and complex topic.

One of the most exciting things about the study of birds is that it is not yet complete. We may smile at the beliefs of our ancestors – such as the notion that swallows spent their winter hibernating underwater – yet there is still so much that we don't know. Writing almost a century ago, the German-American ornithologist Paul Bartsch drew attention to our ignorance about many aspects of bird behaviour: 'There are still many unsolved problems about bird life. Little, too, is known about the laws and routes of migration, and much less about the final disposition of the untold thousands which are annually produced.' **10** .... For, despite great progress, modern bird studies often give rise to new and even more complex inquiries.

Tim Birkhead is well qualified to examine the ways successive generations have tried to answer the fundamental questions about birds. A professor at the University of Sheffield, he specializes in two very different disciplines: the study of animal behaviour and the history of science. **11** .... In it, he ranges from Aristotle to modern scientists such as Peter Berthold, whose migration studies have revealed much about how birds migrate round the world.

Unlike other histories of the subject, *The Wisdom of Birds* does not take a chronological approach. **12** .... In other hands this might have been confusing, but Birkhead steers his narrative through this complex structure to tell a compelling story.

He is clearly passionate, not just about the birds themselves, but also about the people who have studied them, and the works they have produced. So *The Wisdom of Birds* is lavishly illustrated with examples of bird art, including many from the early works of ornithology. **13** ....

If the book has a hero, it is an unlikely but deserving one. Birkhead begins and ends with a challenge to his colleagues: who is the greatest ever ornithologist? **14** .... But Birkhead's own choice is an often neglected seventeenth-century Englishman, John Ray. He launched the revolutionary concept of studying living birds in the field, rather than dead ones in a museum.

15 .... John Ray travels through time to be the guest of honour at an International Ornithological Congress. As Birkhead says: 'He would be amazed by how much we know and, of course, by how much more there is still to learn about birds.' This is a fitting ending to a book that is one of the most entertaining, informative and enthusiastic accounts of the history of ornithology, and of the many different ways in which we have observed, studied and wondered about birds.

A These two interests come together in *The Wisdom of Birds*.

B *The Wisdom of Birds* concludes with a striking image.

C Much the same could be said today.

D Some of them come in for particular criticism in the book.

E These, and the fine production of the book itself, add immensely to the reader's satisfaction.

F The subject was neglected for decades.

G The names they come up with are strong contenders.

H Instead, Birkhead explores ornithological themes such as birdsong, the breeding cycle and migration, moving back and forth across the centuries.

Part 3

You are going to read a magazine article in which four people talk about their careers in engineering. For questions **16–30**, choose from the people (**A–D**). The people may be chosen more than once.

Mark your answers **on the separate answer sheet**.

Which person

talks about how important engineers in general can be?	16
gives evidence of the success of something he/she was involved in creating?	17
was not sure which subject to choose at one point?	18
mentions being the leader of a group of people?	19
refers to having two roles at the same time?	20
made a decision as a result of going to a certain event?	21
has not yet completed his/her studies?	22
gives reasons why engineers have a high reputation?	23
mentions the need to attract certain people to engineering?	24
says that creating something led to a desire for a certain career?	25
is currently trying to produce different versions of something?	26
refers to always doing the same kind of work after completing his/her studies?	27
says that the demand for people who do what he/she does is growing?	28
enjoys using something that he/she produces?	29
says why he/she has not lost enthusiasm for his/her work?	30

The world of engineering

A THE SNOWBOARD DESIGNER

Liza Brooks, 24, is still studying for her engineering doctorate in advanced snowboard design, but she is already technical director of the UK's biggest snowboarding company, True Snowboards.

I'm a keen snowboarder so it seemed like a good idea to specialize in building great snowboards. I set up True Snowboards in 2006 with two other colleagues, so now I'm an engineer and an entrepreneur. We now sell snowboards throughout Europe and, next season, we'll be launching in North America. True Snowboards now sponsors some of the best UK snowboarders, including 17-year-old Samantha Rogers, who took the silver medal at this year's British Big Air Championships, a key snowboarding event. Riders at the event who used our boards achieved a 74 per cent medal rate, which says something about how good they are. Our speciality is designing boards that can cope with dry slopes. These surfaces are very abrasive, so they can cause a lot of friction and literally melt conventional boards. I used my engineering skills to come up with a workable solution to dissipate the heat so that the boards don't melt and so that they last longer. Right now, I am experimenting to find new shapes to make the boards perform even better. And I get to go outside and play with the prototypes.

B THE SPACE EXPERT

Maggie Aderin, 39, is a scientist for Astrium Ltd, the UK's largest space systems and services company. With a background in mechanical engineering, she oversees projects for the European Space Agency as well as NASA.

My job is great fun. I head up a team that makes optical instruments for space satellites. We are currently working on an amazing instrument for the Aeolus Satellite which is going to measure wind speed through the Earth's atmosphere. It has to be tough and very accurate, so we need to design and build it with great care. It will need to withstand temperatures that range from between minus 50 and plus 50 degrees centigrade, and will help us to understand more about global warming. I knew I wanted to work in space technology when I made my first telescope at the age of 15. When I left school I studied physics at Imperial College London and then did a PhD in mechanical engineering. I have been engineering instruments ever since. Now I use my engineering skills to solve problems and I am aware of how my job can help preserve the planet in the future.

C THE RELIEF WORKER

Engineer Andrew Lamb, 26, works for the not-for-profit organization RedR, which specializes in disaster relief. Lamb was keen to use his skills for the greater good.

Did you know that 40 per cent of people who work for the international aid organization Médecins Sans Frontières are engineers and not doctors? That's because engineers are absolutely essential in a crisis. They are the ones who can make the water run again and get the power on. They can construct roads and shelters. Aid agencies really value engineers for their management skills in stressful situations, because we work as a team. We are also taught how to break down problems into smaller pieces. Workers who can contribute to disaster relief plans are increasingly sought after as earthquakes, floods and conflict destroy communities. It is vital we get young people into this sector. They can help save lives. It's extremely rewarding when you help get people back on their feet.

D THE ENVIRONMENTALIST

Vicki Stevenson, 37, is a chartered energy engineer specializing in renewable energy.

I love the fact that I am doing something practical which makes a difference. I research practical ways to reduce carbon emissions and use sustainable energy sources instead of fossil fuels. My latest project is working on a solar air heater that captures the heat that strikes off the walls of buildings and uses it to heat offices and to provide ventilation. When I went to university, I was torn between studying astrophysics and laser physics. Lasers won because I attended an open day at an engineering company which showed how the use of lasers and fibre optics made equipment safer for people working in mines. The results of the work I do will have far-reaching relevance, meaning we could all benefit in the long run. Knowing that what I do is useful really keeps me motivated.

PAPER 2 WRITING 1 hour 20 minutes

Part 1

Before you answer the test question, go on to the Further Practice and Guidance pages which follow.

You **must** answer this question. Write your answer in **120–150** words in an appropriate style.

---

1   Your English-speaking friend, David, recently came to stay with you for a week. Read David's letter and the notes you have made. Then write a letter to David, using **all** your notes.

> Thanks very much for having me to stay with you. It was very kind of you and your family and I'm very grateful.
>
> I really enjoyed my stay with you. We went to lots of interesting places and I saw lots of fascinating things. We certainly did a lot in one week!
>
> It was great meeting your family. Please say hello from me and thank them for looking after me so well. I've got some really good photos of them and of the things we did while I was there – would you like me to send them to you?
>
> As I said, I hope you'll come and stay with me soon. Let me know when you want to come.
>
> All the best,
>
> David

o problem (note pointing to first paragraph)

Come for longer next time (note pointing to second paragraph)

Yes please (note pointing to third paragraph)

'es, arrange ater (note pointing to fourth paragraph)

Write your **letter**. You must use grammatically correct sentences with accurate spelling and punctuation in a style appropriate for the situation.

WHAT'S TESTED

In Part 1 of the Writing Paper, you must write a **letter** or **email**. You read some material that tells you the situation and the context of your letter or email. Some notes have been added to the material, and you must include what is stated in these notes in the letter or email you produce. There is no difference between a letter and email concerning the kind of language you are required to produce – if you are writing an email, you must form grammatically correct full sentences and not use the style of language often used in text messages (eg you must not use shortened words or leave out important parts of the sentence grammatically).

Your answer will be marked according to the following categories:

- **Content**: you must include in your letter or email everything you have been told to include in the instructions.

- **Organization and cohesion**: your letter or email must be organized in a clear and logical way, with appropriate linking between and within sentences and paragraphs.

- **Range**: you must use the appropriate structures and language for the different things you are required to do in your letter or email. For example, you will need to use appropriate structures and vocabulary for thanking, suggesting, agreeing, describing, explaining, apologizing, giving opinions, expressing feelings, comparing, etc.

- **Accuracy**: the number of language mistakes you make, especially serious mistakes, will affect the mark you get!

- **Appropriacy of register and format**: your letter or email must be as informal or formal as the situation requires – for example, if you are writing to a friend, it should be informal. It must also be in an appropriate format, with a suitable opening and closing (but no postal addresses for the letter) and suitable paragraphing.

- **Target reader**: the reader of the letter or email should be completely clear about the purpose of the letter or email and understand fully everything it contains.

TIPS

- Make sure that you include everything you are required to include. Read the opening instructions carefully, read the material presented very carefully and make sure that you use all of the notes.

- Make sure that your answer follows a logical sequence, with one point following another clearly. To do this, you can usually follow the same order as the material you read and the notes added to it.

- Try to use a variety of structures and vocabulary, appropriate for the different things you are required to do in the letter or email. Don't keep repeating the same words and phrases.

- Do not copy big sections of the material you read – use different words and phrases. You will need to use some words and phrases from the material you read, but you will lose marks if you simply copy large amounts of it.

- You can add your own ideas in addition to using the information given to you. If you do this well, you may get a higher mark. However, make sure that what you write is really connected with the task and that it does not make your answer too long.

The following exercises will help you to write your answer for this part of the test. When you have completed all of the exercises, write your answer.

GETTING IDEAS AND PLANNING YOUR ANSWER

1   Which of the following **must** you do in your letter?

A	respond to thanks	**D**	apologize	**G**	explain a problem
B	describe events	**E**	ask for information	**H**	respond to an invitation
C	suggest a future plan	**F**	accept an offer		

Now check your answers to this exercise.

2   Here are some useful phrases and structures which you **could** include in your letter. You do not have to use all of them in your letter but try to use some of them.

it was no problem	I'll give your message to	let's try to arrange ....
I'm glad that you	if you sent	..... to hear from you ....
we really enjoyed –ing	it would be good to see	
you should stay with us	I'd like to	

SAMPLE ANSWER

Read this sample answer carefully and answer these questions. Then check the assessment of this sample answer on page 132.

- **Content**: does the letter include everything that should be included?
- **Organization and cohesion**: is the letter organized in a clear and logical way, with appropriate linking?
- **Range**: is there a range of appropriate structures and vocabulary?
- **Accuracy**: are there any mistakes?
- **Appropriacy of register and format**: is the letter appropriately informal or formal, and is the format suitable?
- **Target reader**: will the reader be completely clear about the purpose of the letter and understand fully everything it contains?

Dear David,

We really enjoyed having you here and it was no problem at all. We are glad you liked the places we showed you. My family and me agreed that you should definatly stay longer next time you come over.

Please say hello to your family as well. I would really like to meet them one day too. Did they like the pictures you took while you were here? By the way, it would be very nice if you sent your photos over to us. We would love to see them!

I will talk to my family about visiting you so we can arrange something later.

Things are going well here again. I am back in school and I can feel that speaking English with you has helped me.

We hope to hear from you soon.

All the best,

Caroline.

Now write your answer to the question in the test.

Part 2

Write an answer to **one** of the questions **2–5** in this part. Write your answer in **120–180** words in an appropriate style.

---

2   Your teacher has asked you to write a story. The story must **begin** with the following words:

   When he found his seat on the plane, Sam recognized the person who was sitting in the seat next to his.

   Write your **story**.

3   You have recently had a discussion in your English class about different age groups. Now your teacher has asked you to write an essay, giving your opinion on the following statement.

   The young can learn a lot about life from older people.

   Write your **essay**.

4   You have had a class discussion about part-time jobs that people at your college do or could do. Your teacher has now asked you to write a report on part-time jobs in the area. You should include information on jobs that students on the course are currently doing and on other possible jobs. You should also include advice on how students can get these jobs.

   Write your **report**.

5   **(a)** or **(b)**. Two questions on the set books.

   There are two set books. There is one question on each set book. You answer **one** of the two questions.

There is more information, and guidance and practice, on set book questions in Test 4.

PAPER 3 USE OF ENGLISH 45 minutes

Part 1

Read the text and the test questions. Before you answer the test questions, go on to the Further Practice and Guidance pages which follow.

For questions **1–12**, read the text below and decide which answer (**A**, **B**, **C** or **D**) best fits each gap. There is an example at the beginning (**0**).

Mark your answers **on the separate answer sheet**.

Example:

    0   **A** threat   **B** risk   **C** danger   **D** warning

0	A	B	C	D
	▢	▢	▬	▢

Polar bears

Polar bears are in (**0**) ………….. of dying out. (**1**) …………. some other endangered animals, it's not hunters that are the problem, it's climate change. Since 1979, the ice cap at the Arctic Circle where the polar bears live has (**2**) …………. in size by about 30 per cent. The temperature in the Arctic has slowly been (**3**) …………. and this is (**4**) …………. the sea ice to melt, endangering the polar bears' home.

The polar bears' main (**5**) …………. of food are the different types of seal found in the Arctic. They catch them by waiting next to the air holes the seals have (**6**) …………. in the ice. (**7**) …………. the bears are very strong swimmers, they could never catch seals in the water. This means that the bears (**8**) …………. do rely on the ice to hunt.

Polar bears also need sea ice to travel. They can (**9**) ……..….. a huge territory and often swim from one part of the ice to another. They have been (**10**) …………. to swim up to 100km, but when there is less ice, they may have to swim further and this can (**11**) ……..….. fatal to the bears. A number of bears have drowned in the last few years and scientists believe that it is because they were not able to (**12**) …………. more sea ice before they became too tired and couldn't swim any further.

1 **A** Opposite   **B** Compared   **C** Unlike   **D** Different

2 **A** cut   **B** reduced   **C** shortened   **D** lost

3 **A** lifting   **B** gaining   **C** advancing   **D** rising

4 **A** resulting   **B** turning   **C** causing   **D** creating

5 **A** sources   **B** means   **C** origins   **D** materials

6 **A** placed   **B** set   **C** brought   **D** made

7 **A** Even   **B** Although   **C** As   **D** Despite

8 **A** really   **B** properly   **C** surely   **D** fully

9 **A** pass   **B** extend   **C** cover   **D** spread

10 **A** learnt   **B** noticed   **C** known   **D** experienced

11 **A** prove   **B** happen   **C** come   **D** end

12 **A** achieve   **B** land   **C** get   **D** reach

WHAT'S TESTED

The questions in Part 1 of the Use of English Paper test you mainly on vocabulary. Questions may focus on any of the following:

- **the meaning of single words:** which choice has the correct meaning in the context.

- **completing phrases:** which choice goes together with the other words to form a phrase (eg a collocation, a fixed phrase, an idiom or a phrasal verb).

- **lexico-grammatical features:** which choice has the correct meaning and fits grammatically (eg which choice goes with a given preposition or verb form, which linking word or phrase fits).

TIPS

- Begin by reading through the whole text to find out what it is about and what it contains. This will help you to know the context for the questions.

- Look carefully at what comes both before and after each gap so that you can decide on the meaning of the choice that correctly fills each gap.

- If there is more than one gap in a sentence, read the whole sentence very carefully so that you are clear about the context and meaning of each choice that correctly fills each gap.

- Look for any grammatical elements that come before or after a gap (prepositions, verb forms, etc). It is possible that more than one choice fits correctly because of its meaning, but only one choice is also grammatically correct.

The following exercises will help you to choose the correct answer to each question in the test. When you have completed each exercise, check your answers and then choose your answer for the question in the test.

In each exercise, choose which of the four options fits into each of the four sentences. (The question numbers below relate to the questions in the test and the options below are the same as those for that question in the test.)

1   A   This programme is .... any other programme on TV at the moment.

    B   I know that I'm quite lucky, ... to a lot of other people.

    C   My opinion on this subject is the .... of yours.

    D   Our house is .... from the others in the road.

> opposite
> compared
> unlike
> different

2   A   Sean has .... a lot of weight and looks quite thin now.

    B   These trousers need to be .... – they're too long for me.

    C   The number of unemployed people .... considerably last month.

    D   I've .... a few words from the paragraph because it's too long.

> cut
> reduced
> shortened
> lost

3   A   I'm .... a lot of knowledge on this course.

    B   The level of the water was .... fast.

    C   People were .... their children onto their shoulders so that they could see.

    D   Technology is .... all the time.

> lifting
> gaining
> advancing
> rising

4   A   The management is currently .... a lot of new jobs at the company.

    B   Pressure at work is .... her to become quite depressed.

    C   The new manager is .... the company into a very successful one.

    D   Economic problems are .... in a lot of job losses.

> resulting
> turning
> causing
> creating

5 A   What are the .... used in making this product?

  B   We need to find more .... of income to increase our profit.

  C   Trams and bikes are the most popular .... of transport in this city.

  D   I've been learning about the .... of the sport of rugby.

> sources
> means
> origins
> materials

6 A   She carefully .... each piece of furniture around the room.

  B   I've just cleaned that window and you've already …................. a mark on it.

  C   When he'd finished cooking, he .... the food to the table.

  D   Somebody .... the building on fire during the night.

> placed
> set
> brought
> made

7 A   .... the weather wasn't very good, we had an enjoyable day.

  B   .... having very little money, they're quite happy.

  C   .... I was feeling very tired, I went to bed early,

  D   .... Georgia was angry, and she doesn't usually get angry.

> Even
> Although
> As
> Despite

8 A   He didn't do the job .... – it was full of mistakes.

  B   The apartment was .... furnished, so we didn't have to buy any furniture.

  C   I .... did try hard, but I wasn't able to do it.

  D   You .... don't intend to do such a stupid thing, do you?

> really
> properly
> surely
> fully

9 A   The news will .... quickly and soon everyone will know what happened.

  B   She was enjoying herself in Paris and she decided to .... her stay there.

  C   We're going to .... a distance of about 1000km on our trip.

  D   You .... the university as you drive along that road.

> pass
> extend
> cover
> spread

10 A   I've .... recently that Mia seems a lot happier than she used to be.

  B   Jack is an honest person but he's been .... to tell lies occasionally.

  C   I've .... a lot about the past from talking to my grandparents.

  D   The same feeling of shock was .... by everyone in the room.

> learnt
> noticed
> known
> experienced

11 A   How did this problem .... about?

  B   She was worried about what was going to .... to her in that dangerous situation.

  C   The treatment is likely to .... successful and he will probably recover completely.

  D   He's very clever and he'll probably .... up with a very good job.

> prove
> happen
> come
> end

12 A   Because of the delay, we didn't .... our destination on time.

  B   That insect is going to .... on our food in a moment.

  C   She's very happy because she's managed to .... her ambition.

  D   We have to .... to the airport two hours before our flight.

> achieve
> land
> get
> reach

Now check your answers to the questions in the test.

Part 2

For questions **13–24**, read the text below and think of the word which best fits each gap. Use only **one** word in each gap. There is an example at the beginning (**0**).

Write your answers **IN CAPITAL LETTERS on the separate answer sheet**.

Example: 0   BEEN

Scientists explain excitement of children

The reason children become more excited than adults at receiving gifts has (**0**) ………….. identified

by scientists. They found that the areas of the brain involved in processing rewards were far more

active in younger people (**13**) …………. they received a prize. This explained why children found

(**14**) …………. almost impossible to contain (**15**) …………. excitement on birthdays.

(**16**) …………. team from the US National Institute of Mental Health used scans to study

(**17**) …………. parts of the brain were stimulated when rewards (**18**) …………. presented to

participants. Younger people showed more activity in key brain areas while they viewed a video game

(**19**) ………….received money.

Dopamine, a chemical that carries messages between brain cells, is believed (**20**) …………. act as a

'currency' in the brain's reward processing areas. However, the brain's dopamine system declines with

age. The study suggested that this is (**21**) …………. receiving presents feels less thrilling as people

(**22**) …………. older.

The scientists say that targeting these dopamine mechanisms may help in the development

(**23**) …………. ways of treating various disorders of the reward system, (**24**) ………. as pathological

gambling and drug addiction.

Part 3

For questions **25–34**, read the text below. Use the word given in capitals at the end of some of the lines to form a word that fits in the gap **in the same line**. There is an example at the beginning (**0**).

Write your answers **IN CAPITAL LETTERS on the separate answer sheet**.

Example: 0   GLOBAL

The ultimate challenge

Do you have the mental and physical strength to enter the ultimate

(**0**) …………… race? If so, there is still time to apply for the free-to-   **GLOBE**

enter Land Rover G4 Challenge – the adventure of a (**25**) ……………   **LIFE**

that combines off-road driving with kayaking, mountain biking, abseiling,

climbing and orienteering across some of the most remote and extreme

terrain in the world.

The (**26**) ……….……. process is currently underway to choose one man   **SELECT**

and one woman to represent the UK in the competition. The (**27**) ………   **SUCCEED**

applicants will form a two-strong British team which will then battle

against teams from 17 other countries in this extremely (**28**) …………….   **DEMAND**

three-week event in one of the most sparsely (**29**) ……..……… countries   **POPULATION**

on the planet – Mongolia. A (**30**) ………..…… of terrains including   **VARIOUS**

steppes, mountains and the extreme climate of one of the world's largest

deserts, the Gobi, makes Mongolia the ultimate test.

Race organizer John Edwards says: 'Mongolia is a (**31**) ……………….   **SPECTACLE**

country which will enable us to create a truly (**32**) ………….……. event.   **ORDINARY**

We have been working hard to find routes that will push the vehicles and

the (**33**) …….....……. to their limits.'   **COMPETE**

If you're a very (**34**) …………..… person and you think you're tough   **ADVENTURE**

enough, log on to the website as soon as possible!

Part 4

For questions **35–42**, complete the second sentence so that it has a similar meaning to the first sentence, using the word given. **Do not change the word given**. You must use between **two** and **five** words, including the word given. Here is an example (**0**).

Example: **0**   It took me a fairly long time to answer all my emails.

               QUITE

               I spent .... all my emails.

The gap can be filled with the words 'quite a long time answering', so you write:

Example: **0**   QUITE A LONG TIME ANSWERING

Write only the missing words **IN CAPITAL LETTERS on the separate answer sheet**.

---

35   That's the most ridiculous thing I've ever heard!

      SUCH

      I've .... ridiculous thing!

36   I didn't think carefully enough about the situation.

      MORE

      I should .... about the situation.

37   Gill hasn't contacted me for weeks.

      HEARD

      I last .... weeks ago.

38   He didn't make a mistake when he played the song.

      WITHOUT

      He played the song .... mistakes at all.

39   It's possible that Jana can take you in her car.

      ABLE

      Jana might .... a lift in her car.

40   I asked him to explain his behaviour.

      EXPLANATION

      I asked him .... his behaviour.

41   If we don't leave before 8, we won't get there on time.

      SET

      We won't get there on time unless .... before 8.

42   The assistant said that it was not possible for me to get a refund.

      GIVEN

      The assistant said that I couldn't .... back.

PAPER 4 LISTENING approximately 40 minutes

Part 1

Before you listen to the CD, read the test questions and go on to the Further Practice and Guidance pages which follow.

You will hear people talking in eight different situations. For questions **1–8**, choose the best answer (**A**, **B** or **C**).

1   You hear a woman on the radio talking about a politician. What is her opinion of the politician?

   A   He can be trusted.

   B   He keeps changing his mind.

   C   He is not like other politicians.

2   You hear a woman talking about a song. What does she say about the song?

   A   The performer didn't write it.

   B   It has been recorded by lots of other performers.

   C   It deserves to be more popular.

3   You hear two characters talking in a radio play. Where are they?

   A   in a hotel

   B   at home

   C   at an airport

4   You hear a writer talking on the radio about criticism. What is his attitude to criticism?

   A   He rarely pays attention to it.

   B   He thinks about it.

   C   He gets upset by it.

5   You hear someone talking about learning to play a musical instrument. What is her main point?

   A   Everyone should learn an instrument.

   B   Some instruments are harder to learn than others.

   C   She wishes she could play an instrument.

6   You hear two people talking about a reality TV programme. What do the two speakers agree about?

   A   There are too many programmes of that kind.

   B   It won't be as good as other programmes of that kind.

   C   It will be very popular.

7   You hear someone talking about a sports stadium. What does he say about the stadium?

   A   It's difficult to get to it.

   B   It can be hard to get tickets for it.

   C   It has replaced another stadium.

8   You overhear a manager talking to an employee at work. What is the manager doing?

   A   accusing her of doing something wrong

   B   sympathizing with her about a problem

   C   apologizing for a mistake

WHAT'S TESTED

The questions in Part 1 of the Listening Paper test you on your ability to understand what speakers say in short recordings. A recording may consist of one speaker or it may be a short conversation between two speakers. Questions focus on a wide variety of things, including the following:

- **detail:** a specific piece of information given
- **an opinion/attitude** expressed or described
- **a feeling** expressed or described
- **function:** what a speaker is doing while speaking (eg complaining, apologizing, etc)
- **purpose:** a speaker's intention when speaking, what the speaker wants
- **general gist:** the general meaning or the main point made
- **topic:** what the short recording is about
- the **relationship** between speakers
- **place:** where the recording is happening, where the speakers are
- **situation:** what happened before the recording, the context or circumstances of the recording
- **genre:** what kind of recording it is (eg what kind of programme)
- **agreement:** something that both speakers agree about (not something only one speaker says)
- **speaker/addressee**: who is speaking/who the speaker is talking to.

TIPS

- Use the time given to read the questions very carefully before you listen to the recordings. This will show you what you need to identify in each one of them.

- Don't choose an option simply because it contains words that you hear in the recording. An option may contain words used in the recording but not be the correct answer.

- Don't feel that you must answer every question the first time you hear the recording. It may be better to wait until you have heard it twice before choosing your answer.

- If you are able to answer a question the first time you hear the recording, listen carefully when it is played for the second time. You may discover that you made a mistake which you can now correct.

- If you find a question particularly difficult, do not spend too much time thinking about it. Put the best answer you can and concentrate on the next recording. If you are still thinking about the previous question, you may get lost and fail to answer the next question correctly.

The following exercises will help you to choose the correct answer to each question in the test. When you have completed each exercise, check your answer(s) and then choose your answer for the question in the test.

The choices below for each question are in the same order as what you hear in each recording.

Question 1 Listen to the recording twice. Which of the following does the speaker say?
   A   She agreed with many of the politician's views.
   B   She didn't like the politician very much before the speech.
   C   Some politicians can be trusted.
   D   Her opinion of the politician has changed.
   E   He is likely to express different opinions in the future.
   F   He has changed his mind many times in the past.

Question 2 Listen to the recording twice. Which of the following does the speaker say?
   A   Most people know him because of the song.
   B   The song was very successful and well-known.
   C   Something about the song is not generally known.

    D   Other people have recorded songs he has written.

    E   All the songs he has written have been very popular.

    F   Some of the songs he has written should be more popular.

Question 3 Listen to the recording twice. Which of the following do the speakers mention?

    A   problems during a journey

    B   looking forward to completing a journey

    C   returning to a place

    D   being on holiday at the moment

    E   somewhere they have been before now

    F   doing something with their luggage

Question 4 Listen to the recording twice. Which of the following does the speaker say?

    A   Some reviews of his work are negative.

    B   He is not as sensitive to criticism as he used to be.

    C   He hardly ever reads reviews of his work.

    D   He thinks most reviewers are stupid.

    E   He sometimes agrees with comments about his work.

    F   He sometimes disagrees with comments about his work.

Question 5 Listen to the recording twice. Which of the following is the speaker talking about?

    A   her experiences of learning to play instruments

    B   how learning one instrument differs from learning another

    C   her inability to learn different instruments

    D   how people can learn to play instruments

    E   people not taking advantage of opportunities to learn to play instruments

    F   her feelings about other people being able to play instruments

Question 6 Listen to the recording twice. Which of the following do both speakers mention?

    A   a belief that the new programme will be good

    B   an intention to watch the new programme

    C   their enjoyment of this kind of programme

    D   how this programme differs from others

    E   the number of reality TV programmes on TV

    F   other people watching this programme

Question 7 Listen to the recording twice. Which of the following does the speaker mention?

    A   a comparison between stadiums

    B   going to another stadium in the past

    C   an increase in the number of people going to games at the stadium

    D   the location of the stadium

    E   a problem connected with getting to the stadium

    F   not being able to go to a game there

Question 8 Listen to the recording twice. Which of the following does the manager say?

    A   A client says that Jenny did something wrong.

    B   Jenny said something that she should not have said.

    C   He is aware of what the client is like.

    D   Jenny has treated the client well previously.

    E   He will deal with the client when he phones again.

    F   He should have spoken to the client himself.

Now check your answers to the questions in the test.

Part 2

You will hear a talk about the song 'Happy Birthday'. For questions **9–18**, complete the sentences.

HAPPY BIRTHDAY

The song was first called 'Good Morning [_____ **9**]'.

It was originally intended that [_____ **10**] would sing the song every morning.

The song then became known as 'Good Morning [_____ **11**]'.

Children began to sing the song with 'Happy Birthday' words when they were [_____ **12**].

The song was sung with 'Happy Birthday' words in a [_____ **13**] in 1931 and then in another one in 1934.

The legal situation concerning the song remains valid [_____ **14**].

The song is among the [_____ **15**] songs most frequently sung in English.

Money has to be paid for using the song in any [_____ **16**], eg a TV show, a toy, etc.

The Hill sisters set up [_____ **17**] that receives money for use of the song.

The song consists of just four [_____ **18**] but it is one of the most famous songs in the world.

Part 3

You will hear five different people talking about phone calls they received. For questions **19–23**, choose from the list (**A–F**) how each speaker felt during the phone call. Use the letters only once. There is one extra letter which you do not need to use.

A   annoyed

B   relieved   Speaker 1   [   ] **19**

C   confused   Speaker 2   [   ] **20**

D   disappointed   Speaker 3   [   ] **21**

E   worried   Speaker 4   [   ] **22**

F   sympathetic   Speaker 5   [   ] **23**

Part 4

You will hear an interview with an American actress who recently made a film in Britain. For questions 24–30, choose the best answer (A, B or C).

24 What does Emma say about the weather in Britain?

    A   It took her some time to get used to it.

    B   Her character in the film was wrong about it.

    C   It was quite a pleasant change for her.

25 What does Emma say about her relationship with the actors who played her roommates?

    A   It was the same in real life as in the film.

    B   She was surprised by how good it was.

    C   It has been difficult to continue it.

26 What does Emma say about English and British accents?

    A   She was able to copy one of the other actor's accents.

    B   She cannot do a range of English and British accents.

    C   She doesn't like the sound of the Welsh accent.

27 What does Emma say about her American accent?

    A   She didn't like comments that were made about it.

    B   She isn't really aware of having one.

    C   Lots of people don't notice it.

28 What does Emma say about boarding schools?

    A   She thinks they are the best kind of school.

    B   She has changed her opinion of them.

    C   She only knows about them from books and films.

29 What does Emma say about the dancing scene in the movie?

    A   She had to repeat it several times.

    B   She finds it embarrassing to watch it.

    C   She had done that kind of thing before.

30 Emma says that if you're a movie star,

    A   you will receive a lot of unfair criticism.

    B   you cannot expect to be popular with everyone.

    C   you are likely to become sensitive to negative comments.

PAPER 5 SPEAKING 14 minutes

Part 1 (3 minutes)

Before you do the Part 1 tasks, go on to the Further Practice and Guidance page which follows.

Personal history

- How many different places have you lived in during your life so far?
- Describe the home or homes you have lived in during your life.
- What kind of education and/or jobs have you had in your life so far?
- What do you like most and least about the town/village/area where you live at the moment?
- Do you think you will continue to live in the same place for a long time? (Why?/Why not?)

Reading

- How much time do you spend reading?
- Do you read a newspaper regularly? (Why/Why not?)
- What kind of magazines do you like reading? (Why?)
- What kind of books do you like reading? Do you prefer fiction or non-fiction? (Why?)
- Describe a book that you particularly enjoyed. What was good about it?

Part 2 (4 minutes)

1 Crowds

Candidate A: Look at photographs 1A and 1B on page 121. They show **crowds of people at different events.**

Compare the photographs and say **what kind of experience you think the different crowds of people are having.**

Candidate A talks on his/her own for about 1 minute.

Candidate B: Which crowd would you prefer to be a member of?

Candidate B talks on his/her own for about 20 seconds.

2 Celebrations

Candidate B: Look at photographs 2A and 2B on page 121. They show **different groups of people celebrating somebody's birthday**.

Compare the photographs and say **what you think people did in order to organize the different birthday celebrations**.

Candidate B talks on his/her own for about 1 minute.

Candidate A: What kind of celebration would you prefer for your birthday?

Candidate A talks on his/her own for about 20 seconds.

WHAT'S TESTED

In Part 1 of the Speaking Paper, you answer spoken questions by giving personal information, for example about your life, your interests, your experiences, your plans, your country, etc.

TIPS

*   Do not try to prepare fixed answers for this part of the Paper. It is possible that you will not be able to use these prepared answers because you will not be asked questions connected with them. Secondly, these prepared answers will not sound natural and may not be logical answers to the questions you are asked. As a result, preparing fixed answers is likely to mean that you do not perform well in this part of the Paper.

*   However, it is a good idea to do the right kind of preparation. Practise with a partner asking and answering questions about yourself, your life, your interests, etc. In addition to the practice of the topics in the tests in this book, think of other areas of your life and life in general and practise talking about them.

The following exercises will help you to answer the questions in this part of the test. When you have completed each exercise, answer the questions in the test.

Which of the following answers/statements are in correct English? If a sentence is incorrect, say or write it correctly.

Personal history

A   I've lived in three different places during my life.

B   I've always lived in same place.

C   I lived in an apartment in the city centre from the age of four until I was 12.

D   I'm living there since five years.

E   I've been studying at college since six months.

F   I was waiter in a restaurant during the college holidays.

G   The best thing about this city is that there is a lot to do.

H   I don't like this place because it's too much people here.

I   I think I'll stay here for several years because I've got a good job here.

J   I'm only planning to stay here for a short time because I go back to my own country.

Reading

A   I don't read much time.

B   I usually spend a few hours each week reading.

C   I read a newspaper every day because I like to know what's happening in the world.

D   I don't read a newspaper regularly because I'm not very interesting in them.

E   I like reading music magazines because listen to the music is my favourite thing.

F   I like reading celebrity magazines because I like reading a gossip about famous people.

G   I prefer fiction because I like reading exciting stories.

H   I read a lot of biographies because I like learning about the lives of famous people.

I   I enjoyed really this book because it made me laugh a lot.

J   I thought that this book it was very good because of the characters.

Now do the Part 1 tasks in the test.

Parts 3 and 4 (7 minutes) Photography competition

Part 3

Imagine that you are the judges of a photography competition. The title of the competition is 'Perfect Surroundings'. Look at the photographs that you have to consider as possible winners of the competition on page 122.

First, talk to each other **about what each entry shows and how effective each photograph is in showing 'perfect surroundings'.** Then decide **which photograph should win the competition and which should come second.**

Candidates A and B discuss this together for about 3 minutes.

Part 4

- Do you take a lot of photographs? (Why?/Why not?)
- What are your favourite photographs that you possess? Why are they your favourites?
- When do you/your friends/your family take photographs? What do you/they do with these photographs?
- Some people say that taking lots of photographs is a waste of time. What do you think?
- What kind of surroundings do you particularly like to be in? (Why?)
- What kind of surroundings do/would you dislike being in? (Why?)

FCE TEST 2

PAPER 1 READING 1 hour

Part 1

You are going to read an article about children's memories. For questions **1–8**, choose the answer (**A, B, C** or **D**) which you think fits best according to the text.

Mark your answers **on the separate answer sheet**.

What children remember

Whether it's holidays, great days out or lazy days at home, you hope your children will retain happy memories of their childhoods. But often their treasured recollections don't match parental expectations.

Take my exasperated friend Sarah. Back on the train after a day at both the Natural History and the Science museums with three children under 10, she asked: 'So what did you all learn?' 'That if I bang my head on something hard, it's going to hurt,' came the reply from her six-year-old daughter. Roaring dinosaurs and an expensive lunch had little impact, but the bump on a banister was destined to become family legend. After I'd helped out on a school trip to Tate Modern art gallery, the teacher told me that three of my five-year-old charges drew the escalators as their most memorable bit of the day. 'On a zoo trip, Luca liked the caterpillar best,' says my friend Barbara. 'Forget lions, giraffes and gorillas. What made the most impression (and what he still talks about five years later) is the time he found a caterpillar at the zoo.'

My children are masters of odd-memory syndrome, recalling the minutiae and looking blank-faced at major events. The self-catering cottage of last year is 'the yellow house that smelled funny'. A skiing holiday is 'remember when we had burgers for breakfast?' and a summer holiday is 'when we had two ice creams every night'.

Food features large in other children's memories. 'Did you like going on the plane?' a friend asked her three-year-old daughter after her first flight. 'I liked the crisps,' came the reply. Four years on, another friend's daughter still remembers Menorca for the tomato-flavoured crisps and Pembrokeshire for the dragon ice cream (ice cream in a dragon-shaped pot). Last summer, Janey and her husband took their three children on a three-week train trip around Europe. 'We wanted to open their minds to the joys of travel and experiencing different cultures,' she says. 'But the high point for them was the Mickey Mouse-shaped ice cream. That was in Rome. I wonder whether the Coliseum made any sort of impression.'

But parenting expert Suzie Hayman is reassuring. 'I think food figures high in everybody's memories,' she says. 'I just have to think of hot chocolate and I'm transported back to Paris. Adults tend to be less direct or simply try hard to come up to other people's expectations. The important thing is that you give your children lots of stimulation. If you visit a museum, you can convey your appreciation for something. Just don't expect them to share it. It's all about laying out the buffet and letting children pick. What children want most is you – your attention, your approval, your time. They may prefer the box to the present, but you're still giving them variety for their memory pool. It's also important that they don't grow up expecting that happy times only equate with spending money on expensive days out.'

My nine-year-old has a memory theory: the more uncomfortable the bed, the better the holiday. So sleeping on bathroom floors and bending Z-beds make for a fantastic time and fluffy pillows and soft mattresses (more expensive) equal boring. This is one unexpected memory I plan to nurture for years to come.

1   What do all of the memories mentioned in the second paragraph have in common?

   A   They concerned something unexpected that happened during a trip.

   B   They were not connected with the main purpose of the trip.

   C   They concerned trips that adults particularly enjoyed.

   D   They were not things that the children remembered for long.

2   What does the writer suggest about 'major events' in the third paragraph?

   A   Her children's memories of them are different from hers.

   B   Her children's memories of them change over time.

   C   Her children are unable to remember them at all.

   D   Her children remember only certain parts of them.

3   The food examples in the fourth paragraph illustrate the fact that

   A   food is often what children remember about journeys.

   B   children's memories of past events frequently involve food.

   C   children like talking about unusual food they have had.

   D   children keep their memories of unusual food for a long time.

4   What does Suzie Hayman say about memories of food?

   A   Children are more likely to mention food than adults.

   B   Adults forget what food they have had after a while.

   C   The fact that children remember food is not important.

   D   All her best memories of childhood involve food.

5   What does Suzie Hayman say about parents?

   A   They should not expect their children to enjoy the same things that they enjoy.

   B   They should not take their children on expensive days out.

   C   They should not pay attention to what their children can remember.

   D   They should not take their children to places that will not interest them.

6   The writer says that her child's memory theory

   A   is different from that of other children.

   B   has an advantage for the writer.

   C   makes logical sense to the writer.

   D   is something that she shares with her child.

7   Which of the following phrases from the article would make a suitable title for it?

   A   Great days out (first paragraph)

   B   Family legend (second paragraph)

   C   Odd-memory syndrome (third paragraph)

   D   Other children's memories (fourth paragraph)

8   The writer's purpose in the article is to point out

   A   how difficult it is for children to remember the kind of things that adults remember.

   B   how annoying children's memories of past events can be for adults.

   C   how happy children's own memories of past events make them feel.

   D   how different children's memories are from what adults want them to remember.

Part 2

Read the text and the test questions. Before you answer the test questions, go on to the Further Practice and Guidance pages which follow.

You are going to read a magazine article about the sport of climbing. Seven sentences have been removed from the article. Choose from the sentences **A–H** the one which fits each gap (**9–15**). There is one extra sentence which you do not need to use.

Mark your answers **on the separate answer sheet**.

Aiming high

Looking for a new sport that keeps you fit and gets the adrenaline flowing? How about climbing? You can climb indoors or out, from small walls or boulders to peaks anywhere in the world – once you get the hang of it!

'It's a sport that involves your mind, body and emotions,' John Gibbons of London's Westway sports centre says. 'It's one of the few sports where you compete against yourself. You may be part of a club and climbing with others but you are seeing how good *you* can be. **9** ....'

Indoor walls can be from 7 to 16 metres, although some centres have walls of 20 metres or more. Each wall has bolt-on holds (to place your feet and hands) of different shapes and sizes. These can be moved around and varied to make the climb more or less challenging – and routes can be changed every few months. 'Big holds, spaced comfortably apart so that you can easily move your feet and hands from one to the other without too much trouble, are the easiest,' John explains. '**10** .... That kind of climb is called a Slab.'

Trickier climbs have smaller holds that are harder to grip, and they are spaced more awkwardly apart. **11** .... The angle of the wall can also make the climb more difficult.

Is the idea to find the fastest way to the top? 'It's to find the route to the top!' laughs Graeme Alderson of the British Mountaineering Council. 'Just as when you're skiing, the idea can be to find the best way to get to the bottom without falling over – not necessarily the fastest.' **12** .... The challenge can be to climb the highest you can get without falling off!

Falling is not a problem at climbing centres, though. When you climb, you are attached by a harness to a rope looped to a firm anchor at the top of the wall and held by your instructor or one of your team mates at the bottom. A device called a belay holds it taut, so while you are climbing, the rope is kept firm in case you slip. **13** .... Instead, you dangle safely in your harness away from the climbing wall.

You can enjoy climbing on indoor walls as a sport. **14** .... 'Many people have started off with climbing walls and then climbed all over the world. You can climb anything from a small boulder to Mount Everest, naming the new peaks you scale,' says Neil Wightwick of the Glasgow Climbing Centre. 'A group of us named five peaks in Chile,' he continues. 'One member of the team named a peak after himself!'

15 .... Well, you can find out on our website. We've found an online Extreme Climbing game to test your skills and get you started. You will also find lots of great links to sites with videos of climbers in action, as well as links to nationwide climbing centres, both inside and out, to help you get climbing yourself.

A   Maybe you'd like a go at climbing but don't know where to start.

B   If you do one of those, you have to think more about how to move.

C   That's because some climbs look easier than they really are.

D   And, unlike other sports, friends of all abilities can climb together and enjoy it.

E   Or you can use it to work out what level of climb you would be able to do outside.

F   If that happens, you don't plunge to the ground.

G   With them, you can gently climb to the top without any difficulty.

H   Not everyone gets to the top of their climbs.

WHAT'S TESTED

The questions in Part 2 of the Reading Paper require you to work out how parts of a text fit together. You must make sure that each sentence you choose for each gap fits into that gap for the following reasons:

- **text structure:** the sentence fits because it is logical at that point in the text in relation to the overall content and structure of the text.

- **cohesion:** the sentence fits because it contains something that matches grammatically with something mentioned before and/or after the gap.

- **coherence:** the sentence fits because its meaning or topic makes sense in relation to what comes before and/or after the gap.

TIPS

- Begin by reading the whole text with the gaps in it but don't look at the choices at this point. If you get a general idea of what the text is about and what each paragraph of it contains, this will help you to choose the correct sentences for the gaps later.

- Then try to fill each gap. As you do so, remember that each sentence you choose must fit **both grammatically and because of its meaning or topic.**

- Look carefully at the text before and/or after each gap. Look at each sentence. If one of the sentences seems to fit because of its meaning or topic, make sure that it also fits grammatically. Look for any grammatical features (for example pronouns, linking words and phrases, etc) in the sentences. When choosing the correct sentence, look for a sentence that has a grammatical feature that fits with something mentioned before or after the gap.

- More than one sentence may seem to fit into a gap because of its topic or meaning. More than one sentence may fit into a gap grammatically. The correct sentence will be the only one that fits for both reasons.

- Continue to look at all the sentences as you go through. You may discover that you chose a sentence for a gap incorrectly, and that sentence really fits into another gap.

The following exercises will help you to choose the correct answers to each question in the test. When you have completed each exercise, check your answer(s) and then choose your answer for the question in the test.

Question 9

Read the text *until gap 9*.

1   What is mentioned before the gap?

   A   a difference between wall climbing and other sports

   B   how easy or difficult wall climbing is

   C   a particular experience while wall climbing

2   What is the sentence that goes into gap 9 likely to contain?

   A   a reason for a problem

   B   a reference to an event that has already been described

   C   an advantage of wall climbing

Question 10

Read the sentences *before and after gap 10*. The subject of the sentence before the gap is 'Big holds'. In the sentence after the gap, 'That' must refer to something mentioned previously.

What is the sentence that goes into gap 10 most likely to contain?

> **A** a reference to several different kinds of climb
>
> **B** a reference to a particular problem while climbing
>
> **C** a reference to things that help people to climb

Question 11

Read the sentences *before and after gap 11*. The subject of the sentence before the gap is 'Trickier climbs'. The word 'also' in the sentence after the gap must add to something mentioned previously.

What is the sentence that goes into gap 11 likely to be about?

> **A** dealing with a difficult task
>
> **B** taking up wall climbing
>
> **C** completing a climb easily

Question 12

Read the whole paragraph that contains *gap 12*.

What is most likely to be the topic of the missing sentence?

> **A** a particular kind of climb mentioned previously
>
> **B** climbing that is not done indoors
>
> **C** whether people complete a climb or not

Question 13

Read the whole paragraph that contains *gap 13*. The sentence before the gap ends with 'in case ...'. The sentence after the gap begins with 'Instead'.

What is the sentence that fills the gap most likely to refer to?

> **A** a type of climb and what it involves
>
> **B** not realizing that a climb will be difficult
>
> **C** a possible event and an impossible result of it

Question 14

Read the sentence *before gap 14* and the rest of the paragraph *after gap 14*.

What is the main topic of the paragraph and therefore what the missing sentence is likely to mention?

> **A** finding out how to take part in climbing
>
> **B** climbing that is not wall climbing
>
> **C** climbing in comparison with other sports

Question 15

The sentence that goes into gap 15 begins a new topic and a new paragraph. Read the rest of the paragraph *after gap 15*.

What topic is the missing sentence introducing?

> **A** succeeding or failing when climbing
>
> **B** getting information on climbing
>
> **C** differences between climbing and other sports

Now check your answers to the questions in the test.

Part 3

You are going to read a magazine article about a fashion show organized by a clothes company. For questions **16–30**, choose from the sections of the article (**A–F**). The sections may be chosen more than once.

Mark your answers **on the separate answer sheet**.

In which section of the article are the following mentioned?

negative comments about clothes shown at a show	16
people who decide not to attend a show	17
when Burberry makes its clothes in large quantities	18
information about the show that Burberry is unwilling to give	19
the building where sales of the clothes from the show are made to shops	20
the need to be different from other clothes companies	21
what people attending the show bring with them	22
what the audience does as soon as the show finishes	23
where Burberry sells its products to the public	24
a comparison between how long it takes to plan the show and how long the show lasts	25
people wanting to speak to someone involved in the show	26
where various categories of people watch the show from	27
a false impression that people may have of fashion events like this one	28
how quickly reactions to the show appear	29
the effect of a single show on certain people's futures	30

How fashion shows work

Sales can depend on just 18 minutes under the spotlight. James Hall reports

A   It is Burberry's catwalk show during Milan Fashion Week. The tent, pitched in a courtyard in an exquisite building on Milan's Corso Venezia, gradually fills with 1000 fashion editors and representatives from the world's smartest department stores, all clutching invites as thick as slices of bread. At the end of the catwalk, hundreds of photographers jostle for the best position. The room is packed. The lights dim and the show gets under way. The models strut their stuff to pastoral music. The theme is gardening. The show, which has taken more than six months to plan at the cost of tens of thousands of pounds, is over in 18 minutes. The lights rise and the crowd dashes to the next event.

B   Welcome to the sausage factory of high fashion. Burberry's show is one of about 100 that take place during Milan Fashion Week. To the outside world, fashion weeks like Milan's appear to be little more than a love-in for the luxury goods sector. However, beneath the glitzy exterior, there is serious business going on. Fashion editors can make or break a brand with a favourable or cruel review. Designers' entire careers can hang on one collection. But, most crucially, retail executives will place orders worth hundreds of millions of pounds based on what they see.

C   So how does the business of Fashion Week work? What are the mechanics of the event? And how immediate are the benefits if the show is deemed a hit? For Burberry, Milan Fashion Week is the zenith of the year. Although Burberry is known in the UK as a retailer, over 40 per cent of its annual sales come from selling its clothes through other people's shops around the world. Its four annual shows at Milan are its main chance to show retailers what it has to offer. Creating a buzz in the fashion press is equally important as these same collections will be on sale at Burberry's own shops. Burberry has just minutes to do this in each show.

D   Christopher Bailey, Burberry's creative director, starts picking out fabrics for the clothes months before the show. The ranges are only mass-produced once the orders come in after Fashion Week, so getting the looks right for the catwalk is absolutely key. Mr Bailey explains that Milan is his chance to set out Burberry's stall for the rest of the year. Standing out from the crowd is the name of the game. 'When you are up against some of the biggest names in fashion on the same night, you have to make an impression,' he says.

E   Burberry starts to fit out the venue about two weeks before the show. Lighting, seating, sound system, décor, backstage area, they are all planned in minute detail and designed by Mr Bailey to echo the show's theme. Store windows around the world are also co-ordinated to mirror the themes. The company does not disclose the event's budget, but it is clearly huge. The seating arrangement has a strict hierarchy. There are blocks of seats for different groups: a block for the most important fashion editors (around and opposite the company's management), a block for retail buyers from Europe, a block for emerging markets and so on. An early indicator of a show's success is who turns up – or pointedly fails to.

F   Fortunately, Burberry's show is exceptionally well-attended. Although the 18 minutes of the show are crucial, the 24 hours following the event are arguably more important. This is when the hard sell occurs and the money is effectively banked. As soon as Mr Bailey takes his bow at the end of the show, dozens of fashion journalists and TV crews rush backstage to grab a word with him. Clips, quotes and reviews are online and on newswires within minutes. At 9am the morning after the show, Burberry opens its showroom above its store in Milan. This is the most important part of the entire process as it is when department store buyers place their orders. The clothes from the night before are on rails and film and music from the show plays on a loop. A trickle of buyers soon becomes a torrent. Just five hours later, Mr Bailey returns to London to start the entire process again.

PAPER 2 WRITING 1 hour 20 minutes

Part 1

You **must** answer this question. Write your answer in **120–150** words in an appropriate style.

---

1   You have received an email from your English-speaking friend, Richard, who is going to start a new job. Read Richard's email and the notes you have made. Then write an email to Richard, using **all** your notes.

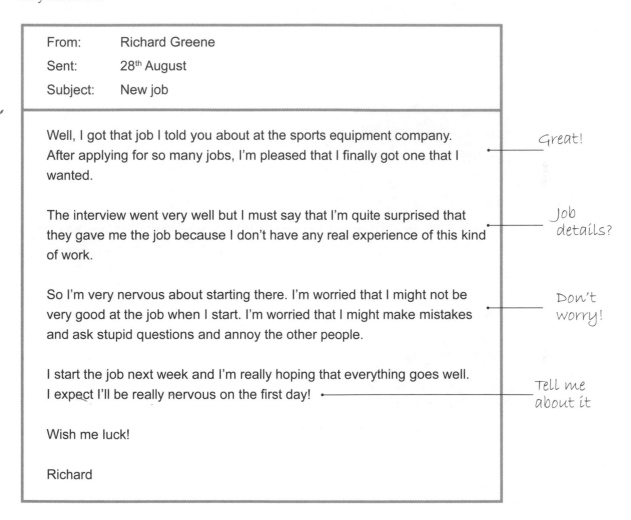

From:	Richard Greene
Sent:	28th August
Subject:	New job

Well, I got that job I told you about at the sports equipment company. After applying for so many jobs, I'm pleased that I finally got one that I wanted.   *Great!*

The interview went very well but I must say that I'm quite surprised that they gave me the job because I don't have any real experience of this kind of work.   *Job details?*

So I'm very nervous about starting there. I'm worried that I might not be very good at the job when I start. I'm worried that I might make mistakes and ask stupid questions and annoy the other people.   *Don't worry!*

I start the job next week and I'm really hoping that everything goes well. I expect I'll be really nervous on the first day!   *Tell me about it*

Wish me luck!

Richard

Write your **email**. You must use grammatically correct sentences with accurate spelling and punctuation in a style appropriate for the situation.

Part 2

Before you answer the test questions, go on to the Further Practice and Guidance pages which follow.

Write an answer to **one** of the questions 2–5 in this part. Write your answer in **120–180** words in an appropriate style.

2   You have seen this announcement in an English-language magazine.

> WHAT DO YOU THINK OF THIS MAGAZINE?
>
> We're going to have a special Letters page containing your views on this magazine. Write to us and tell us what you think. What's good about our magazine and why do you like it? Do you have any criticisms? Is there anything that you think we should have in the magazine that we don't have? We'll publish some of your letters.

Write your **letter**.

3   Your teacher has asked you to write an essay, giving your opinion on the following statement.

Money is not the most important thing in life.

Write your **essay**.

4   You recently saw this notice in an English-language magazine.

> BRILLIANT BUT NOT WELL-KNOWN
>
> Is there a book or some music that you think should be much more well-known than it is? A book or some music that you think is really brilliant, but that most people don't know about? What's so good about it? Why does it deserve to be more successful than it is? We want reviews of books or music that you love but that haven't become really popular. The book or music doesn't have to be new.

Write your **review**.

5   **(a)** or **(b).** Two questions on the set books.

There are two set books. There is one question on each set book. You answer **one** of the two questions.

There is more information, and guidance and practice, on set book questions in Test 4.

WHAT'S TESTED

In this test, for questions 2–4 in Part 2 of the Writing Paper, you must write **one** of the following:

- **a letter**: this may be informal (to a friend or colleague) or formal (to someone in authority, eg a possible employer, a magazine editor, a college principal, or any kind of official). It may require you to give information, express opinions and/or feelings, apply for something, etc.

- **an essay**: this is usually written for a teacher. It must be clearly organized so that clear points are made with appropriate linking of ideas. It requires you to discuss a particular topic and give your opinions and the reasons for those opinions.

- **a review**: this is written for a publication (eg a magazine or website). It requires you to describe something (eg a film, book, play, concert, place visited, product, etc) and to give clear opinions on it.

Your answer will be marked according to the same categories as for Part 1:

- **Content**: you must include everything you have been told to include in the instructions.

- **Organization and cohesion**: your answer must be organized in a clear and logical way, with appropriate linking between and within sentences and paragraphs.

- **Range**: you must use appropriate structures and language for what you are required to do in your answer (eg, giving opinions, advising, explaining, suggesting, comparing, expressing feelings, describing, etc) and you will need to use a range of appropriate vocabulary for the topic.

- **Accuracy**: the number of language mistakes you make, especially serious mistakes, will affect the mark you get!

- **Appropriacy of register and format**: your answer must be as informal or formal as the situation requires. It must also be in an appropriate format, with a suitable opening and closing and suitable paragraphing.

- **Target reader**: the reader should fully understand what is in the answer (eg, the writer's views, the information given, etc).

TIPS

Letter

- Make sure that your letter is appropriately formal or informal, depending on the situation and who the reader of the letter will be.

- Read the instructions very carefully and make sure that you include everything in your letter that you are told to include.

Essay

- Plan your ideas before you start writing so that you produce an essay which makes points in a clear and logical way. Make sure your essay has an introduction, then various points and reasons and then a clear conclusion. Try to think of a variety of linking words and phrases to connect the points you make and to link opinions with reasons for them.

- You can agree with the statement you are given, disagree with it or both agree and disagree.

Review

- Try to think of a variety of vocabulary for describing the thing you are reviewing, rather than always using simple words.

- Make sure that you explain why you liked/disliked it. A review must include personal opinions as well as description.

The following exercises will help you to write answers for Questions 2, 3 and 4 in this part of the test. When you have completed all of the exercises for each question, write your answer for that question.

QUESTION 2 LETTER

GETTING IDEAS AND PLANNING YOUR ANSWER

1   Which of the following **must** you do in your letter?

    A   make general comments about the magazine

    B   compare the magazine with other magazines

    C   give examples of things in the magazine that you like

    D   give reasons for liking the magazine

    E   say how often you read the magazine

    F   offer to write something for the magazine

    G   say whether there is something you dislike about the magazine

    H   suggest something to include in the magazine

Now check your answers to this exercise.

2   Look at this list of words and phrases, which **could** all be used in your letter. If there are any that you don't know, look them up in a dictionary. You do not have to use all of them in your letter but try to use some of them.

(not) keen on	features	criticize	readers
entertaining	section	boring	regular
favourite	improvement	aspect	fault
impressive	look forward to	make a suggestion	on the whole
style of writing	pleasure	issue	informative

SAMPLE ANSWER

Read this sample answer carefully and answer the questions that follow. Then check the assessment of this sample answer on page 141.

I am really honoured to be one of the first to make comments about my favourite magazine of all.

Firstly, I love all aspects of it, every issue comes as a surprise and I always jump with joy when the next one is released.

I can't put down all the interesting articles about celebrities real life. They make me realize that even well known people have the same fears, anxieties and boredom, just like us simple human beings, apart from the luxurious lifestyle, obviously!

The endless tips on makeup, waxing, hair and facial treatments are so invaluable I just can't see myself without attempting one of the techniques displayed in every issue.

I believe that the magazine covers a great range of information, providing a very pleasurable and entertaining reading.

Finally, I would like to suggest a new section of job opportunities as well as hints about what career to choose in this extreme competitive world. I am sure it will be very helpful for everyone who are still having doubts about job prospectives.

Thanks for this opportunity and I am really looking forward to the next issue.

- **Content**: does the letter include everything that should be included?

- **Organization and cohesion**: is the letter organized in a clear and logical way, with appropriate sections and linking?

- **Range**: is there a range of appropriate structures and vocabulary?

- **Accuracy**: are there any mistakes?

- **Appropriacy of register and format**: is the letter appropriately informal or formal, and is the format suitable?

- **Target reader**: will the reader be completely clear about the purpose of the letter and understand fully everything it contains?

Now write your answer to the question in the test.

QUESTION 3 ESSAY

GETTING IDEAS AND PLANNING YOUR ANSWER

1   Here are some things that your essay **might** include. Decide which ones you are going to include.

people who think that money is the most important thing in life

the advantages of having a lot of money

the disadvantages of not having money

the disadvantages of being rich

the difficulties of getting money

things that are more important in life than money

things that money does not give you

your personal attitude to money in comparison with other things in life

2   Look at this list of linking words and phrases, which you **could** use in your essay. If there are any that you don't know, look them up in a dictionary. You do not have to use all of them in your essay but try to use some of them.

firstly	however	instead of	in addition to
because of	rather than	although	furthermore
in conclusion	secondly	despite	so
because	so that	since	in spite of
on the other hand	besides	as well as	as
even if	unless	finally	of course
as long as	no matter	moreover	to sum up

SAMPLE ANSWER

Read the sample answer carefully and answer these questions. Then check the assessment of this sample answer on page 141.

- **Content**: does the essay include everything that should be included?
- **Organization and cohesion**: is the essay organized in a clear and logical way, with appropriate sections and linking?
- **Range**: is there a range of appropriate structures and vocabulary?
- **Accuracy**: are there any mistakes?
- **Appropriacy of register and format**: is the essay appropriately informal or formal, and is the format suitable?
- **Target reader**: will the reader be completely clear about the views expressed in the essay?

Money is not the most important thing in the world. Because there are so many priceless things which money cannot buy.

Everyone wants to live in high living standard. Having a big house, driving a fast, comfortable and expensive car, all these such things shape our dreams since our childhood. Money can supply a happy and comfortable life, but up to a point.

Society always shows more respect to rich people than poor people. Money represents power, happiness and prosperity. However, money does not bring the happiness every time. In addition, most of people realize that being healthy is undoubtedly more important than being rich, as they lose their health. Furthermore, money only able to buy commercial and materialistic things, not emotional things such as love, affection, etc.

In conclusion, despite money is described as one of the most important things in the world, there are many things that impossible to get even if we are rich. Feeling confident and happy as being of a member of a nice family is one of the most important things, besides being healthy and getting love.

Now write your answer to the question in the test.

QUESTION 4 REVIEW

GETTING IDEAS AND PLANNING YOUR ANSWER

1   Which of the following **must** you include in your review?

   A   the title of the book or music and who wrote/performed it

   B   a description of the book or music

   C   how well-known the book or music is/was

   D   when you read the book/first heard the music

   E   why you think the book/music is excellent

   F   why the book/music will become more popular

   G   why other people would like the book/music

   H   other books/music by the same person/people

Now check your answers to this exercise.

2   Look at this list of phrases, which you **could** use in your review. Complete the phrases by filling in the correct verbs from the list. Try to use some of these phrases in your review.

made   didn't get   had   didn't do   came   found
didn't pay   didn't catch   gave   didn't become

A   It .... a big effect on me.

B   Some critics .... it very good reviews.

C   I .... it extremely impressive.

D   It .... much publicity.

E   It didn't sell very well when it first .... out.

F   It .... a big hit.

G   It .... me feel good when I read/heard it.

H   People .... much attention to it.

I   It .... very well but I don't know why it wasn't successful.

J   I thought it was great but it .... on with people in general.

Now check your answers to this exercise.

SAMPLE ANSWER

Read this sample answer carefully and answer these questions. Then check the assessment of this sample answer on page 142.

*   **Content**: does the review include everything that should be included?
*   **Organization and cohesion**: is the review organized in a clear and logical way, with appropriate sections and linking?
*   **Range**: is there a range of appropriate structures and vocabulary?
*   **Accuracy**: are there any mistakes?
*   **Appropriacy of register and format**: is the review appropriately informal or formal, and is the format suitable?
*   **Target reader**: will the reader be completely clear about what the writer describes and the opinions expressed in the review?

Swallowing Grandma by Kate Long is a book that surprised me in a very positive way – I did not have any expectations about it when I started reading it, but soon I found myself really enjoying every page of it.

It is a story of an 18-year-old Katherine living in a small town with her grandmother, not knowing much what had happened to her parents. We follow her everyday life, struggling with everything that being an overweight lonely teenager involves. As the plot unwinds, the family mystery begins to unravel and there are some unexpected twists in the end.

What I find very interesting is the narrative structure of the book – besides Katherine there is another narrator telling part of the story, taking turns with her. However, most of the time we do not know who this other narrator is, only in the end we understand everything.

The reason I liked this book so much is because it is written very beautifully, often funnily but still sensitively.

Now write your answer to the question in the test.

PAPER 3 USE OF ENGLISH 45 minutes

Part 1

For questions **1–12**, read the text below and decide which answer (**A, B, C** or **D**) best fits each gap. There is an example at the beginning (**0**).

Mark your answers **on the separate answer sheet**.

Example:

    0   **A** ended   **B** completed   **C** stopped   **D** left

0	A	B	C	D
	☐	☐	☐	▬

Proactive job hunting

Once upon a time, people (**0**) .... school or university, joined a company and stayed with

it until they retired. The concept of a job for life is now long (**1**) .... , and nowadays many

employees find it hard to stay loyal to their companies for even a relatively short (**2**) .... of

time. According to a recent survey, this is particularly (**3**) .... in London, where more than

half of those asked said that they constantly (**4**) .... one eye on other job opportunities,

(**5**) .... they are fairly happy in their existing jobs. A high number of London workers say

that they are always on the (**6**) .... , although they are content and motivated in their

current position.

Job seekers find that the internet (**7**) .... them with a quick and easy way to find out what's

available, and 53 per cent said that they had applied for a job or (**8**) .... with an employment

agency in the past 12 months. This proactive (**9**) .... means that people can look for a perfect

job match with the (**10**) .... of effort. But while this is good for job hunters, the growing

lack of company loyalty could (**11**) .... up being a big problem for employers. Perhaps

surprisingly, the (**12**) .... factor attracting job seekers was not more money, but challenging

and interesting work.

1 A gone   B over   C done   D finished

2 A stage   B point   C section   D period

3 A right   B true   C actual   D real

4 A hold   B put   C keep   D place

5 A just as   B as well   C so that   D even if

6 A lookout   B search   C watch   D pursuit

7 A serves   B delivers   C provides   D fulfils

8 A engaged   B registered   C appointed   D recorded

9 A manner   B approach   C style   D custom

10 A least   B smallest   C lowest   D minimum

11 A come   B end   C lead   D run

12 A biggest   B widest   C largest   D highest

Part 2

Read the text. Before you answer the test questions, go on to the Further Practice and Guidance page which follows.

For questions **13–24**, read the text below and think of the word which best fits each gap. Use only **one** word in each gap. There is an example at the beginning (**0**).

Write your answers **IN CAPITAL LETTERS on the separate answer sheet**.

Example: 0   IN

Kite surfing

It's the fastest-growing watersport (**0**) …………….… the world. Five years ago, (**13**) ………..…. were a few hundred kite surfers in the UK. Now the number (**14**) ……………….. nearer 10 000.

Kite surfers use the wind to sail across the water on a surfboard. The kite is attached (**15**) …………. the rider's waist by a harness and controlled by a bar. It's thrilling to watch the brightly coloured kites zipping through the skies, pulling their riders at enormous speed. But it's even (**16**) ……………. thrilling to do it. Aaron Hadlow, the wonderkid of the sport, explains the appeal. 'There's so (**17**) …………….. you can do. You can ride waves, jump high or just cruise around. You can also go out in risky conditions and scare yourself – it's definitely high adrenalin.' Hadlow tried it out at the (**18**) ……………. of 10 and started competing when he was 12. Three years (**19**) ……………….. , he was world champion, a title he has held (**20**) ………………… four years.

Richard Gowers, chairman of the British Kite Surfing Association, says the sport is popular (**21**) ……………... it is so easy to learn. 'You don't have to be superhuman to do it. It normally (**22**) ……………. two to three days to master the basics. (**23**) ………………. of the best things is that you don't need a lot of equipment. You can pack (**24**) ………..……. all in the back of a car.'

WHAT'S TESTED

The questions in Part 2 of the Use of English Paper test you mainly on grammar. Common grammatical areas tested include **verb tenses and verb forms, prepositions, articles, pronouns, comparative structures, quantifiers, determiners, etc**. Some questions may focus on the vocabulary areas tested in Part 1 (see page 21).

TIPS

- Begin by reading through the whole text to find out what it is about and what it contains. This will help you to know the context for filling each gap.

- Look carefully at what comes both before and after each gap so that you can decide on the meaning of the sentence or phrase with the gap in it, and therefore what the word that goes into the gap refers to.

- If there is more than one gap in a sentence, read the whole sentence very carefully so that you are clear about the context and meaning of each word that correctly fills each gap.

- When you have filled a gap, read the sentence that contains it again – make sure that it makes sense and is grammatically correct with the word you have put into the gap.

The following exercises will help you to write the correct answer to each question in the test. When you have completed each exercise, check your answer and then write your answer for the question in the test.

For each question, decide what the sentence or phrase containing the gap describes or refers to.

Question 13

A   types of people who were kite surfers

B   how many kite surfers existed

Question 14

A   a change in the number

B   the present number

Question 15

A   the connection between one thing and another

B   one thing being on top of another

Question 16

A   a comparison between activities

B   a change in something

Question 17

A   how good doing kite surfing is

B   the large number of things you can do

Question 18

A   the other people who were with him

B   how old he was

Question 19

A   a time after a time in the past

B   how long in the past

Question 20

A   a point in time in the past

B   a period of time

Question 21

A   a reason

B   an additional piece of information

Question 22

A   the beginning of a process

B   an amount of time required

Question 23

A   a very good thing

B   good things mentioned previously

Question 24

A   the action of packing

B   the equipment

Now check your answers to the questions in the test.

Part 3

For questions **25–34**, read the text below. Use the word given in capitals at the end of some of the lines to form a word that fits in the gap **in the same line**. There is an example at the beginning (**0**).

Write your answers **IN CAPITAL LETTERS on the separate answer sheet**.

Example: 0   PROUD

Life on a Native American reservation

There are around 800 reservations in ̇e US where Native American

tribes live and they are (**0**) .... people. Over 30 000 members of the   **PRIDE**

Lakota tribe live on the Pine Ridge Reservation, but life there is not easy.

Some people do not have a car or telephone and many live in simple

(**25**) .... houses. There are only one or two stores where they can   **WOOD**

buy things. Lots of people are (**26**) .... and times are tough. Despite   **EMPLOY**

the many (**27**) .... of life on the reservation, people still choose to   **DIFFICULT**

live there and want to stay. Some Native Americans are trying to attract

(**28**) .... to come and learn more about their lives, their traditions and   **VISIT**

their music. On some reservations, people are opening shops selling Native

American (**29**) .... and modern Native American music on CD.   **JEWEL**

Children of the Lakota learn from their elders, who hold the (**30**) ....   **WISE**

of the tribe. (**31**) .... stories are very important to Native   **TRADITION**

Americans. The elders tell their children and (**32**) .... about their people   **CHILD**

and their tribal history. It is important that the tradition of storytelling is

continued by the younger members if these stories are not to be

(**33**) .... Even writing down the stories or putting them onto a   **FORGET**

computer may not prevent them from being lost (**34**) ....   **EVER**

Part 4

For questions **35–42**, complete the second sentence so that it has a similar meaning to the first sentence, using the word given. **Do not change the word given.** You must use between **two** and **five** words, including the word given. Here is an example (0).

Example: **0**   It took me a fairly long time to answer all my emails.

           QUITE

           I spent .... all my emails.

The gap can be filled with the words 'quite a long time answering', so you write:

Example: **0**   QUITE A LONG TIME ANSWERING

Write only the missing words **IN CAPITAL LETTERS on the separate answer sheet**.

---

35   You're a better cook than me.

     COOKING

     I'm not .... you are.

36   I shouted at her because she annoyed me.

     MADE

     If .... angry, I wouldn't have shouted at her.

37   Let's eat something now, I'm hungry.

     HAVE

     Why .... to eat now? I'm hungry.

38   We couldn't swim because the water was so cold.

     US

     The water was .... go swimming.

39   I don't understand the meaning of that sentence – it's very confusing.

     MEANS

     I don't know .... – it's very confusing.

40   She didn't want to discuss the problem.

     KEEN

     She .... about the problem.

41   It's strange for me to eat at this time of the day.

     USED

     I'm .... at this time of the day.

42   Have you always taken an interest in politics?

     INTERESTED

     Has .... you?

PAPER 4 LISTENING approximately 40 minutes

Part 1

You will hear people talking in eight different situations. For questions **1–8**, choose the best answer
(**A**, **B** or **C**).

1   You overhear two people talking about a disagreement. What feeling does the woman express?

   A   willingness to discuss the matter again

   B   regret at what she said

   C   annoyance at what happened

2   You hear a football supporter talking about a player. What is his opinion of the player?

   A   He's getting better.

   B   He's not as good as he was.

   C   He's never been very good.

3   You overhear a college administrator talking on the phone about a lesson. What does she tell the caller?

   A   The cost of one lesson will be refunded.

   B   The lesson will happen at a later date.

   C   A different teacher will take the lesson.

4   You hear a man talking about a company. Who is the speaker?

   A   a manager at the company

   B   a business journalist

   C   a worker at the company

5   You hear a man and a woman discussing a social arrangement. What is the woman's purpose?

   A   to find out information

   B   to change the arrangement

   C   to avoid going

6   You hear someone on the radio talking about recycling. What is the speaker's main topic?

   A   problems associated with recycling

   B   why recycling is necessary

   C   the amount of recycling that is happening

7   You overhear two people talking in an airport waiting area. What is the situation?

   A   They're going on a business trip.

   B   They're going to live in another country.

   C   They're going on holiday.

8   You hear a man talking about a phone call. What does he say about the call?

   A   It took longer than it should have taken.

   B   He was told something surprising during it.

   C   He had not expected the call.

Part 2

Before you listen to the CD, read the test questions and go on to the Further Practice and Guidance page which follows.

You will hear an interview with someone who works in a museum in London. For questions **9–18**, complete the sentences.

THE PETRIE MUSUEM

Sir William Petrie died in ▢ **9** .

He mainly collected the ▢ **10** used by people in ancient Egypt.

The curator's favourite object is a ▢ **11** which has two letters written on it.

Petrie ▢ **12** the objects well before sending them from Egypt.

The museum contains ▢ **13** objects that people cannot see.

In the new building, the objects will be displayed in ▢ **14** .

A small area of the new museum will be about Petrie and ▢ **15** .

The new museum will not have ▢ **16** for objects.

The museum is discussing with people what the ▢ **17** in the new museum will contain.

Petrie described his collection as ' ▢ **18** '.

WHAT'S TESTED

The questions in Part 2 of the Listening Paper test you on your ability to identify, understand and write down facts and pieces of information stated in a recording, in order to fill gaps in sentences. The recording may involve one or two speakers.

TIPS

- The questions follow the same order as what you hear in the recording.
- Use the time given to read the questions very carefully before you listen to the recording. This will give you an idea of what kind of information is required in each gap. Read the whole of each sentence carefully, both before and after the gap. This will help you to decide what each answer should be grammatically (eg a noun phrase, a singular or plural noun, a date, a number, etc). It will also give you an idea of what the missing word or phrase is likely to mean in the context.
- No answer will be more than three words. Don't write more than three words.
- Every answer will be a word or phrase that you actually hear in the recording. Do not try to change the words and phrases that are said by the speakers – if you do this, you may make unnecessary mistakes, even though you have understood and identified the correct answer.
- Don't spend too much time thinking about one question - this may cause you to miss the information for later questions.

The following exercises will help you to write the correct answer to each question in the test.

Listen to the whole recording once to get a general idea about what is said in it. Then listen for a second time, and answer the questions below. When you have completed each exercise, check your answer(s) and then write your answer for the question in the test.

Stop the recording when the interviewer says 'what does he or she do?'

Question 9
The gap should be filled by
A a place. B a year.

Question 10
The gap should be filled by a phrase meaning
A common objects. B valuable objects.

Stop the recording when the curator says 'who were buried in the tomb'.

Question 11
The gap should be filled by
A a small object. B a structure for the dead.

Stop the recording when the curator says 'Not all archaeologists did that in those days!'

Question 12
The gap should be filled by a verb describing
A an action. B an experience.

Stop the recording when the curator says 'where they can be seen'.

Question 13
The gap should be filled by
A a number. B an adjective.

Question 14
The gap should be filled by a phrase describing
A parts of a building. B pieces of furniture.

Stop the recording when the curator says 'just in store at the moment'.

Question 15
The gap should be filled by a phrase describing
A what Petrie did. B how objects are kept.

Stop the recording when the curator says 'our plans for the move'.

Question 16
The gap should be filled by a word or phrase describing
A something consisting of words.
B something consisting of pictures.

Question 17
The gap should be filled by a word describing
A pieces of equipment. B intentions.

Stop the recording at the end.

Question 18
The gap should be filled by a phrase describing
A the value of the collection.
B the size of the collection.

Now check your answers to the questions in the test.

Part 3

You will hear five different people talking about trips they went on. For questions **19–23**, choose from the list (**A–F**) what each person says about their trip. Use the letters only once. There is one extra letter which you do not need to use.

A It started badly.

Speaker 1   **19**

B It was exciting.

Speaker 2   **20**

C It lasted too long.

Speaker 3   **21**

D It was better than I had expected.

Speaker 4   **22**

E It finished early.

Speaker 5   **23**

F It was badly organized.

Part 4

You will hear an interview with someone who started the activity known as 'free running'. For questions **24–30**, choose the best answer (**A**, **B** or **C**).

24 Sébastien says that he does free running because

    A other activities became boring for him.

    B if feels like a natural activity to him.

    C it is an individual activity.

25 What does Sébastien say about fitness and taking up free running?

    A Fit people are keen to do difficult things immediately.

    B People who are not fit don't learn very quickly.

    C Free running is a good way of getting fit.

26 What does Sébastien say about the danger of free running?

    A It is not as great as some people think.

    B Most free runners pay no attention to it.

    C It is reduced as much as possible.

27 What does Sébastien say about taking risks?

    A He used to take more risks than he does now.

    B He always tries to take the minimum amount of risk.

    C Some of the things he does involve no risk.

28 When Sébastien jumped across the stadium roof,

    A he felt that he could easily jump the required distance.

    B he had to control his nerves before he did the jump.

    C he knew that he would land on a mat if he fell.

29 What does Sébastien say about his fear of heights?

    A People don't believe that he has it.

    B He always has to overcome it.

    C It is not as great as it used to be.

30 What does Sébastien say about where free running can be done?

    A People's opinions on this are changing.

    B His own opinions on this have changed.

    C Some people have the wrong opinion on this.

PAPER 5 SPEAKING 14 minutes

Part 1 (3 minutes)

Habits and routines

- What happens on a typical day for you?
- Describe a journey that you often make.
- What do you usually do at weekends/in your free time?
- What do you usually do/eat at mealtimes?
- Do you have any habits that annoy other people? (What?)

Games and sports

- Which indoor games do you play regularly?
- Which indoor games are common in your country?
- Do you take part in any outdoor sports regularly? (Which?)
- Do you like watching any outdoor sports, live or on TV? (Which?)
- Which game(s) or sport(s) do you dislike? (Why?)

Part 2 (4 minutes)

Before you do the Part 2 tasks, go on to the Further Practice and Guidance Pages which follow.

1 Travelling to work

Candidate A: Look at photographs 1A and 1B on page 123. They show **people travelling to work in different ways.**

Compare the photographs and say **what you think are the advantages and disadvantages of the different ways of travelling to work**.

Candidate A talks on his/her own for about 1 minute.

Candidate B: Which way of travelling to work would you prefer?

Candidate B talks on his/her own for about 20 seconds.

2 Shouting

Candidate B: Look at photographs 2A and 2B on page 123. They show **different people shouting in different situations.**

Compare the photographs and say **why you think the people are shouting**.

Candidate B talks on his/her own for about 1 minute.

Candidate A: In what sort of situations do you shout?

Candidate A talks on his/her own for about 20 seconds.

WHAT'S TESTED

In Part 2 of the Speaking Paper, you talk about two pairs of photographs, as follows:

- Firstly, you talk about the pair of photographs that you are given.
- You **describe** and **compare** the two photographs. You also answer a specific question about them. To do this, you talk on your own for **1 minute**.
- Then the other candidate answers a question relating to your photographs. This question requires a **personal response** lasting **20 seconds**.
- Then the other candidate **describes** and **compares** his/her pair of photographs for **1 minute**.
- Then you give a **personal response** to a question about the other candidate's photographs. You talk for **20 seconds**.

TIPS

- When you look at the two photographs that you must describe and compare, also look carefully at the question that appears above them. This question will also be asked by the interlocutor. When you talk about the photographs, you must focus on this question and give an answer to it.
- Think of appropriate vocabulary to **describe** the photographs.
- Use correct phrases and grammatical structures for **comparing**.
- You may not be sure what is happening in the photographs or why it is happening, so you will need to **guess and suggest** what you think is possibly or probably true. To do this, try to use a variety of words and phrases, don't keep repeating 'I think'.
- Organize your thoughts before you begin to talk about your photographs. One minute can feel like a long time when you have to speak alone! Try to make sure that you can think of enough things to say. There will be several similarities and differences between the photographs, so look for as many as you can find. The question about the photographs requires you not only to talk about what is in the photographs but also to give your opinions about what you can see and to express ideas connected with what is in the photographs. Keep calm and don't talk too fast! Use the tests in this book and the exercises below for this test to practise talking about photographs for one minute.
- The question you are asked about the other candidate's photographs may ask you to express a **preference**. Practise using correct phrases and grammatical structures for talking about preferences and for expressing likes and dislikes.
- The question about the other candidate's photographs may ask you to relate the photographs to **your own life and experience**.

The following exercises will help you to answer the questions in this part of the test. When you have completed all of the exercises, answer the questions in the test.

Photographs 1A and 1B

Describing

Which of these words relates to photograph 1A and which to 1B? Write A or B. Some words may relate to both photographs.

traffic .....   bars .....   crowded .....   lanes .....   holding .....

queue .....   stationary .....   carriage .....   busy .....   congested .....

Comparing

Decide whether each of these sentences comparing the photos is grammatically correct or not. If a sentence is incorrect, say or write it correctly.

1   This person is outdoors, whereas those people are not.

2   That journey isn't as easy than this one.

3   This person is getting more of exercise than those people.

4   Those people are experiencing much more stress than that person.

5   The person on the bike might get to work more quickly that the people in the cars.

6   The person on the bike looks like happier than the people on the train.

7   Those people's journey is a lot worse than that person's journey.

8   Whereas that person being relaxed, those people are not.

Personal response – preference

Choose the correct word or phrase to complete each of these sentences.

1   I'd prefer *to go/going* by bike because it's healthier.

2   I'd rather *going/go* by train because it's easier.

3   I wouldn't like *to be/be* one of the people on that train.

4   I enjoy *to cycle/cycling* so the bike would be better for me.

5   I'd hate *to go/go to* work every day on a train like that.

Photographs 2A and 2B

Describing

Which of these words relates to photograph 2A and which to 2B? Write A or B. Some words may relate to both photographs.

team .....   coach .....   furious .....   encouraging .....   yelling .....

crowd .....   meeting .....   pointing .....   fist .....   argument .....

Guessing and suggesting

For each of the sentences, decide which one of the choices A–D means the same as the underlined word or phrase and therefore could be used instead of the underlined word or phrase.

1   I <u>guess</u> that they disagree about something.

    A calculate   B imagine   C estimate   D tell

2   That person <u>seems</u> to be very angry about something.

    A looks like   B regards as   C resembles   D appears

3   In my <u>opinion</u>, that person is in charge of the group.

    A idea   B view   C thought   D belief

4   I think it's <u>likely</u> that they are discussing an important issue at work.

    A probable   B sure   C perhaps   D possibly

5   I get the <u>impression</u> that this person is the team's coach.

    A sense   B feeling   C opinion   D thought

6   It looks to me <u>as if</u> he isn't at all relaxed.

    A as though   B just as   C in case   D so that

7   I <u>assume</u> that he's shouting at the players.

    A hold   B view   C suppose   D take

8   I <u>think</u> that those people are the other team members.

    A regard   B judge   C reckon   D identify

Personal response – your own life and experience

In these sentences, the underlined words are incorrect. Say or write the correct words.

1   I try <u>to don't</u> lose my temper very often.

2   I get angry when people are rude <u>with</u> me.

3   I only shout at people if they have done <u>anything</u> really bad.

4   My friends <u>say</u> me that I shout when I'm using my phone.

5   I shout <u>lot</u> when I'm supporting my team at a football match.

Now do the Part 2 tasks in the test.

Parts 3 and 4 (7 minutes) Skills for life

Part 3

Look at the pictures on page 124, which show various skills.

First, talk to each other **about the advantages of having each of these skills**. Then decide **which two skills are the most important for people to have**.

Candidates A and B discuss this together for about 3 minutes.

Part 4

- Which of these skills do you have?

- Is there a skill that you would like to learn? (Which? Why?)

- Are there any skills that you have tried to learn but been unable to learn? (Which? Why?)

- How do people learn the skills that are useful in life?

- Which practical skills do you think people should learn at school and which practical skills do people learn at school in your country?

- Some people say that practical skills are more important than academic ability. What do you think?

FCE TEST 3

PAPER 1 READING 1 hour

Part 1

You are going to read an extract from a novel. For questions 1–8, choose the answer (**A, B, C** or **D**) which you think fits best according to the text.

Mark your answers **on the separate answer sheet**.

Brunetti was at the post office at seven-thirty the next morning, located the person in charge of the postmen, showed his warrant card, and explained that he wanted to speak to the postman who delivered mail to the area in Cannaregio near the Palazzo del Cammello. She told him to go to the first floor and ask in the second room on the left, where the Cannaregio postmen sorted their mail. The room was high-ceilinged, the entire space filled with long counters with sorting racks behind them. Ten or twelve people stood around, putting letters into slots or pulling them out and packing them into leather satchels. He asked the first person he encountered, a long-haired woman with a strangely reddened complexion, where he could find the person who delivered the mail to the Canale della Misericordia area. She looked at him with open curiosity, then pointed to a man halfway along the table and called out, 'Mario, someone wants to talk to you.'

The man called Mario looked at them, then down at the letters in his hands. One by one, merely glancing at the names and addresses, he slipped them quickly into the slots in front of him, then walked over to Brunetti. He was in his late thirties, Brunetti guessed, with light brown hair that fell in a thick wedge across his forehead. Brunetti introduced himself and started to take his warrant card out again, but the postman stopped him with a gesture and suggested they talk over coffee.

They walked down to the bar, where Mario ordered two coffees and asked Brunetti what he could do for him.

'Did you deliver mail to Maria Battestini at Cannaregio …?'

'Yes. I delivered her mail for three years. I must have taken her, in that time, thirty or forty items of registered mail, had to climb all those steps to get her to sign for them.'

Brunetti anticipated his anger at never having been tipped and waited for him to give voice to it, but the man simply said, 'I don't expect to be tipped, especially by old people, but she never even said thank you.'

'Isn't that a lot of registered mail? Brunetti asked. 'How often did they come?'

'Once a month,' the postman answered. 'As regular as a Swiss watch. And it wasn't letters, but those padded envelopes, you know, the sort you send photos or CDs in.'

Or money, thought Brunetti, and asked, 'Do you remember where they came from?'

'There were a couple of addresses, I think,' Mario answered. 'They sounded like charity things, you know, Care and Share, and Child Aid. That sort of thing.'

'Can you remember any of them exactly?'

'I deliver mail to almost four hundred people,' he said by way of answer.

'Do you remember when they started?'

'Oh, she was getting them already when I started on that route.'

'Who had the route before you?' Brunetti asked.

'Nicolo Matucci, but he retired and went back to Sicily.'

Brunetti left the subject of the registered packages and asked, 'Did you bring her bank statements?'

'Yes, every month,' he said, and recited the names of the banks. 'Those and the bills were the only things she ever got, except for some other registered letters.'

'Do you remember where those were from?'

'Most of them came from people in the neighbourhood, complaining about the television.'

Before Brunetti could ask him about how he knew this, Mario said, 'They all told me about them, wanted to be sure that the letters were delivered. Everyone heard it, that noise, but there was nothing they could do. She's old. That is, she was old, and the police wouldn't do anything. They're useless.' He looked up suddenly at Brunetti and said, 'Excuse me.'

Brunetti smiled and waved it away with an easy smile. 'No, you're right,' Brunetti went on, 'there's nothing we can do, not really. The person who complains can bring a case, but that means that people from some department – I don't know what its name is, but it takes care of complaints about noise –

have to go in to measure the decibels of the noise to see if it's really something called 'aural aggression', but they don't work at night, or if they get called at night, they don't come until the next morning, by which time whatever it was has been turned down.' Like all policemen in the city, he was familiar with the situation, and like them, he knew it had no solution.

1   Which of the following happens in the first paragraph?

   A   Everyone stops working when Brunetti enters the room.

   B   Someone wonders why Brunetti is looking for Mario.

   C   Brunetti is confused by something he is told.

   D   Brunetti becomes impatient with someone.

2   What do we learn about Mario in the second paragraph?

   A   He was older than Brunetti had expected.

   B   He found his work boring.

   C   He was very experienced at his work.

   D   He was surprised by Brunetti's arrival.

3   When Mario mentioned getting Maria Battestini to sign for registered mail,

   A   he said that most old people weren't polite to postmen.

   B   Brunetti asked him if her reaction had annoyed him.

   C   he said that his efforts deserved a tip.

   D   Brunetti formed an incorrect opinion about how he had felt.

4   Mario mentions a Swiss watch to give an idea of

   A   how similar the registered envelopes were.

   B   the neat appearance of the registered envelopes.

   C   the constant pattern of the arrival of the registered envelopes.

   D   how unusual the registered envelopes were.

5   When asked exactly where the registered envelopes came from, Mario

   A   indicated that he could not be expected to remember that information.

   B   suggested that the addresses had seemed strange to him at first.

   C   said that someone else might have that information.

   D   replied that there were too many addresses for him to remember.

6   When they discussed other mail that Maria Battestini received, Mario

   A   explained why he knew what some of it contained.

   B   wasn't sure where some of the bank statements came from.

   C   expressed surprise at the amount of it.

   D   said that he had asked other people about it.

7   When Mario mentioned the problem of noise, he made it clear that

   A   he sympathized with the police in that situation.

   B   he didn't want to criticize Brunetti personally.

   C   nothing would have had any effect on the old woman.

   D   he had discussed the matter with the police himself.

8   When he talks about complaints about noise, Brunetti

   A   suggests that he finds the system for dealing with them ridiculous.

   B   explains that he is not sure what the system for dealing with them is.

   C   says that he wishes that the police could deal with them.

   D   says that the people who deal with them are always very busy.

Part 2

You are going to read an article about a series of events in Britain which aim to encourage people to draw. Seven sentences have been removed from the article. Choose from the sentences **A–H** the one which fits each gap (**9–15**). There is one extra sentence which you do not need to use.

Mark your answers **on the separate answer sheet**.

<hr>

The Big Draw

Emily Baker rediscovers the simple joy of putting pencil to paper

I don't draw. I'm intimidated by the idea of putting pencil to paper in the privacy of my own home, let alone in public. **9** .... I've come with Zoe, my 14-year-old daughter, who is just as daunted but better at pretending she isn't, to a weekend of art workshops launching Britain's ninth annual Big Draw. This month, hundreds of venues across Britain, including libraries, museums, historic sites and schools will be hosting free events designed to encourage people to draw.

'The Big Draw is not about perfecting your artistic technique. It's about recognizing that drawing is a way of engaging with the world,' says Sue Grayson Ford, who runs the Campaign for Drawing, the charity that sponsors the Big Draw and other events. '**10** .... It's our universal language.'

Her words are echoed by our first workshop leader, who says. 'It's less about what you put on the paper than what you see.' Well, that's a relief. We are drawing pictures inspired by words listed on a card. As I move coloured pencils around the paper, I begin to feel relaxed. I look around the room. **11** .... When we are finished, our works are hung on the wall among a weekend's worth of contributions to form a canvas.

Later, professional artists show us how to draw cartoon characters. We then learn how to make them move under the guidance of an animator. **12** .... I find I am thinking less about my artistic output and more about how we see the world.

This would delight the founders of the Campaign for Drawing. The charity is dedicated to the principles of the nineteenth-century critic John Ruskin. He believed that art was more about what you see than what is drawn. He felt that if we observed the world more closely, we would take better care of it. I'm not sure how many of those at the workshops are thinking about John Ruskin, but many, including me, are inspired. One elderly woman, there with her two granddaughters, pauses to note: 'I haven't drawn for years. **13** .... In fact, I think I'm going to do that straight away.'

Parents often notice that as children grow up, they become self-conscious about drawing and give up. '**14** .... Drawing is such a natural form of expression,' says Grayson Ford. 'The Big Draw, hopefully, will encourage people to return to that uninhibited age.'

Nine years ago the Campaign for Drawing launched the first Big Draw in the subway tunnel beneath the Science and Victoria and Albert Museums in London. Grayson Ford didn't imagine that it would expand to include 1000 British events this year, as well as programmes in America and Europe. **15** ....

I'm still pretty inhibited at the end of the day, but I can't forget the peace. On the way home Zoe asks me why I'm smiling. 'I was just thinking I might invest in a sketch pad,' I say.

A In another session, we design placards about how the media portrays body image.

B But here I am in a drawing workshop, surrounded by strangers and professional artists.

C However, some require advance registration.

D But this has made me feel like taking it up again.

E Workshop topics range from an Etch-a-Sketch competition in Newcastle to making pop-up buildings for a paper city in Manchester.

F Virtually every discipline from drama to science uses drawing as a basic form of communication.

G It's a shame that that happens.

H Children and adults sit engrossed in what they are doing.

Part 3

Read the test questions and the text. Before you answer the test questions, go on to the Further Practice and Guidance pages which follow.

You are going to read a magazine article about children performing in musical shows in theatres. For questions **16–30**, choose from the people (**A–D**). The people may be chosen more than once.

Mark your answers **on the separate answer sheet**.

Which person mentions…

children getting upset if they are not chosen for a show?   **16** ☐

the number of children performing in a show?   **17** ☐

children providing assistance during a show?   **18** ☐

the need for a child performer to be noticeable during a show?   **19** ☐

a desire to continue being involved in shows?   **20** ☐

a common opinion of child performers?   **21** ☐

the maximum amount of time children spend performing in a show?   **22** ☐

an example of how a child being in a show can cause inconvenience?   **23** ☐

different feelings experienced during a performance?   **24** ☐

the range of abilities children acquire from performing in a show?   **25** ☐

finding out what happens after a child is chosen for a show?   **26** ☐

a reason for not continuing to be involved in shows?   **27** ☐

a belief that it is not a good idea for children to be performers?   **28** ☐

the fact that a child may suddenly be required for a performance?   **29** ☐

an unfortunate result of being a performer concerning school?   **30** ☐

Kids on stage

Children are performing in popular musicals in many London theatres. We talked to various people about the phenomenon of children on stage.

A   THE DIRECTOR

Andrew Tyler chooses children to appear in stage musicals

I'm not only looking for children who can sing, dance and act, they also have to have lively personalities and a lot of confidence – it's essential that they grab the audience's attention and if they can't do that, I don't choose them. When I'm working on a show, I start by contacting agents and telling them what I need, and then I hold auditions for as many children as I can. When the children have been chosen, I draw up the contracts for them and the schedule for performances – there are usually three teams of children for each show and they perform according to a rota system. No child is in a show for more than six months. Being in a show is tiring for the children because they have to combine it with going to school, but they have a great time and they learn an enormous amount about discipline, teamwork and concentration, as well as special skills such as choreography and singing.

B   THE YOUNG PERFORMER

Emily Gould is currently appearing in a popular London show

I love musicals and I'm thrilled to be in this one. I've got quite a big part and have to sing a song all by myself in one scene. I'm always pretty nervous during each performance because I'm worried that I might make a mistake. But at the same time I'm excited about doing it and I feel quite proud of myself when I'm on the stage. I'm one of the youngest children in the show – the age range is five to thirteen. The older children are good to me – they remind me about what I have to do next and encourage me a lot. I don't have time to be in any of the sports teams at school, which is a shame because I'd like to do that too, but acting and singing are great. I want to keep on performing in musicals for the next few years at least, though I'm not sure I want it to be my career.

C   THE STAGE MOTHER

Anita Benfield's son Tom is currently appearing in a popular musical in London

Tom started going to a local drama school when he was five. Last year, the head of the school suggested that he was good enough to audition for this musical. I took him to a series of four auditions and he got the part. We'd had no experience of the audition process and although he got the part, I thought it was horrible. The vast majority of the children get rejected. At the end of each audition, dozens of children burst into tears when they were told that they hadn't been successful – they were absolutely devastated. When Tom got chosen, we were given the schedule for the ten weeks of rehearsals – I hadn't realized how much time would be taken up. It's all rather exhausting – for the parents as much as the children. When the performances start, you get a timetable of the performances the child will be appearing in. But he also has to be available at short notice to replace a child who is ill, and this makes it hard to plan anything. Because of that, we can't book a holiday and recently we weren't able to attend a family wedding.

D   THE EX-CHILD STAR

Ian Miller was a child star in the 1980s

My parents were very keen for me to be on the stage and I showed a lot of talent for it when I was a child. By the time I was ten, I'd been in a number of stage musicals and also appeared in various TV series. When I went to secondary school, I stopped performing because I developed other interests and lost my enthusiasm for it – I didn't want to give up so much time to do it, I wanted to do what my friends were doing. I enjoyed my time as a child performer but I didn't miss it when I stopped. Lots of child performers don't go on to become successful adult performers even if they want to. People in the business tend to think that they aren't capable of developing into good adult performers and they aren't taken seriously when they're older. I don't want my own children to do it – I think performing can be very stressful for children and I think it's much better for children to concentrate on getting a good education and then train to be a performer when they're older, if they want to.

WHAT'S TESTED

Part 3 of the Reading Paper requires you to match questions or statements with short texts or sections of a text. The text may consist of a series of short texts (for example a series of short texts connected with different people, places, etc) or it may be a continuous text divided into sections. You have to decide which short text or section of the text contains the exact information that is in the question or statement. You will be required to match the following:

- **specific information/details** included in the text

- **opinions and attitudes** expressed in the text.

TIPS

- Begin by reading quickly through each text or section of the text. This will give you a general idea about what each one contains and the differences between the content of each one, and it will help you when you come to answer the questions. If you start with the questions, you may quickly become confused.

- There are two approaches you can take. You can look at each question and then look through the text to find the short text or section that matches it. Or you can read each short text or section and go through all of the questions to find which questions match that short text or section.

- Be careful. More than one short text or section may contain something closely related to the question. But only one will contain something that precisely matches the question.

- The numbered questions/statements rephrase what is stated in the text. Do not try to match exact words and phrases in the question with the same words and phrases in the text. Words and phrases used in the question may appear in a section of the text, but that section may not be the answer to the question. What you have to do is to match ideas. So look for the place in the text where the same idea is expressed in different words and phrases.

The following exercises will help you to choose the correct answer to each question in the test. When you have completed each exercise, check your answer(s) and then choose your answer for the question in the test. The letters in brackets refer to the people/sections of the text A–D.

Question 16

Which word from the text refers to the process for choosing performers for a show?

A   auditions (A, C)

B   rota (A)

C   scene (B)

D   rehearsals (C)

Question 17

There are several numbers in the text. What do the following numbers in the text refer to – the age of children or the number of children?

A   three (A)

B   five to thirteen (B)

C   dozens (C)

D   ten (D)

Question 18

Which **two** people talk about what happens while children are on stage and performing in a show?

Question 19

Which **two** people mention a child's individual performance in a show?

Question 20

Which **three** people mention their current involvement in shows?

Question 21

1   Which person mentions a negative opinion of child performers?

2   Which person gives a positive opinion of children appearing in shows?

Question 22

1   Which **two** people mention specific periods of time?

2   What specific periods of time do they mention?

Question 23

Which **two** people mention something not being possible because of involvement in a show?

Question 24

Which of the following refer to feelings experienced while performing on stage?

A   nervous (B)

B   excited (B)

C   proud (B)

D   devastated (C)

E   exhausting (C)

Question 25

Which **two** people mention getting the abilities required to be a good performer?

Question 26

Which **two** people mention what happens after the process of choosing children to perform in a show?

Question 27

Which **two** people mention continuing or not continuing to be involved in shows?

Question 28

Which **two** people talk about child performers in general?

Question 29

Which **two** people talk about the arrangements connected with when a child performs in a show?

Question 30

Which **two** people mention a problem caused by performing during school time?

Now check your answers to the questions in the test.

PAPER 2 WRITING 1 hour 20 minutes

Part 1

You **must** answer this question. Write your answer in **120–150** words in an appropriate style.

1   Your English-speaking friend, Clare, has recently gone to live in another country. Read Clare's letter and the notes you have made. Then write a letter to Clare, using **all** your notes.

> Well, I've now been here for two weeks and I'm beginning to get used to my new life here. I've certainly been very busy since I moved here – there have been all sorts of things happening! ——— **What?**
>
> I'm quite happy in my new home, although lots of my belongings are still in bags and boxes! I'm hoping to find time to unpack everything soon. **escribe?**
>
> I'm glad I decided to come and live here – it's a really good city. But there are some things and people that I miss of course! ——— **For example?**
>
> It would be really good if you could come and stay with me here, perhaps in a couple of months when I've really settled down. What do you think? ——— **Suggest**
>
> Keep in touch.
>
> Clare

Write your **letter**. You must use grammatically correct sentences with accurate spelling and punctuation in a style appropriate for the situation.

Part 2

Before you answer the test questions, go on to the Further Practice and Guidance pages which follow.

Write an answer to **one** of the questions 2–5 in this part. Write your answer in **120–180** words in an appropriate style.

2   You have had a class discussion about a future class trip for a day and talked about places that your class could go for that trip. Your teacher has now asked you to write a report on possible places to go. You should include information on why the places you mention would be good to visit and how a trip to these places could be organized.

Write your **report**.

3   You have decided to enter an international short story competition. The competition rules say that the story must **begin** with the words:

Carla was very excited as she opened the letter.

Write your **story**.

4   You have seen this announcement in an English-language magazine.

WHAT REALLY ANNOYS YOU?

What annoys you the most? Tell us what makes you really angry. Why does it make you so angry? It could be anything, something really serious or something that isn't so important. If you want to, you can talk about more than one thing that really annoys you.

We'll publish the most interesting articles in a special section.

Write your **article**.

5   **(a)** or **(b)**. Two questions on the set books.

There are two set books. There is one question on each set book. You answer **one** of the two questions.

There is more information, and guidance and practice, on set book questions in Test 4.

WHAT'S TESTED

In this test, for questions 2–4 in Part 2 of the Writing Paper, you must write **one** of the following:

- **a report**: this is written for someone in authority (eg a teacher), or for people who belong to the same group as the writer (eg other members of a class or club). It should be in sections and each section should probably have a heading. It will include facts and information and may also involve recommending or suggesting something.
- **a story**: this is written for a publication (eg a magazine or website) or a competition. It must describe a clear and logical series of events, and it requires you to use your imagination.
- **an article**: this is written for a publication (eg a magazine) and should be as interesting and entertaining as possible. It must include your opinions and it requires you to make points effectively.

Your answer will be marked according to the categories listed in Test 2 (see page 45).

TIPS

Report
- Make sure that you divide the report into sections. If possible, use headings for each section.
- The report should begin with a short introduction giving the background to it (the reason why it is being written) and end with a conclusion/recommendation.

Story
- Plan your story carefully so that it makes sense! It must be clear to the reader what happened and what the order of events was. Be careful to use the correct verb tenses.
- Try to think of good and appropriate vocabulary for the story to describe people and events. The story gives you a chance to use vocabulary you have learnt that is not very simple.

Article
- Try to make the article as interesting as possible for the reader by using a lively style, for example to express strong feelings or opinions.
- Make sure that your article makes sense as a whole and your ideas are linked logically.

SAMPLE ANSWERS

Read the sample answers carefully and answer these questions for each one. Then check the assessment of each sample answer on pages 150 and 151.

- **Content**: does the answer include everything that should be included or make sense as a story?
- **Organization and cohesion**: is the answer organized in a clear and logical way, with appropriate sections and linking?
- **Range**: is there a range of appropriate structures and vocabulary?
- **Accuracy**: are there any mistakes?
- **Appropriacy of register and format**: is the answer appropriately informal or formal, and is the format suitable?
- **Target reader**: will the reader be completely clear about:
  - the purpose of the report and understand fully everything it contains?
  - what happens in the story?
  - what the writer describes in the article and fully understand the writer's feelings and opinions?

The following exercises will help you to write answers for Questions 2, 3 and 4 in this part of the test. When you have completed all of the exercises for each question, write your answer for that question.

QUESTION 2 REPORT
GETTING IDEAS AND PLANNING YOUR ANSWER

1   Which of the following **must** you include in your report?

   A a reference to the class discussion   **C** opinions on more than one place

   B a description of past trips   **D** the disadvantages of going to certain places

E   reasons for visiting certain places   G   a request for more information
F   advice on planning the trip   H   ideas for more than one trip

Now check your answers to this exercise.

2   Look at this list of words and phrases, which **could** all be used in your report. If there are any that
     you don't know, look them up in a dictionary. You do not have to use all of them in your report but
     try to use some of them.

discussed	enjoyable	recommend	in connection with
possibilities	appeal to	advantage	in addition
suitable	interested in	journey	is supposed to be
costly	fun	in groups	exciting
educational	option	schedule	probably

SAMPLE ANSWER

```
Purpose:
The aim of this report is to summarize the opinions of students on the
destination of a day trip. We have discussed about this from many angles.
Firstly, it has to be fun. Secondly, it should contain educational elements.
Thirdly, it will not be costly. Bearing these aspects in mind, Windsor area
seems an ideal place for a day out.
Windsor Castle:
We are planning to visit this historical as well as the current Royal Family's
residential castle to look into the English history.
Windsor Great Park:
This park is said to have great charm with its leafy tranquillity and
picturesquely scattered gardens, cottages, farms and a fetching lake, according
to Notes from a Small Island by Bill Bryson. We are having a picnic lunch at
Chiltern Hill with great views.
Windsor Safari Park:
After a long walk and a lunch, it will be fun and relaxing to drive through
half-wild animals.
Transport:
Hiring a minibus is the most cost-effective and the easiest option to visit all
the places.
Conclusion:
This course seems ideal for a day out with full activities.
```

Now write your answer to the question in the test.

QUESTION 3 STORY

GETTING IDEAS AND PLANNING YOUR ANSWER

1   Here are some things that your story **might** include. Decide which ones you are going to include.
     • what happened before the letter arrived   • how Carla felt as she read the letter
     • why Carla was excited about the letter   • what Carla did after reading the letter
     • Carla's feelings as she opened the letter   • what Carla said to someone else about the letter
     • what the letter contained   • what happened as a result of the letter

2   Here are some adjectives describing happy and unhappy feelings, which you **might** include in
     your story. Which adjectives describe happy feelings and which ones describe unhappy feelings?

pleased	miserable	enthusiastic	tearful	glad	awful
devastated	shocked	disappointed	concerned	disturbed	relieved
upset	delighted	dreadful	satisfied	thrilled	depressed
fed up	sad				

SAMPLE ANSWER

Carla was very excited as she opened the letter. After all, she had been waiting for it for weeks, and all this time she could not think of anything else.

Her hands were shaking, her palms were sweating. Carla closed her eyes while she slowly took the letter out of the envelope and held it very close to her. What went through her mind at that moment was how this white piece of paper could change her life completely. She really wanted this change to happen and she thought that there was nothing else on this world which would make her happier.

She finally opened her eyes and started to read the letter. Tears were rolling down her cheeks. When she had finished, she put the letter down on the table and jumped out of joy. She said to her mum, who was right next to her, excitedly: 'I got the job and I am moving to New Zealand!'

Now write your answer to the question in the test.

QUESTION 4 ARTICLE

GETTING IDEAS AND PLANNING YOUR ANSWER

1   Here are some things that your article **might** be about. Decide which of them your article is going to be about. You may choose more than one.

Something that:

- a particular group of people does
- is very common in your country
- a person/people you know does/do
- happens in the place where you study or work

- happens in another part of the world
- affects you personally
- has started happening recently
- you have read about or seen in the media

2   Look at this list of words and phrases, which are all connected with being angry and which **could** all be used in your article. If there are any that you don't know, look them up in a dictionary. You do not have to use all of them in your article but try to use some of them.

makes me furious/very cross	drives me mad	I can't bear
I can't stand	gets on my nerves	I'm sick/tired of
irritates me	lose my temper	in a bad mood
is annoying		

SAMPLE ANSWER

What annoys me the most is that our next door neighbour always puts large pieces of unwanted household items such as a toilet seat, a flush tank, tables and chairs in our front courtyard. I find this behaviour selfish, unacceptable and upsetting.

My neighbour has a big front garden of which she keeps clean and tidy. Instead of leaving any useless stuff in her own garden, she puts them in ours! Only because ours is in such a state, muddy patches of worn-out lawn, it does not mean she has the right to leave her rubbish there, making the place look unsightly. The worst of all, she simply expects someone to come along and collect them. Rubbish like that will not be picked up by the local council. In addition, they could be left there for a long time before they are finally removed.

Selfish people really irritate me. Thoughtless people like her simply show no respect to others, and make other people's life a misery.

PAPER 3 USE OF ENGLISH 45 minutes

Part 1

For questions **1–12**, read the text below and decide which answer (**A**, **B**, **C** or **D**) best fits each gap. There is an example at the beginning (**0**).

Mark your answers **on the separate answer sheet**.

Example:

0   **A** people   **B** creatures   **C** individuals   **D** beings

0	A	B	C	D
	▢	▢	▢	▬

It's cool to camp

For many of us, life is full of man-made sounds: traffic, machinery, television and other human

(**0**) .... It is not surprising (**1**) .... that camping continues to (**2**) .... in

popularity, as it teaches us to take our focus off these distractions and (**3**) .... to enrich our lives.

According to a recent report, one holiday (**4**) .... eight in Europe is a camping holiday. Despite

that, some would still have you believe that camping should be considered an alternative holiday

that you are driven towards because money is (**5**) .... Nonsense. It is a lifestyle choice

to be embraced and enjoyed, for it (**6**) .... us the freedom to explore in our own time and

(**7**) .... our own speed.

The opportunities available for (**8**) .... camping with some form of recreational activity are as

varied as Europe's many thousands of miles of hiking trails, cycling routes, canals, rivers and lakes.

Whether your chosen form of activity is recreational or competitive, a sociable hobby or a way of

(**9**) .... the crowds, there can be nothing more pleasurable than sitting outside your tent after a

day of activity with only the hum of dragonflies and the gas stove (**10**) .... the peace.

And just remember: whatever form of camping you choose, (**11**) .... you are out there enjoying

yourself and the surroundings, the (**12**) .... of the world can wait.

1   **A** therefore   **B** nevertheless   **C** so   **D** though

2   **A** enlarge   **B** grow   **C** raise   **D** stretch

3   **A** contributes   **B** gives   **C** supplies   **D** helps

4   **A** from   **B** on   **C** for   **D** in

5   **A** hard   **B** rare   **C** tight   **D** slim

6   **A** lets   **B** opens   **C** allows   **D** enables

7   **A** of   **B** at   **C** by   **D** to

8   **A** mixing   **B** attaching   **C** adding   **D** uniting

9   **A** escaping   **B** separating   **C** clearing   **D** departing

10 **A** stopping   **B** annoying   **C** disturbing   **D** breaking

11 **A** in case   **B** as long as   **C** even if   **D** whereas

12 **A** outside   **B** rest   **C** other   **D** remains

Part 2

For questions **13–24**, read the text below and think of the word which best fits each gap. Use only **one** word in each gap. There is an example at the beginning (**0**).

Write your answers **IN CAPITAL LETTERS on the separate answer sheet**.

Example: 0   FOR

Puzzles can increase intelligence

Brain training puzzles really can boost intelligence, a study shows (**0**) ……..…… the first time.

While previous studies have suggested that number puzzles can improve memory and crosswords

can expand vocabulary, scientists (**13**) ……..…… now proved that mental exercise really does

(**14**) ……………. us more quick-witted. A Swiss-American team reports in a leading scientific journal

how computer-based mental exercises were used (**15**) ……..…… improve overall problem-solving

ability.

(**16**) …………..… team gave 35 volunteers a series of mental exercises designed to improve their memory.

A control group of 35 subjects did not take these tests. Members of the first group were shown a

different type (**17**) ……………. square every three seconds and asked if a certain square matched

(**18**) …………..… shown earlier. Participants also heard a series of spoken letters and had to decide

(**19**) ……………. each was the same as one presented two or three steps earlier in the sequence. If they

did well, the task became harder and if they did badly, (**20**) ……..…… became easier. They repeated

the exercises for between eight (**21**) ……..…… nineteen days. Their problem-solving ability was then

compared with the group who (**22**) ……………. not done the exercises.

The results of the studies, published in *The Proceedings of the National Academy of Sciences*, showed

that the group who took part (**23**) ……………. the brain training exercises had a significantly better

problem-solving ability than the other group. Moreover, the more the participants trained, the more

problems (**24**) ……..……. could solve.

Part 3

Read the text and look at the test questions. Before you answer the test questions, go on to the Further Practice and Guidance page which follows.

For questions **25–34**, read the text below. Use the word given in capitals at the end of some of the lines to form a word that fits in the gap **in the same line**. There is an example at the beginning (**0**).

Write your answers **IN CAPITAL LETTERS on the separate answer sheet**.

Example: **0**   ACCORDING

The backache generation

Young people are suffering ten times more back pain than their parents

did at the same age, (**0**) .... to a survey. It found that they are   **ACCORD**

suffering from long hours spent hunched over PCs and computer games.

Creaking knees and stooped shoulders are also affecting teenagers and

young people, not just the (**25**) .... Figures from the survey show   **ELDER**

that (**26**) .... knees are afflicting 63 per cent of under-18s, in   **PAIN**

(**27**) .... with only three per cent of 55-year-olds who had knee   **COMPARE**

problems in their (**28**) .... The survey blames lack of exercise,   **YOUNG**

(**29**) .... lifestyles and longer working hours.   **ACT**

Lack of opportunity to get off the (**30**) .... and walk on a natural   **PAVE**

landscape is also responsible for problems like backache, ankle

(**31**) .... and joint pain, it says. More than eight out of ten of those   **INJURE**

surveyed only ever walk on concrete. Joshua Wies, a physiotherapist

said: 'It is very (**32**) .... that under-18s are experiencing problems   **WORRY**

that are usually associated with the pensioners. Are we going to start

seeing teenagers having (**33**) .... for hip problems, something that   **TREAT**

was completely (**34**) .... just a decade ago?'   **KNOW**

WHAT'S TESTED

The questions in Part 3 of the Use of English Paper test you mainly on vocabulary. You are required to form a range of kinds of word from the words given – in any gap you may be required to form **an adjective**, **a noun**, **a verb** or **an adverb**. Some questions require you to use **prefixes** and many questions require you to use **suffixes**.

Sometimes, a question may require another kind of change to the word given – an **internal change** (not adding a prefix or suffix to make a longer word, but changing the form of the word, for example changing the verb 'speak' to the noun 'speech'), or forming a **compound** (a word formed by putting together two or more separate words, for example, changing the noun 'class' to the compound noun 'classroom').

TIPS

- Begin by reading through the whole text to find out what it is about and what it contains. This will help you to know the context for filling each gap.

- When you form each word, decide first of all what kind of word it must be (an adjective, a noun, a verb or an adverb). Look carefully at what comes both before and after each gap so that you can decide what kind of word is required.

- Then decide what the required word must mean. For example, if it is an adjective, is it a negative adjective requiring a prefix? If it is a noun, should it be plural?

- When you have filled a gap, read the sentence that contains it again – make sure that it makes sense and is grammatically correct with the word you have put into the gap.

The following exercises will help you to write the correct answer to each question in the test. When you have completed each exercise, check your answers and then write your answer for the question in the test.

1   For each question, decide what kind of word (A–I) you need to put into each gap. Some of the choices are required more than once, and some of the choices are not required at all.

Question 25 ....   **Question 26** ....   **Question 27** ....   **Question 28** ....

Question 29 ....   **Question 30** ....   **Question 31** ....   **Question 32** ....

Question 33 ....   **Question 34** ....

A   plural noun with suffix   F   verb with prefix
B   adverb with suffix   G   adjective with suffix
C   adjective with prefix   H   adjective used as noun
D   singular/uncountable noun with suffix   I   noun with internal change
E   adjective with prefix and suffix

2   Now look at this table of prefixes and suffixes and decide which ones are required in the words you have to form. Some of the choices here are not required in any answer; some may be required more than once.

PREFIXES	SUFFIXES/ENDINGS					
un-	-ful	-ly	-ence	-ive	-able	-ians
dis-	-ists	-dom	-ily	-ed	-ous	-ers
in-	-itive	-ing	-al	-ison	-ity	-n
mis-	-ment	-ation	-ies	-th		

Now check your answers to the questions in the test.

Part 4

For questions **35–42**, complete the second sentence so that it has a similar meaning to the first sentence, using the word given. **Do not change the word given**. You must use between **two** and **five** words, including the word given. Here is an example (**0**).

Example: 0   It took me a fairly long time to answer all my emails.

> **QUITE**
>
> I spent ………………………………………………… all my emails.

The gap can be filled with the words 'quite a long time answering', so you write:

Example: 0   QUITE A LONG TIME ANSWERING

Write only the missing words **IN CAPITAL LETTERS on the separate answer sheet**.

---

35 We really enjoyed visiting London.

> **GREAT**
>
> Our ……………………………………………… fun.

36 My department at work consists of six people, including me.

> **US**
>
> In my department at work…………………………………..………… , including me.

37 Whose idea was it to organize a party for her?

> **CAME**
>
> Who ………………………………………….. of organizing a party for her?

38 She's never had a job in management before now.

> **EVER**
>
> This is the first ………………………………………… a job in management.

39 Despite knowing the correct answer, he didn't say anything.

> **ALTHOUGH**
>
> He didn't say anything, …………………………………… the correct answer was.

40 'I don't think you should give up the course,' she said to him.

> **NOT**
>
> She advised ………………………………………….. the course.

41 It's not a problem for me to change our arrangement.

> **MIND**
>
> I …………………………………………… our arrangement.

42 This hotel is cheaper than the others in the brochure.

> **COMPARED**
>
> This hotel is cheap ……………………………… ones in the brochure.

PAPER 4 LISTENING approximately 40 minutes

Part 1

You will hear people talking in eight different situations. For questions **1–8**, choose the best answer
(**A**, **B** or **C**).

1   You hear someone talking about a festival. What does she say about the festival?

   A   Some bands were better than others.

   B   The crowd was happy all the time.

   C   The weather spoiled it.

2   You hear two people talking about a teacher on a course they are taking. What is the man's opinion
   of the teacher?

   A   She is too strict.

   B   She may be rather nervous.

   C   She is well organized.

3   You overhear someone talking on the phone. Who is she talking to?

   A   a manager

   B   a friend

   C   an assistant

4   You hear two people talking about having a lot of money. What is the man's attitude to having a lot
   of money?

   A   He thinks it would have a big effect on him.

   B   He thinks it is unlikely to happen.

   C   He thinks he would waste the money.

5   You hear a woman talking about her education. What does she say about her education?

   A   Teachers did not encourage her.

   B   Her friends also did poorly at school.

   C   She regrets her attitude in the past.

6   You hear someone talking to a colleague about a problem at work. What is the speaker's purpose?

   A   to make her position clear

   B   to get advice

   C   to suggest a solution

7   You hear someone on the radio talking about modern life. What is the speaker's main topic?

   A   research methods

   B   social developments

   C   the benefits of technology

8   You overhear two people talking about a restaurant. What does the man say about the restaurant?

   A   It isn't particularly expensive.

   B   The food was better than he had expected.

   C   He had difficulty getting a table.

Part 2

You will hear a talk about someone called Grace Darling. For questions **9–18**, complete the sentences.

GRACE DARLING

Grace's father worked as a lighthouse [| **9**] on Longstone island.

Grace and her brothers and sisters checked the [| **10**] and made sure they were always full.

The island was surrounded by dangerous [*and* | **11**].

One night, a ship's engines stopped because of a problem with its [| **12**].

Some people got away by using a [| **13**].

In the morning, Grace and her father didn't see the other people because it was [| **14**].

Grace and her father used a little [| **15**] to go to the people.

Grace and her father brought [| **16**] back to the land.

Grace became famous and several artists painted [| **17**].

Some people wanted pieces of [| **18**].

Part 3

Before you listen to the CD, read the test questions and go on to the Further Practice and Guidance page which follows.

You will hear five different people speaking on the phone. For questions **19–23**, choose from the list (**A–F**) what each speaker's purpose is. Use the letters only once. There is one extra letter which you do not need to use.

A   to change some information

                                                Speaker 1   **19**

B   to confirm an arrangement

                                                Speaker 2   **20**

C   to report a problem

                                                Speaker 3   **21**

D   to make a complaint

                                                Speaker 4   **22**

E   to check some details

                                                Speaker 5   **23**

F   to request advice

WHAT'S TESTED

The questions in Part 3 of the Listening Paper test you on your ability to understand what speakers say in five short recordings that are connected in some way, and to match each speaker with the correct choice. The set of questions may focus on any of the things listed for Part 1 of the Listening Paper: **detail**, **opinion/attitude**, **feeling**, **function**, **purpose**, **general gist**, **topic**, etc (see page 27).

TIPS

- Use the time given to read the questions very carefully before you listen to the recordings. This will show you what the focus of the set of questions is and therefore what you need to identify when you listen to each speaker.

- Don't choose an option simply because it contains a word or words that a speaker uses – this option may not be the correct answer.

- Speakers will say things that are connected with more than one of the options – you must decide which option exactly matches what a particular speaker says.

- Don't choose your answers too quickly when listening for the first time. You may discover that an answer you have chosen for one speaker really matches with another speaker and you may then become confused. Use the second listening to make your final decisions on your answers.

The following exercises will help you to choose the correct answer to each question in the test. When you have completed each exercise, check your answer(s) and then choose your answer for the question in the test.

Question 19

Listen to Speaker 1 twice.

1 Has the speaker already made an arrangement?

2 Has the speaker already been told the cost?

3 Does the speaker know how and when to pay?

4 Has the company done something wrong?

Question 20

Listen to Speaker 2 twice.

1 Is the speaker talking about incorrect information?

2 Is the speaker talking about the content of the course?

3 Has the speaker decided not to do the course?

4 Is the speaker angry about something that has happened?

Question 21

Listen to Speaker 3 twice.

1 Does the speaker want to replace something?

2 Is the speaker having a problem?

3 Is the speaker annoyed with the company?

4 Is the speaker asking for help?

Question 22

Listen to Speaker 4 twice.

1 Has the speaker already agreed to do something?

2 Is the speaker thinking of doing something?

3 Is the speaker unable to understand some information?

4 Does the speaker need help?

Question 23

Listen to Speaker 5 twice.

1 Has the speaker failed to make contact previously?

2 Does the speaker want to discuss something that has previously been discussed?

3 Is the speaker asking for immediate action?

4 Is the speaker asking what to do?

Now check your answers to the questions in the test.

Part 4

You will hear an interview with someone who trains whales for public performances. For questions **24–30**, choose the best answer (**A**, **B** or **C**).

24 When Laura first swam with a whale,

    A she immediately changed her opinion of whales.

    B the experience was different from what she had expected.

    C she thought about what was happening to her.

25 Laura says that being in the water with whales is a 'miracle' because

    A the whales show that they each have different personalities.

    B other animals do not behave in the same way as whales.

    C the whales make a conscious decision to be friendly.

26 Laura says that when you approach a whale,

    A you should think of it as someone you don't know well.

    B it may suddenly change its attitude towards you.

    C you should not expect it to understand what you are saying.

27 Laura says that 'secondary reinforcers' are used

    A if a whale has not understood an instruction.

    B after a particular action has been completed.

    C to tell a whale to repeat an action.

28 What does Laura say about giving the whales food?

    A It has less effect on them than physical contact.

    B It works best when it is combined with a game.

    C The whales often wonder when this will happen.

29 Laura says that a successful relationship between a whale and a trainer

    A is based on genuine affection between the two.

    B requires strong discipline from the trainer.

    C can take a very long time to develop.

30 When asked about the skills a trainer needs, Laura mentions

    A losing confidence when something goes wrong.

    B reacting to the frightening appearance of a whale.

    C forgetting what to say to the spectators.

PAPER 5 SPEAKING 14 minutes

Part 1 (3 minutes)

Jobs and careers

- What kind of job would you like to have in the future?
- How easy/difficult will it be for you to get that job? (Why?)
- What kind of jobs and careers do young people in your country want to have?
- Which job(s) would you really not want to do? (Why?)
- Which jobs do you think are particularly easy to do and which are very difficult? (Why?)

Fashion

- Do you like to wear fashionable clothes? (Why?/Why not?)
- What are the current fashions in clothes in your country?
- What kind of music is fashionable among young people in your country?
- Do you think that young people pay too much attention to fashions in general? (Why?/Why not?)
- Which fashion(s) do you think is/are particularly bad for young people? (Why?)

Part 2 (4 minutes)

1 Waiting

Candidate A: Look at photographs 1A and 1B on page 125. They show **people waiting in different situations.**

Compare the photographs and say **how the people might be feeling**.

Candidate A talks on his/her own for about 1 minute.

Candidate B: How would you feel in these situations?

Candidate B talks on his/her own for about 20 seconds.

2 TV shows

Candidate B: Look at photographs 2A and 2B on page 125. They show **people appearing in different kinds of TV programme.**

Compare the photographs and say **what you think people enjoy about watching these kinds of TV programmes.**

Candidate B talks on his/her own for about 1 minute.

Candidate A: Which kind of programme do you prefer to watch?

Candidate A talks on his/her own for about 20 seconds.

Parts 3 and 4 (7 minutes) Helping at an event

Before you do these tasks, go on to the Further Practice and Guidance Pages which follow.

Part 3

Imagine that your school, college or workplace is organizing an Open Day, when visitors will come to see and find out about the place. People have been asked to help with various aspects of the event. Look at the pictures of things connected with the event on page 126.

First, talk to each other about **what each aspect of the event will involve**. Then decide **which one you will offer to help with.**

Candidates A and B discuss this together for about 3 minutes.

Part 4

- Would you enjoy helping at an event like this? (Why?/Why not?)

- Have you ever organized or helped to organize an event? (Which? How?)

- What kinds of events are organized at the place where you study or work?

- Is it common for people to organize events for charities in your country? (What events? Which charities?)

- Do many people in your country do voluntary work to help others? (Why?/Why not? What kinds?)

- Some people say that governments and not voluntary organizations should provide money for everyone who needs it. What do you think?

WHAT'S TESTED

In Parts 3 and 4 of the Speaking Paper, you have a discussion with the other candidate, as follows:

- In Part 3, you are both shown a set of visuals and you are given both spoken and written instructions for the task that you have to do. You are required to **discuss together all of the pictures** and to **make a decision** connected with them. This discussion lasts for **3 minutes**.

- In Part 4, you discuss together **various topics connected with the topic of Part 3**. The interlocutor asks these questions. This discussion lasts for **4 minutes**.

TIPS

- When you look at the set of visuals for Part 3, also look carefully at the questions that appear above them. These questions will also be asked by the interlocutor. When you **discuss the pictures** with the other candidate, you must focus on these questions.
- Think of appropriate **vocabulary** to talk about each of the visuals and to discuss the topic and related topics.
- Remember that you must discuss all of the pictures in Part 3, so make sure that you don't spend too long talking about one or two of them and fail to talk about the others at all. And don't try to agree on a decision until you have discussed all the visuals.
- Discuss your decision, but don't worry if the two of you cannot agree on one. And remember, there is no 'correct answer'.
- In Part 3, you will need to use appropriate and correct language for **making suggestions** and **asking for opinions and suggestions**. Try not to repeat the same phrases all the time when you are doing these things, try to do them using as many different structures and phrases as you can. For example, don't use 'should' all the time when making suggestions, use other structures and phrases too.
- In both Parts 3 and 4, you will need to use appropriate and correct language for **agreeing and disagreeing** and for **giving reasons**. Again, try to use a variety of words and phrases when doing these things, don't repeat the same words and phrases all the time.
- In both Parts 3 and 4, try to make a full contribution to the discussion. Don't simply make short statements or say 'yes' or 'no' after the other candidate speaks or when you are asked a question. Make suggestions, express opinions and give reasons in more than simple language.

The following exercises will help you to do the tasks in these parts of the test. When you have completed all of the exercises, do the tasks in the test.

Discussing the visuals

Which of these words relate to each of the seven pictures? Write the number of the picture next to each word. A word might relate to more than one of the pictures.

tidy up   .....   refreshments .....   publicity .....   promote   .....   take round .....

tour (noun) .....   display   .....   leaflet   .....   change (noun)/coins .....

stall (noun) .....   guide (noun) .....   clear up   .....   sign (noun)   .....   print (verb) .....

bin (noun)   .....   spaces   .....   hand out .....   direct (verb) .....

Making suggestions

Complete the rewritten suggestions using no more than two words.

1   I think we should offer to do that.

    I suggest .... to do that.

2   I think we should choose that one.

    Why don't .... that one?

3   I think we should discuss one of the other possibilities.

    Let's .... one of the other possibilities.

4   We shouldn't do that one, it will be very hard work.

We'd better .... that one, it will be very hard work.

5   I think we should look at one of the other choices.

It would be a good idea .... at one of the other choices.

6   I don't think we should choose that one.

I don't think we ought .... that one.

Asking for opinions and suggestions

Complete these questions by putting one word into each gap.

1   ....'s your opinion on this one?

2   Does this one seem .... a good idea to you?

3   .... about this one? What do you think it would involve?

4   .... me what you think about this one.

5   Can you think .... a reason for choosing this one? I can't.

6   Do you .... an opinion on this one?

Agreeing and disagreeing

Choose the correct word or phrase to complete each of these sentences.

1   I think *you're/you've* right about that.

2   Are we *agree/agreed* that we're not going to choose that one?

3   I'm in favour *for/of* helping with this one.

4   You think this one isn't a good idea and I think *same thing/the same*.

5   I'm *against/opposed* the idea of doing that.

6   OK, are we *with/in* agreement about what we're going to do?

Topic vocabulary

Complete these sentences connected to each of the questions in Part 4 by putting in the correct prepositions.

1   I think it might be fun to take part .... that kind of event.

2   I wouldn't be capable .... organizing an event on my own.

3   The college sometimes puts .... special events, such as concerts and dances.

4   Big events to raise money for charities happen .... time to time in my country.

5   Lots of people don't care .... other people's problems.

6   I think the government is responsible .... helping people in that situation.

Giving reasons

Complete each of these sentences connected to the questions in Part 4, using a linking word or phrase from the list below.

so that	because	why	to	for	because of

1   I wouldn't want to help at that event .... it would be boring.

2   My reason .... helping with that event was that some friends organized it.

3   I usually go to those events .... meet new people.

4   It's a charity that raises money .... people can have better water supplies.

5   The reason .... young people do voluntary work is that they want to help others.

6   People want to help .... things they read in the papers or see on TV.

Now do the Parts 3 and 4 tasks in the test.

FCE TEST 4

PAPER 1 READING 1 hour

Part 1

You are going to read an article about a family holiday. For questions **1–8**, choose the answer (**A**, **B**, **C** or **D**) which you think fits best according to the text.

Mark your answers **on the separate answer sheet**.

The cycling holiday that went wrong

Picture the scene: it is twilight and my wife, my eight-year-old son and I are pushing our bicycles up a busy country road in Austria, when three supercharged motorbikes whip by like bats out of hell. Ahead, there's an oncoming juggernaut so, without dropping below 50kph, the motorbikes swerve within inches of us, leaving us frozen with fear. The roaring horn of another giant lorry charging up behind us sends us into the ditch. Except that there isn't a ditch, just a dense forest, so we hold our breath at the edge of the tarmac as the monster machine rattles past. My wife and son burst into tears and I feel vulnerable – and very angry. Welcome to the first day of the Morris family cycling holiday.

It wasn't meant to be like this. The idea had been to introduce my loved ones gently to the joys of exploring a country on two wheels, but after just 11 hours it was doubtful they would ever get back on a bike again. Before this, my son, Ben, hadn't cycled much further than to his local school; my wife had given up pedal power after a nasty encounter with a van when she was a student. To win them over, I had to make sure our first family trip would be as stress-free, safe and pleasure-packed as possible.

I began my research by excluding any tours that included hills, heavy luggage and – most important of all – terrifying traffic. I came across a specialist travel company which suggested the River Danube Cycle Way in northern Austria as the best route for beginners. Ninety per cent of the journey would be on dedicated cycle paths – flattish and car-free. Better still, the seven-night package included cycle hire, maps, decent hotels, luggage transfers and a back-up team, all at a reasonable price. It sounded perfect for cycle-tour newcomers.

The first day's ride was not only terrifying, but also too long for beginners: 26½ miles not 19, as advised. As a result, we missed the last bike ferry across to our hotel for the night and were then redirected by our route map on to a busy road where we encountered the juggernauts. Grim first impressions are difficult to wipe out.

As for the problems of the rest of the trip, I mostly blame myself. I hadn't taken on board that a week's cycling does involve a lot of cycling. I remember reading the itinerary and thinking that 165 miles in seven days did seem a bit ambitious, but not impossible. In isolation, a full day's cycling of about 22 miles was fine, it was the cumulative effect of several days on the bike that was the problem. So for my poor wife, tired legs, sore hands and the discomfort of being on a saddle for so long turned a potentially relaxing holiday into more of an endurance challenge.

My own difficulty lay with the luggage. The prospect of having our bags transported for us had seemed luxurious, but it soon became a daily chore. By 8.30am, our luggage had to be ready for collection, no mean feat for a family with a totally disorganized approach to packing. With our belongings on their way to the next hotel, we were tied into covering a certain distance just to catch up with a clean pair of underpants. The rigid schedule is, of course, essential for the safe transportation of hundreds of pieces of luggage. It just didn't fit in with the spontaneity and freedom I normally associate with cycling. Similarly, dragging my son away from the many excellent playgrounds and outdoor swimming pools along the route in order to keep up didn't feel nice.

Admittedly, the journey wasn't all traffic terror and damaged bottoms. The steep-sided Danube Ring was stunning, and whizzing through the cornfields as high as a cyclist's eye around Feldkirchen was well worth the detour. But the real discovery of the holiday was the Wachau district. Winding between medieval towns, the Wachau Valley is stuffed full of fairy-tale castles, monasteries, abbeys and rolling vineyards. It's a rich landscape that is best savoured from the saddle of a bicycle. But if we – or maybe that should be I – were to do the trip again, there are several things I would change. For a start, I would limit the packing. We would have been far more relaxed if we had carried our own bags.

1   In the first paragraph, the writer describes

    A   something that happened while they were riding their bicycles.

    B   nearly being hit by more than one vehicle.

    C   a mistake they made while they were on a busy road.

    D   getting lost while making a journey.

2   The writer says in the second paragraph that the experience on the country road

    A   was the same as something that had happened to his wife.

    B   made him think that the cycling holiday might not continue.

    C   was something that he had feared might happen.

    D   was something that he could have prevented from happening.

3   What does the writer emphasize in the third paragraph?

    A   how much research he did before choosing a holiday

    B   how suitable the holiday he chose seemed

    C   how much advice he got before booking the holiday

    D   how hard it was to find a suitable holiday

4   What does the writer say about the first day's ride?

    A   It took them longer than necessary to cover the distance.

    B   They read their map incorrectly during it.

    C   It affected their attitude to the whole holiday.

    D   They had not noticed what the scheduled distance was.

5   What does the writer say about the other problems they had on the trip?

    A   His wife had warned him that they were likely to happen.

    B   After a while they weren't quite so bad.

    C   He had expected the amount of cycling to be a serious problem.

    D   He should have expected them to happen.

6   What does the writer mean by 'no mean feat' in line 31?

    A   something that didn't happen

    B   a big achievement

    C   something impossible

    D   a waste of time

7   What does the writer say about the rigid schedule?

    A   He felt that it was inappropriate for cycling.

    B   His son often complained about it.

    C   He could not see the need for it.

    D   They did not always manage to stick to it.

8   The writer mentions the Wachau district as an example of

    A   a place they intend to return to one day.

    B   an experience that was better than he had expected.

    C   one of the positive experiences of the holiday.

    D   somewhere that attracts a lot of cyclists.

Part 2

You are going to read an article about a course for people whose jobs involve talking to customers on the telephone. Seven sentences have been removed from the article. Choose from the sentences **A–H** the one which fits each gap (**9–15**). There is one extra sentence which you do not need to use.

Mark your answers **on the separate answer sheet**.

Taking tele-sales to a new level

A telephone skills course offers employees a professional qualification, writes Andrew Cave

The students wore gowns and mortar boards and received their qualifications at an official presentation. But the 10 graduates who picked up their certificates in Cheltenham were no usual students. **9** .... The members of this class were all call centre and branch employees who had studied one day a month in formal, work-based training, reinforcing this with regular measurement and assessment in their daily jobs. They became Britain's first graduates in advanced telephone skills, courtesy of a level-five diploma in sales.

The course is run by Simon Bell, who has 20 years of experience in sales and training, and says he has created a course that focuses on 'enjoyable, manageable and sustainable selling'. **10** .... The graduation ceremony marked the end of the first pilot scheme by Chelsea Building Society. Mark Higgins, the building society's head of people development, said the training had an 'astounding' and 'outstanding' effect on the company's best salespeople.

The course combines 30 hours of tutorial with 350 hours of desk-based, practical learning. **11** .... The remainder of the course takes place at work, monitored by a process that takes up to 15 minutes at the end of each day and requires people on the course to record their day's call experiences.

Mr Higgins did not disclose the actual increase in sales performances achieved by the course's graduates but said they were encouraging enough for the company to want to roll out the scheme across its 300-strong workforce, call centre of 120 staff and 33 branches. **12** .... The rest did so and felt that they learnt a lot.

These graduates from the pilot course said it had taught them a new approach. Chris Howell, a telephone sales agent, said, 'What the course has taught us is that what we've been doing is just one way of doing things. It has shown us that we can do it a lot better, a lot more easily and gain a lot more success from it.' One thing in particular that he said he had learned is how to compliment people over the phone. 'People appreciate it,' he said. '**13** ....'

Neil Gurney, a sales manager, added, 'I thought I was very successful on the telephone in presenting information and selling to our customers. **14** .... I didn't know about this failing on my part until I took the course. I realized that what I hadn't been doing was asking our customers what their thoughts and feelings were in relation to the facts that I was presenting. Now I really engage with them, getting their feedback so that I can best meet the needs of the customer.'

Gethin Evans, the company's training manager, said, 'This training deals with something that on the surface is very straightforward – making telephone calls and engaging customers in conversation. What could be simpler? **15** .... From my perspective, the depth of academic study that we've covered is unbelievable. I had no idea there would be so much information that enriches a telephone conversation. Our customers are responding and the impact that it's having on them is probably as profound as it is on the people taking the course.'

A   The idea is that this results from developing a good relationship with customers.

B   But in fact there's an awful lot more to it than meets the eye.

C   It's easy and you get great results from it.

D   Only one of the original 11 people on the course failed to complete it.

E   Instead of carrying out a three-year degree course, they had toiled for just five months.

F   For this reason, there is a need for professional qualifications.

G   Each module includes a day of formal training.

H   However, there was something missing.

Part 3

You are going to read a magazine article about learning how to play the drums. For questions **16–30**, choose from the sections of the article (**A–E**). The sections may be chosen more than once.

Mark your answers **on the separate answer sheet**.

___

In which section of the article are the following mentioned?

the writer's children being shocked by her behaviour | 16 |

what the drumming teacher did previously | 17 |

a statistic concerning the amount of energy used in drumming | 18 |

a belief that drumming can be satisfying for almost everybody | 19 |

the fact that the writer's family learnt something quite quickly | 20 |

a desire to attract certain kinds of children to drumming | 21 |

a theory concerning how drumming makes people feel better | 22 |

when the writer realized how enjoyable drumming is | 23 |

a comparison illustrating how complicated drumming is | 24 |

a reason why learning how to drum involves another subject | 25 |

a feeling that children should not be the only ones to enjoy playing music | 26 |

the attitudes of children in general towards drumming | 27 |

people who are not keen to take up drumming | 28 |

a reason why drumming does not have to disturb other people | 29 |

something that the writer's children were not happy to hear | 30 |

The joys of drumming

Drumming is a perfect, healthy family activity, says Lucy Atkins

A There can be few things more therapeutic than hitting something for an hour. Rock drumming lessons may not seem an obvious family activity, but an hour with teacher Nigel Ralf turns out to be the best entertainment money can buy – not just for me, but for my children too. The benefits of rock drumming are many. First, there is the simple therapeutic joy of hitting something very hard. Then there are the newly discovered health effects. Researchers recently studied a drummer in a well-known rock band and discovered that he burned off up to 600 calories per hour. His fitness, they found, was similar to that of a professional footballer. The researchers now plan to develop rock-drumming programmes in schools as an ingenious way to get non-sporty, computer-obsessed children to burn off the calories.

B Ralf, of course, is already doing this. 'Drumming is seen as cool,' he says, 'and although you work up a definite sweat, no child thinks of it as exercise.' They are, after all, still sitting down. There are also many psychological benefits – drumming (usually of the tribal rather than the rock type) is used to treat depression and other mental illnesses. The idea is that banging a drum activates the brain's pleasure centres, tackles stress, takes you out of your self-obsessed rut and promotes a sense of community. Best of all, it is enormous fun – for all ages. I first discovered this at the school summer fete, where Ralf put on a drumming competition for the children. Having elbowed my offspring out of the way, I became hooked. My children may have been horrified to see their mother transform into a wild person on a drum kit, but they still agreed to come to a family lesson.

C Our hour-long session begins with maths. Not a good start – I see my children's horrified faces – but, says Ralf, 'in drumming maths is easy.' It is all about recognizing multiples of four so you can go at different speeds. We are using electronic drum sets, which are more compact and, crucially, have volume control (you can even plug in headphones to avoid upsetting the neighbours). Next, Ralf introduces us to the basic 'four-beat rock rhythm'. This involves a surprising degree of mental agility: two hands and a bass-drum foot, each doing something different while your brain keeps a one-two-three-four rhythm. Ralf likens this to rubbing your tummy and patting your head at the same time while introducing yourself to a group. It is a brain-aching exercise in coordination, which, he points out, must have knock-on effects in sport, not to mention boosting the brain's synapses.

D With loud rock music blaring, it is not long before we all get the hang of the beat. I can see the concentration on the faces of Sam, seven, and Isabella, nine. Their faces light up as they realize they are actually doing it right. At the end of the song we are all out of breath and laughing. 'Virtually any child – or adult – can get some sense of achievement from drumming,' says Ralf, who left a job in electronics to teach drumming in primary and secondary schools. 'It's also a great way to get them interested in other musical instruments.' Though he offers private lessons, most pupils come to group tutorials after school or to holiday rock schools.

E It also turns out that I am not the only mother with a yearning for drumsticks. 'I get lots of mad mummies wanting a go,' Ralf says. 'The dads are often more reticent. Perhaps they don't want to look as if they don't know what they're doing.' One of Ralf's weekly rock schools (aimed at children) has now spawned a band of mothers, F:rock. 'We thought 'if they can have fun, why can't we?'' says Annabel Dunstan, 42, the lead guitarist of this six-strong outfit, which meets weekly. They have now played two gigs and are starting to write their own material. 'It has been brilliant learning something new,' she says. All in all, our family rock drumming lesson is a roaring success. We leave relaxed and smiling, energy spent. My children have signed up for Ralf's weekly rock school and I am obsessed.

PAPER 2 WRITING 1 hour 20 minutes

Part 1

You **must** answer this question. Write your answer in **120–150** words in an appropriate style.

1   You have received an email from your English-speaking friend, Judy, who is going to get married. Read Judy's email and the notes you have made. Then write an email to Judy, using **all** your notes.

From:	Judy Graham
Sent:	4th March
Subject:	Wedding

Well, I've got some very exciting news. Harry and I have finally decided to get married. I'm so happy about this!

Congratulations!

We've spent the last couple of weeks getting everything organized. We've fixed the date for the wedding – it's going to be on Saturday 21st September and I'm really hoping you'll be able to come.

Of course!

The wedding's going to be a pretty big event – we're inviting about 100 people and, after the ceremony, the reception will be in a big hotel. It's a lovely place and I'm sure you'll like it.

Present?

If you can come (and I really hope you can!), would you like me to organize accommodation for you? There are lots of good small hotels in the town.

Yes, you choose

Hope to hear from you soon,

Judy

Write your **email**. You must use grammatically correct sentences with accurate spelling and punctuation in a style appropriate for the situation.

Part 2

Write an answer to **one** of the questions **2–5** in this part. Write your answer in **120–180** words in an appropriate style.

2   You recently saw this notice in an English-language magazine.

A FILM THAT MADE YOU THINK

Have you seen a film that really made you think? A film with a serious message that changed your opinion of something? A film that caused you to feel that you had learnt something about life, people, the world? A film that you thought about and discussed after you'd seen it? We'd like a review of that film, to be published in a special reviews section soon.

Write your **review**.

3   You are applying to take a course in an English-speaking country. In addition to filling in the application form, you are required to write a letter to the college principal, explaining why you want to take the particular course you have applied for. You should explain in your letter your reasons for applying for the course and why you feel that you would be a good student on that course.

Write your **letter**.

4   You have seen this notice in an English-language magazine.

MY PERFECT DAY

What would be the perfect day for you? What would happen on that day? What would you do? Why would it be the perfect day for you? We'll publish the best articles.

Write your **article**.

5   **(a)** or **(b).** Two questions on the set books.

There are two set books. There is one question on each set book. You answer **one** of the two questions.

For more about the set book questions, go on to the Further Practice and Guidance pages which follow.

WHAT'S TESTED

For question 5 in Part 2 of the Writing Paper, you can choose to write about one of the two set books that are specified each year in the Exam regulations (available on the Cambridge ESOL website). There is a choice of two questions on the set books and you must write **one** of the following:

- **an article:** this might be for a magazine, for example describing your feelings about the book, discussing important features of the book, saying whether you recommend it to others, etc.

- **an essay:** this might require you, for example, to write about the plot or characters and give details and opinions about various aspects of the book.

- **a letter:** this might be to a friend, describing the book and giving your opinions on it.

- **a report:** this might be for a teacher or for a club, for example giving reasons for recommending the book or discussing what is interesting about the book.

- **a review:** this might be for a magazine, for example giving opinions on the book and saying whether or not you recommend it to other people.

Your answer will be marked according to the same categories as for all questions in the Writing Paper.

TIPS

Writing about a set book may involve any of the following aspects.

The plot

- What happens in the book?
- How does it begin and end?
- How would you summarize the sequence of events?
- What are the most important events?
- What happens to a particular character through the book?

The characters

- How would you describe the main character(s)?
- How would you describe other characters?
- What are the relationships between characters in the book?
- Which characters do you like/dislike most?
- How would you compare different characters in the book?

Feelings

- What feelings do characters in the book have?
- What feelings did you experience when reading the book?

Opinions

- Why would you recommend/not recommend the book to a friend or to a particular group of people (eg learners of English, magazine readers, etc)?
- How would you compare the book with another book or other books?
- What are your opinions on the writer's style?
- How realistic is the book?

NOTE: You can write about a film of the book.

PREPARATION

Practise doing the following, either about the current exam set books or any book you choose.

- Write a brief summary of what happens in the book. Choose only the most important events.

- Describe one important event in the book, giving details of it.

- Describe the main character(s) in the book, using as many appropriate adjectives as you can.

- Describe a character who interested you but is not one of the main characters and say why this character is interesting.

- Describe the relationship between two of the main characters, using appropriate vocabulary.

- Compare two of the characters, using appropriate comparative structures.

- Describe the feelings of the main character(s) during the book, using a variety of adjectives.

- Describe your own reaction when you read the book, using appropriate vocabulary.

- Say whether or not you would recommend the book, and who you would/would not recommend it to, giving reasons and using appropriate structures.

PAPER 3 USE OF ENGLISH 45 minutes

Part 1

For questions **1–12**, read the text below and decide which answer (**A**, **B**, **C** or **D**) best fits each gap. There is an example at the beginning (**0**).

Mark your answers **on the separate answer sheet**.

> **Example:**
>
> 0   **A** possibility   **B** chance   **C** moment   **D** occasion
>
> | 0 | A | B | C | D |
> |---|---|---|---|---|
> | | ☐ | ▬ | ☐ | ☐ |

Setting sail

Many young people dream about sailing on oceans around the world, but few actually get the

(**0**) .... to do it. Last year, the call went out for young people (**1**) .... in joining the

crew of the Gypsy Moth IV (GMIV). The boat had originally been sailed by Sir Francis Chichester

during his record-breaking 1966 voyage round the world.

Amie Mayers had (**2**) .... about the GMIV project at school and was doing work experience

at the United Kingdom Sailing Academy when the call for crew went out. She had enjoyed her week

of work experience and was (**3**) .... about the prospect of doing something she'd never

done before, (**4**) .... she applied to join the crew, and was accepted. Before setting sail, Amie

had to make sure she was (**5**) .... prepared for her time at sea. Her training included sea

survival, health and safety, and (**6**) .... the ins and outs of sailing a yacht. Amie wasn't

scared throughout the journey. Luckily, she always had another crew member to (**7**) .... her

company and was under the watchful eye of the skipper.

Amie says her experience at sea changed her life, and it seems it has because (**8**) .... after

her voyage she was (**9**) .... a scholarship by the UKSA. She is now training to become a

professional watersports instructor. 'I'm very, very (**10**) .... of what I've done,' says Amie. She

now wants others to take any opportunities for challenging experiences that (**11**) .... their

way. 'Grab the opportunity with both hands, because (**12**) .... you're going to regret it,' she says.

1   **A** willing   **B** attracted   **C** eager   **D** interested

2   **A** gathered   **B** heard   **C** grasped   **D** found

3   **A** keen   **B** fond   **C** excited   **D** fascinated

4   **A** that   **B** as   **C** so   **D** then

5   **A** properly   **B** accurately   **C** rightly   **D** precisely

6   **A** in fact   **B** with regard to **C** surely   **D** of course

7   **A** take   **B** keep   **C** provide   **D** mind

8   **A** recently   **B** soon   **C** quickly   **D** little

9   **A** rewarded   **B** assigned   **C** awarded   **D** donated

10 **A** proud   **B** satisfied   **C** delighted   **D** pleased

11 **A** come   **B** fall   **C** appear   **D** get

12 **A** else   **B** unless   **C** without   **D** otherwise

Part 2

For questions **13–24**, read the text below and think of the word which best fits each gap. Use only **one** word in each gap. There is an example at the beginning (**0**).

Write your answers **IN CAPITAL LETTERS on the separate answer sheet**.

Example   0   THEM

Not the only extinct creature

They were all wiped out before science had a chance to discover (**0**) .... , but only the dodo's

name has lived on. However, experts have now (**13**) .... able to reconstruct the appearance

of dozens of long-extinct birds and animals from the same remote tropical isles (**14**) .... the

dodo lived.

The islands of Mauritius, Réunion and Rodrigues in the Indian Ocean were home to hundreds of

unique and rare creatures before humans first set foot (**15**) .... in 1598. In about 150 years,

(**16**) .... least 45 species had been lost forever (**17**) .... a result of hunting and the

introduction of other species. '(**18**) .... happened on these islands is a sad tale,' says Dr Julian

Hume, a paleobiologist who worked on the project.

Now researchers have recreated what the extinct animals and birds would have looked

(**19**) .... from fragments of bone, fossils and descriptions made by travellers at the time.

Following 30 years of research, they have managed to produce detailed pictures of (**20**) .... the

extinct creatures looked and behaved for a new book called *The Lost Land Of The Dodo*. Among the

species that vanished from the islands were 31 birds found (**21**) .... else. Many of them were

flightless, like the dodo. A combination of hunting by people (**22**) .... the arrival of rats, cats

and monkeys, (**23**) .... attacked and robbed the birds' nests, caused many birds that lived on

the ground (**24**) .... become extinct.

Part 3

For questions **25–34**, read the text below. Use the word given in capitals at the end of some of the lines to form a word that fits in the gap **in the same line**. There is an example at the beginning (**0**).

Write your answers **IN CAPITAL LETTERS on the separate answer sheet**.

Example: **0**   TECHNIQUES

Laughter therapy

A laughter therapist is paid to conduct talks, workshops and one-to-one

sessions using (**0**) ……….…….. that get people to laugh. It is thought   **TECHNICAL**

that laughing may (**25**) ……….……. the body's immune system,   **STRONG**

stimulate blood (**26**) …………..……. , produce endorphins (hormones   **CIRCULATE**

that reduce pain and increase (**27**) ………..…….) and reduce stress.   **HAPPY**

One laughter therapist, Enda Junkins, says, 'Laughter is the human gift

for coping and survival.' As a practising psychotherapist, Enda

(**28**) …………..……. people to use laughter to heal   **COURAGE**

(**29**) …………..……. problems. Other laughter leaders operate more   **PSYCHOLOGY**

relaxed laughter clubs.

Laughter therapists may encounter tears as well as laughter, but most

feel (**30**) …………..……. rewarded by teaching people to tackle their   **GREAT**

problems with laughter. 'It's terrific,' says laughter leader James L Scott.

'You can't think about anything else when you're laughing, which is why it's

such a natural stress (**31**) …………..……. tool that totally clears stress.'   **MANAGE**

Plus, it doesn't need any special (**32**) …………..……. .   **EQUIP**

Are you naturally (**33**) …………..……. at making people laugh? If so,   **GIFT**

that will help. Laughter clinics are held in health centres across the country

– why not try one out to see if it's for you? Then you can get

(**34**) …………..……. training and become a certified laughter leader.   **PROFESSION**

Part 4

Read the questions. Before you answer them, go on to the Further Practice and Guidance page which follows.

For questions **35–42**, complete the second sentence so that it has a similar meaning to the first sentence, using the word given. **Do not change the word given.** You must use between **two** and **five** words, including the word given. Here is an example (**0**).

Example: 0   It took me a fairly long time to answer all my emails.

   QUITE

   I spent .... all my emails.

The gap can be filled with the words 'quite a long time answering', so you write:

Example: 0   QUITE A LONG TIME ANSWERING

Write only the missing words **IN CAPITAL LETTERS on the separate answer sheet**.

---

35 When a group of us went to see that film, I was the only person who didn't enjoy it.
    EXCEPT
    When a group of us went to see that film, ... enjoyed it.

36 I think that your opinion on this subject is wrong.
    AGREE
    I .... your opinion on this subject.

37 A friend of mine took this photograph of me.
    TAKEN
    This photograph of me .... my friends.

38 I don't want you to have any problems because of me.
    CAUSE
    I don't want .... you.

39 I couldn't think of a way of solving the problem.
    HOW
    I couldn't work .... the problem.

40 'Don't make so much noise!' she told them.
    STOP
    She told them .... noisy.

41 We discussed the problem for a long time.
    DISCUSSION
    We .... about the problem.

42 At the end of the party, we all helped with the clearing up.
    OVER
    When the party .... us helped with the clearing up.

WHAT'S TESTED

The questions in Part 4 of the Use of English Paper test you on both grammar and vocabulary. Questions require you to form grammatical structures and/or lexical phrases (eg collocations). There are two marks for each question – each answer is considered to have two parts and there is a mark for each part.

TIPS

• Remember that you must not write more than five words. An answer of more than five words will be marked wrong. A short form of a verb (eg won't) is considered to be two words.

• Remember that you must use the word given and that you must not change that word in any way.

• Make sure that you copy correctly any words in the first sentence that are part of the answer. You will lose marks unnecessarily if you make a careless mistake when writing these words.

• Read the words both before and after the gap very carefully. Your answer must fit with the words before and after the gap to form a grammatically correct sentence that means the same as the first sentence. When you have written your answer, check the full sentence that you have produced very carefully to make sure that it is correct both grammatically and in meaning.

• Remember that there are two marks for each question. If you are not sure of the answer, write a complete answer to fill the gap anyway. Part of your answer may be correct and you may get one of the two marks.

The following exercises will help you to write the correct answer to each question in the test. When you have completed each exercise, check your answer and then write your answer for the question in the test.

For each question, decide what the first word in the gap should be. (It is possible for some questions that another word could also be the first word, but only one of the choices below is correct.)

Question 35
A it
B only
C there
D everyone
E however

Question 36
A agree
B am
C and
D don't
E think

Question 37
A a
B was
C it
D had
E been

Question 38
A you
B for
C any
D that
E to

Question 39
A out
B a
C how
D on
E of

Question 40
A not
B to
C that
D do
E stop

Question 41
A were
B made
C for
D long
E had

Question 42
A came
B end
C was
D became
E ended

Now check your answers to the questions in the test.

PAPER 4 LISTENING approximately 40 minutes

Part 1

You will hear people talking in eight different situations. For questions **1–8**, choose the best answer (**A**, **B** or **C**).

1   You hear someone talking about keeping a diary. What does he say about his diary?

   A   He shows parts of it to other people.

   B   He thinks he might stop doing it.

   C   He doesn't always keep it up to date.

2   You hear a radio announcer talking about a programme. What kind of programme is she talking about?

   A   a drama series

   B   a chat show

   C   a documentary series

3   You overhear two people talking at a bus stop. What is the relationship between them?

   A   They are neighbours.

   B   They work for the same company.

   C   They used to be students together.

4   You hear someone talking about a film. What is her opinion of the film?

   A   It's better than the book.

   B   The critics are wrong about it.

   C   It's too long.

5   You hear a voicemail message. What is the speaker doing in the message?

   A   making an offer

   B   insisting on something

   C   asking for a favour

6   You hear a woman talking about someone she knows. What does she say about him?

   A   He causes problems.

   B   He wants to be popular.

   C   He's always cheerful.

7   You hear someone talking about a mistake he made. How did he feel when he made the mistake?

   A   calm

   B   annoyed

   C   scared

8   You hear a man talking about a newspaper article. What is his main point about the article?

   A   It greatly increased his knowledge.

   B   He couldn't understand it.

   C   He didn't agree with it.

Part 2

You will hear part of an interview with a travel writer about travel blogs on the Internet. For questions **9–18**, complete the sentences.

TRAVEL BLOGS

wayn.com

Members can find out the current location of [   ] **9** .

hotelchatter.com

This is the best site for [   ] **10** .

It includes pictures and films of [   ] **11** .

aluxurytravelblog.com

You can find out how much the [   ] **12** in the world costs.

gridskipper.com

It is about city breaks and includes excellent photographs and [   ] **13** .

travel-rants.com

This blog was started after its writer had a problem with a [   ] **14** .

perrinpost.com

This blog is more [   ] **15** than most other travel blogs.

seat61.com

This includes blogs about travelling in various parts of the world [   ] **16** .

A version of this blog is now available in [   ] **17** form.

tripadvisor.com

This may contain fake reviews that have been written by [   ] **18** .

Part 3

You will hear five different people talking about a famous person. For questions **19–23**, choose from the list (**A–F**) what each speaker's opinion of the celebrity is. Use the letters only once. There is one extra letter which you do not need to use.

A He doesn't have any talent.

B He deserves sympathy.

C He has interesting ideas.

D He won't be famous for long.

E He has a bad influence on young people.

F He annoys a lot of people.

Speaker 1	19
Speaker 2	20
Speaker 3	21
Speaker 4	22
Speaker 5	23

Part 4

Before you listen to the CD, read the test questions and go on to the Further Practice and Guidance pages which follow.

You will hear an interview with someone who runs a company called The Perfume Shop, which sells perfume in a group of shops in the UK. For questions **24–30**, choose the best answer (**A**, **B** or **C**).

24 Which of these statements summarizes Jo's sales philosophy?

    A People care about what they buy.

    B Names don't sell products.

    C People are more important than products.

25 What do we learn about the 'Fish principles'?

    A They are used by many companies.

    B They emphasize enjoyment of work.

    C Jo was told about them by some fish sellers.

26 Jo says that one of the 'Fish principles' concerns

    A thinking of enjoyable activities for staff.

    B deciding to be enthusiastic about your job.

    C persuading customers to buy.

27 Which of the following is true about perfume, according to Jo?

    A It has special connections for some people.

    B People often aren't given the right advice about it.

    C Many people find it hard to decide which one they like best.

28 What problem did the girl in the shopping centre have?

    A She hadn't been able to find the perfume she wanted.

    B She had used all of a certain perfume that she had.

    C She thought she wouldn't be able to buy a certain perfume.

29 Jo's intention when she spoke to the girl was

    A to give her some good news.

    B to sympathize with her problem.

    C to sell her some perfume.

30 Jo says that the man who came into one of The Perfume Shop's stores

    A became a regular customer.

    B wanted a perfume that was no longer available.

    C was amazed when she sent him a bottle of her own perfume.

WHAT'S TESTED

The questions in Part 4 of the Listening Paper test you on your ability to understand what speakers say in a recording lasting approximately three minutes. The recording is usually an interview or conversation, but may also involve only one speaker. Questions focus on the following:

- **an opinion/attitude** expressed or described
- **detail:** a specific piece of information given
- **gist:** the general meaning of what a speaker says or the main point made by a speaker.

TIPS

- The questions follow the same order as what you hear in the recording.
- Use the time given to read the questions very carefully before you listen to the recording. This will show you exactly what you need to focus on as you listen to each part of the recording.
- Don't choose an option simply because it contains words that you hear in the recording. An option may contain words used by a speaker but not be the correct answer.
- The correct options in the questions rephrase what a speaker says using different words and phrases from those used by the speaker, or report or summarize what a speaker says.
- If you are able to answer a question the first time you hear the recording, listen carefully when it is played for the second time. You may discover that you made a mistake which you can now correct.

The following exercises will help you to choose the correct answer to each question in the test. Listen to the whole recording once to get a general idea about what is said in it. Then listen for a second time, and answer the questions below. When you have completed each exercise, check your answer(s) and then choose your answer for the question in the test.

The choices below for each question are in the same order as what you hear in each recording. In each exercise, more than one of the choices is correct.

Stop the recording when Jo says 'The People Shop'.

Question 24

Which of the following does Jo say when asked about her philosophy?

A   She wants customers to buy from her company more than once.

B   She is not only interested in selling products.

C   The quality of a product is more important than its name.

D   Customers want to buy products that they think are special.

E   The name of the shop might change.

F   Another name would be suitable for the shop.

Stop the recording when Jo says 'what the product is'.

Question 25

Which of the following do the interviewer and Jo mention in connection with the 'Fish principles'?

A   the fact that Jo's company uses them

B   the role played by a certain business person in creating them

C   an attitude to work that they are based on

D   how Jo heard about them

E   how widely they are used

F   what they consist of

Stop the recording when Jo says 'at a company event'.

Question 26

Which of the following does Jo mention when she is describing each of the 'Fish principles'?

A   treating customers with kindness

B   customers deciding to buy products

C   telling staff how to behave at work

D   choosing to behave in a certain way while at work

E   something that her own staff did once

F   something she organized for her own staff

Stop the recording when Jo says 'It's very emotional'.

Question 27

Which of the following does Jo say about perfume?

A   Selling perfume involves forming a relationship with a customer.

B   People who sell perfume are sometimes not good at it.

C   Many people don't want to go into a shop and get advice on perfume.

D   People can become confused when trying to choose a perfume.

E   People connect a perfume with someone they know who uses it.

F   A perfume can remind people of a certain event in the past.

Stop the recording when Jo says 'tell her where to get it'.

Question 28

Which of the following did the girl in the shopping centre say about a certain perfume?

A   She had been looking for it in the shopping centre.

B   She used it for a particular reason.

C   She wanted to continue using it.

D   She only had a small amount of it left.

E   She did not expect to be able to buy any more of it.

F   She had been told that it was no longer available.

Question 29

Which of the following did Jo tell the girl?

A   that she was wrong about something

B   that she couldn't buy that particular perfume

C   that The Perfume Shop was a very good shop

D   that she should go to The Perfume Shop

E   that she liked that particular perfume

F   that she would try to get that particular perfume for her

Stop the recording at the end.

Question 30

Which of the following does Jo say about the man?

A   He asked for a perfume that the shop did not have.

B   He asked for a perfume that was no longer made.

C   He had looked in other shops for a certain perfume.

D   He contacted her after she sent him some perfume.

E   He returned to the shop after she sent him some perfume.

F   He told other people about what she did.

Now check your answers to the questions in the test.

PAPER 5 SPEAKING 14 minutes

Part 1 (3 minutes)

Your country

- What is the weather usually like in your country?
- What kind of work do people in your country typically do?
- What kind of things do people talk about in your country?
- What is the difference between life in cities and life in the countryside in your country?
- Would you prefer to live in your own country or in another country? (Why?)

Visiting places

- What's the most exciting place you've visited? (Why?)
- Which place(s) have you been to that were disappointing for you? (Why?)
- Which place(s) would you particularly like to visit? (Why?)
- Which place(s) would you really not like to visit? (Why?)
- Do a lot of tourists visit the place where you live/your country? (Why?/Why not?)

Part 2 (4 minutes)

1 Loading equipment

Candidate A: Look at photographs 1A and 1B on page 127. They show **people putting different equipment into vehicles for transport.**

Compare the photographs and say **why you think the people are transporting the different equipment.**

Candidate A talks on his/her own for about 1 minute.

Candidate B: Which situation would you prefer to be in?

Candidate B talks on his/her own for about 20 seconds.

2 Extreme climates

Candidate B: Look at photographs 2A and 2B on page 127. They show **people in different kinds of extreme climate**.

Compare the photographs and **say what difficulties the people might face in the different places**.

Candidate B talks on his/her own for about 1 minute.

Candidate A: Which of the places would you prefer to go to?

Candidate A talks on his/her own for about 20 seconds.

Parts 3 and 4 (7 minutes) Friendship

Part 3

Look at the pictures that show different images of friendship on page 128.

First, talk to each other about **what aspects of friendship each picture shows.** Then decide **which two pictures show the most important aspects of friendship.**

Candidates A and B discuss this together for about 3 minutes.

Part 4

- Do you find it easy to make friends? (Why?/Why not?)
- Do you prefer to spend time with one friend or with a group of friends? (Why?)
- What qualities do you think are important in a friend? (Why?)
- Some people say that friends are the most important thing in life. Do you agree?
- What kind of person could never become a friend of yours? (Why?)
- Do you think you will always have the same friends? (Why?/Why not?)

Writing Assessment

AND 5

For a Band 5 to be awarded, the candidate's writing fully achieves the desired effect on the target reader. All the content points required in the task are included* and expanded appropriately. Ideas are organised effectively, with the use of a variety of linking devices and a wide range of structure and vocabulary. The language is well developed, and any errors that do occur are minimal and perhaps due to ambitious attempts at more complex language. Register and format which is consistently appropriate to the purpose of the task and the audience is used.

AND 4

For a Band 4 to be awarded, the candidate's writing achieves the desired effect on the target reader. All the content points required in the task are included*. Ideas are clearly organised, with the use of suitable linking devices and a good range of structure and vocabulary. Generally, the language is accurate, and any errors that do occur are mainly due to attempts at more complex language. Register and format which is, on the whole, appropriate to the purpose of the task and the audience is used.

AND 3

For a Band 3 to be awarded, the candidate's writing, on the whole, achieves the desired effect on the target reader. All the content points required in the task are included*. Ideas are organised adequately, with the use of simple linking devices and an adequate range of structure and vocabulary. A number of errors may be present, but they do not impede communication. A reasonable, if not always successful, attempt is made at register and format which is appropriate to the purpose of the task and the audience.

AND 2

For a Band 2 to be awarded, the candidate's writing does not clearly communicate the message to the target reader. Some content points required in the task are inadequately covered or omitted, and/or there is some irrelevant material. Ideas are inadequately organised, linking devices are rarely used, and the range of structure and vocabulary is limited. Errors distract the reader and may obscure communication at times. Attempts at appropriate register and format are unsuccessful or inconsistent.

AND 1

For a Band 1 to be awarded, the candidate's writing has a very negative effect on the target reader. There is notable omission of content points and/or considerable irrelevance, possibly due to misinterpretation of the task. There is a lack of organisation or linking devices, and there is little evidence of language control. The range of structure and vocabulary is narrow, and frequent errors obscure communication. There is little or no awareness of appropriate register and format.

AND 0

For a Band zero to be awarded, there is either too little language for assessment or the candidate's writing is totally irrelevant or totally illegible.

Candidates who do not address all the content points will be penalised for dealing inadequately with the requirements of the task.

Candidates who fully satisfy the Band 3 descriptor will demonstrate an adequate performance in writing at FCE level.

Speaking Assessment

Throughout the test, candidates are assessed on their own individual performance and not in relation to each other, by two examiners. The assessor awards marks according to four analytical criteria:

• Grammar and Vocabulary

• Discourse Management

• Pronunciation

• Interactive Communication.

The interlocutor awards a mark for Global Achievement.

Grammar and Vocabulary

This refers to the accurate and appropriate use of a range of grammatical forms and vocabulary. Performance is viewed in terms of the overall effectiveness of the language used in spoken interaction.

Discourse Management

This refers to the candidate's ability to link utterances together to form coherent speech, without undue hesitation. The utterances should be relevant to the tasks and should be arranged logically to develop the themes or arguments required by the tasks.

Pronunciation

This refers to the candidate's ability to produce intelligible utterances to fulfil the task requirements. This includes stress and intonation as well as individual sounds. Examiners put themselves in the position of a non-ESOL specialist and assess the overall impact of the pronunciation and the degree of effort required to understand the candidate.

Interactive Communication

This refers to the candidate's ability to take an active part in the development of the discourse. This requires an ability to participate in the range of interactive situations in the test and to develop discussions on a range of topics by initiating and responding appropriately. This also refers to the deployment of strategies to maintain interaction at an appropriate level throughout the test so that the tasks can be fulfilled.

Global Achievement

This refers to the candidate's overall effectiveness in dealing with the tasks in the four separate parts of the FCE Speaking test. The global mark is an independent impression mark which reflects the assessment of the candidate's performance from the interlocutor's perspective.

Paper 1: Reading (above) and Paper 3: Use of English (below)

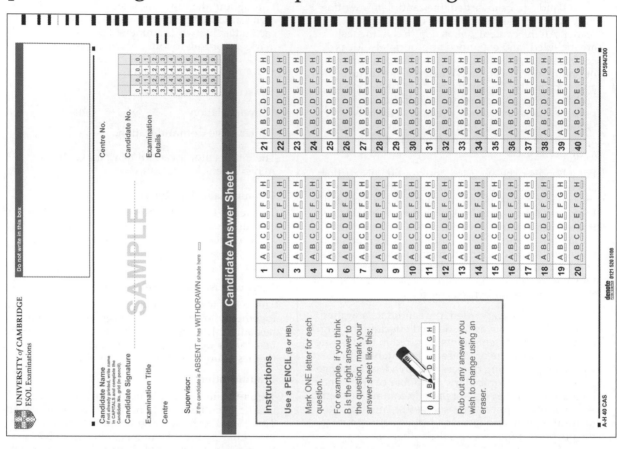

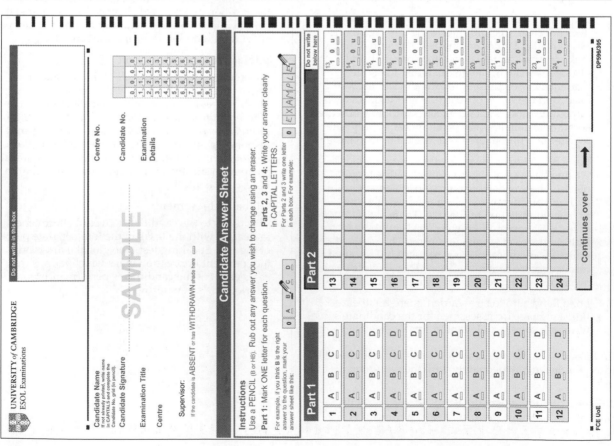

Paper 4: Listening

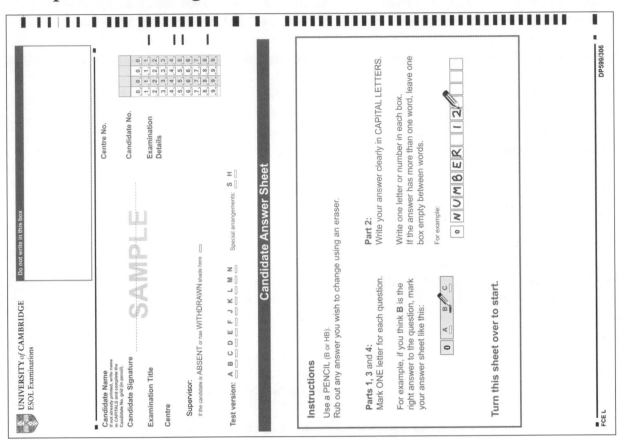

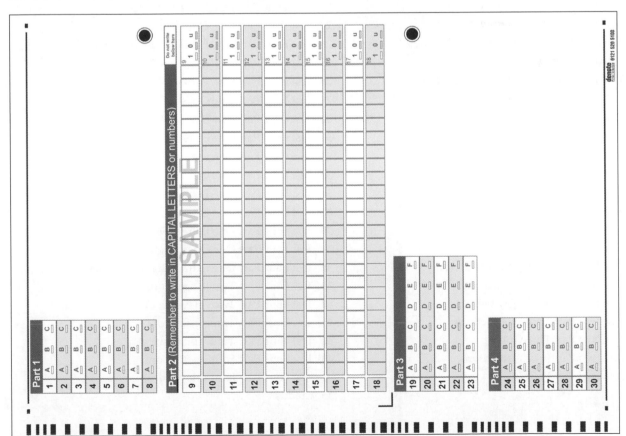

CD1

01 Test One Part One instructions and Question 1
02 Test One Part One Extract One (play twice)
03 Test One Part One Question 2
04 Test One Part One Extract Two (play twice)
05 Test One Part One Question 3
06 Test One Part One Extract Three (play twice)
07 Test One Part One Question 4
08 Test One Part One Extract Four (play twice)
09 Test One Part One Question 5
10 Test One Part One Extract Five (play twice)
11 Test One Part One Question 6
12 Test One Part One Extract Six (play twice)
13 Test One Part One Question 7
14 Test One Part One Extract Seven (play twice)
15 Test One Part One Question 8
16 Test One Part One Extract Eight (play twice)
17 Test One Part Two instructions
18 Test One Part Two (play twice)
19 Test One Part Three instructions
20 Test One Part Three (play twice)
21 Test One Part Four instructions
22 Test One Part Four (play twice)

23 Test Two Part One instructions and Question 1
24 Test Two Part One Extract One (play twice)
25 Test Two Part One Question 2
26 Test Two Part One Extract Two (play twice)
27 Test Two Part One Question 3
28 Test Two Part One Extract Three (play twice)
29 Test Two Part One Question 4
30 Test Two Part One Extract Four (play twice)
31 Test Two Part One Question 5
32 Test Two Part One Extract Five (play twice)
33 Test Two Part One Question 6
34 Test Two Part One Extract Six (play twice)
35 Test Two Part One Question 7
36 Test Two Part One Extract Seven (play twice)
37 Test Two Part One Question 8
38 Test Two Part One Extract Eight (play twice)
39 Test Two Part Two instructions
40 Test Two Part Two (play twice)
41 Test Two Part Three instructions
42 Test Two Part Three (play twice)
43 Test Two Part Four instructions
44 Test Two Part Four (play twice)

CD2

01 Test Three Part One instructions and Question 1
02 Test Three Part One Extract One (play twice)
03 Test Three Part One Question 2
04 Test Three Part One Extract Two (play twice)
05 Test Three Part One Question 3
06 Test Three Part One Extract Three (play twice)
07 Test Three Part One Question 4
08 Test Three Part One Extract Four (play twice)
09 Test Three Part One Question 5
10 Test Three Part One Extract Five (play twice)
11 Test Three Part One Question 6
12 Test Three Part One Extract Six (play twice)
13 Test Three Part One Question 7
14 Test Three Part One Extract Seven (play twice)
15 Test Three Part One Question 8
16 Test Three Part One Extract Eight (play twice)
17 Test Three Part Two instructions
18 Test Three Part Two (play twice)
19 Test Three Part Three instructions
20 Test Three Part Three (play twice)
21 Test Three Part Four instructions
22 Test Three Part Four (play twice)

23 Test Four Part One instructions and Question 1
24 Test Four Part One Extract One (play twice)
25 Test Four Part One Question 2
26 Test Four Part One Extract Two (play twice)
27 Test Four Part One Question 3
28 Test Four Part One Extract Three (play twice)
29 Test Four Part One Question 4
30 Test Four Part One Extract Four (play twice)
31 Test Four Part One Question 5
32 Test Four Part One Extract Five (play twice)
33 Test Four Part One Question 6
34 Test Four Part One Extract Six (play twice)
35 Test Four Part One Question 7
36 Test Four Part One Extract Seven (play twice)
37 Test Four Part One Question 8
38 Test Four Part One Extract Eight (play twice)
39 Test Four Part Two instructions
40 Test Four Part Two (play twice)
41 Test Four Part Three instructions
42 Test Four Part Three (play twice)
43 Test Four Part Four instructions
44 Test Four Part Four (play twice)
45 Credits

Test 1 Part 2 Crowds

- What kind of experience are the different crowds of people having?

1B

Test 1 Part 2 Celebrations

- What did people do in order to organize the different birthday celebrations?

2A

2B

Test 1 Parts 3 and 4 Photography competition

- What does each entry show and how effective is each photograph in showing 'perfect surroundings'?

- Which photograph should win the competition and which should come second?

Test 2 Part 2 Travelling to work

- What are the advantages and disadvantages of the different ways of travelling to work?

1B

1A

Test 2 Part 2 Shouting

- Why are the people shouting?

2A

2B

Test 2 Parts 3 and 4 Skills for life

- What are the advantages of having each of these skills?
- Which two skills are the most important for people to have?

Test 3 Part 2 Waiting

> • How might the people be feeling?

1A

1B

Test 3 Part 2 TV shows

> • What do people enjoy about watching these kinds of TV programmes?

2A

2B

Test 3 Parts 3 and 4 Helping at an event

- What will each aspect of the event involve?
- Which aspect will you offer to help with?

1

2

3

4

5

6

7

Test 4 Part 2 Loading equipment

- Why are the people transporting the equipment?

A

1B

Test 4 Part 2 Extreme climates

- What difficulties might the people face in the different places?

2B

2A

Test 4 Parts 3 and 4 Friendship

- What aspects of friendship are shown in each picture?
- Which two pictures show the most important aspects of friendship?

Age 11   Age 30

KEY AND EXPLANATION

TEST ONE

p.7–10 PAPER 1 Part 1

Further practice and guidance (p.9–10)

Question 1

1 no 2 no 3 yes 4 no 5 no 6 B

Question 2

1 no 2 yes 3 yes 4 yes 5 yes 6 no

Question 3

A, C, F

Question 4

1 B 2 yes 3 no

Question 5

A, C

Question 6

B

Question 7

A, C, D, G, H

Question 8

1 A 2 B 3 no

---

p.7–8 PAPER 1 Part 1 (Test)

1   A   In the first paragraph, the writer repeats the instructions that they were given and then says that all of them arrived on time ('at 9 am precisely'). They were all able to find the place because the instructions were 'idiot-proof' – so easy to understand and follow that nobody could get them wrong or fail to understand them.

The writer's point is that the instructions were clear and easy to understand. There were several parts to the instructions, but everyone found the place without problems, and he is not making the point that the reader might think the instructions were complicated. Obviously, they did want to arrive on time, but he doesn't mention how they felt about arriving on time. And he does not suggest that they did not require these instructions or that they had been to the place before.

2   B   The writer repeats what Tristan Gooley said when he began speaking (the word 'Welcome' makes it clear that these are his first words). The writer says that what he says is 'quite an intro' – an introduction that has a big effect on the audience. The audience reacts with 'oohs and ahs' – sounds that indicate that they are surprised and impressed. He immediately 'has his audience in the palm of his hand' – they are listening to every word he says, he has their full attention. So the audience are very impressed by what he says at the beginning.

The writer says at the end of the paragraph that he knew something about Gooley and what he had done, but he does not say what he had expected Gooley to be like or that he was surprised by Gooley when he met him. The writer was clearly impressed by what Gooley had achieved ('You can't argue with that sort of CV') but he does not mention

a desire to meet him before that day. Gooley tells them that he believes they are certainly 'the only people in the world studying this particular topic today', which means that the topic is a very unusual one, but we are not told that Gooley does not give many talks. He may be the only person who gives talks on the topic, but he may give many talks on it.

3   D   Gooley says that '99.9 per cent of the time', people won't need to use natural navigation, because they 'will have other ways of finding wherever it is you want to get to'. These ways include using maps, compasses and 'the ubiquitous (found everywhere) satnav' (satellite navigation systems).

Gooley says that 'there is a lot to be said for understanding the science of navigation and direction-finding', meaning that it is a good thing. However, this is because people who depend too much on technology 'can lose connection with nature' and Gooley does not say that natural navigation can be more accurate than using technology. Gooley tells them what natural navigation involves and he says that it is a good skill to have, but he does not say that it is complicated or difficult to learn. Gooley says 'But if you don't ...' (if you don't have other ways of navigating, such as maps, compasses and satnav), natural navigation is a good skill to have. He is referring to the 0.1 per cent of the time when you don't have these things. But he does not say that these rare occasions are emergencies (situations when urgent action is required) or that natural navigation should only be used in emergencies.

4   B   The use of the stick involves 'noting the different places where its shadow falls over a short period of time' – recording in some way the different positions of its shadow at different times. This means that you calculate 'the east-west axis' from a number of different pieces of information – the different positions of the shadow. You note the different positions of the shadow at different times during a short period of time.

Gooley mentions the use of the stick in the desert as an example of the use of the sun in natural navigation, but he does not say that this can only be done in the desert. Gooley mentions a time of day ('three in the afternoon') but this is only an example of when the stick can be used – he doesn't say that the stick should only be used at certain times. Gooley is telling them something that they don't know – how to use a stick in this way – but he doesn't say or suggest that this will surprise them or that it has surprised other people.

5   C   The writer says that if you know how to use natural navigation in this situation, you can 'stride (walk quickly) confidently' in any direction 'without fiddling with a map' (you won't need to spend time getting a map out, looking at it, and trying to work out what to do). This is an example of an advantage of having the skill of natural navigation.

Gooley says that the sun 'influences things even if you can't see it', and this is an example of a situation when you cannot see the sun but the sun is still an important factor – identifying that one side of the track 'is getting less sun' and is therefore darker helps you to know which way is south. This is another example of the use of the sun in natural navigation – the desert example is a situation where you can see the sun, and this example is a situation where you can't see it. Gooley is saying that the sun is important in both situations – he is not comparing the desert and the forest in order to show differences between them. Gooley is saying that you don't need map-reading skills if you can do natural navigation in this situation – he is not comparing the skills or talking about using them both in the same situation.

6   D   In the previous sentence, the writer refers to 'the detective work' and this means the process involved in natural navigation – looking for natural signs and clues and evidence that make you able to find your way. 'Just when we think we are getting the hang of it' means 'at the moment when we believe that we are beginning to understand how to do natural navigation'.

Something unexpected does happen – Gooley gives them a particularly difficult task to do – but this task is not what they are 'getting the hang of'. There is a reference to 'the day' in the previous sentence and the writer says that it 'wears on', which means that it continues in a way that is quite difficult or tiring, but this is not what the phrase 'getting the hang of it' refers to. The writer does refer to a particular problem – the difficult task Gooley gives them. However, the phrase 'getting the hang of it' does not refer to this problem or to being unable to deal with it or do the task successfully, it refers to something mentioned previously.

7   B   The writer says that the task was very 'tricky' (difficult) and lists some questions he wanted to ask about the sun, the tree and other things. So he felt that the photograph alone did not give him enough information to answer the question easily.

He only says that the task was 'tricky' – he does not say that he thought it was easy at first and then discovered that it was difficult. He says that he 'analysed the data in minute detail', meaning that he spent time looking carefully at the photograph and the information that it gave him, but he does not say that doing this made him more and more confused. Although he felt that he needed more information, he gave his answer 'firmly' – with certainty, because he believed it was the correct answer. Therefore, he was surprised when he was told that his answer was wrong, and then that his answer was not even 'close' (nearly correct).

8   D   The writer says that he has 'caught the natural navigation bug' – he has become very interested in it and he wants to continue doing it. He says that it is 'fascinating'. However, he also says that it is 'hardly (not really) what you would call a practical skill'. So he personally finds it fascinating but he thinks that it isn't a skill that has much use in life, because there are a lot of 'man-made aids to navigation at our disposal'.

He says that he was 'bottom of the class' (the worst student) and that natural navigation is a 'mysterious' (not easy to understand) science, but he does not mention becoming good at it or how long it would take him to do that. He says that it 'connects us' to the world around us and 'reminds us what it means to be human'. It does this 'thrillingly' (in an exciting way). It also connects us with people a long time in the past who went round the world using only natural navigation. So he believes it is a valuable thing to learn, but not because it is useful in the modern world – in fact it isn't a 'practical skill'. He says that he finds it exciting and that it appeals to him very much, but he does not say that this is because of the kind of person he is and he does not compare the response of different kinds of people to it.

p.11–12 PAPER 1 Part 2

9   F   In the sentence before the gap, the writer is saying that no books on the history of ornithology were published for a long time and now several books on the subject have appeared.

In F, 'The subject' is the 'history of ornithology' from the sentence before the gap. In F, the writer says that this subject was 'neglected' (not given any attention, not given the attention it should have been given) for many years.

In the sentence after the gap, he contrasts this with the attention now given to the subject, and links this contrast with 'However'.

10   C   In the whole of the paragraph before the gap, the writer is saying that we know more about birds than people knew a long time ago, but that there is a lot that we don't know about birds. He quotes someone saying almost 100 years ago that there is a lot we don't know about birds.

In C, the writer is saying that the same thing is true today. The phrase 'Much the same' means 'The same kind of thing that Paul Bartsch said'. The writer is saying that it would be true to say today that there is a lot that people don't know about birds.

In the sentence after the gap 'For' means 'Because' and the writer is saying that the same thing could be said about knowledge of birds because, although there has been a lot of progress in this, studies often produce new questions, rather than answers.

11   A   In the sentence before the gap, the writer mentions the two subjects that Tim Birkhead studies.

In A, 'These two interests' refers back to the two things that Tim Birkhead studies.

At the beginning of the sentence after the gap, 'In it' refers back to the book, mentioned at the end of A ('it' = *The Wisdom of Birds*).

12   H   In the sentence before the gap, the writer mentions something that the book does not do (it differs from other books on the subject because it isn't organized in a chronological way, meaning it doesn't move through time in the order of when things happened).

In H, the writer describes what it does do. H begins with 'Instead' to introduce something that happens after something that does not happen has been mentioned. H then describes how the book is organized.

In the sentence after the gap, the writer says that the way it is organized, described in H, might not have worked if someone else had written the book, but Birkhead does it very well. In the phrase 'this might have been confusing', 'this' means 'the way of organizing the book described in H'.

13   E   In the sentence before the gap, the writer mentions the illustrations in the book.

At the beginning of E, 'These' means the illustrations and refers back to both 'examples' and 'many' in the sentence before the gap, which both refer to the art in the book. In E the writer says that both the pictures and the way the book has been produced (the design, etc) are good things about it, in addition to what is written in it.

14   G   The sentence before the gap ends with a question that Birkhead asks in the book and that is addressed to his colleagues (other people studying the same subject).

In G, the writer is talking about the colleagues' responses to the question Birkhead asks them. In G 'they' refers back to 'his colleagues' in the sentence before the gap, and 'The names they come up with' means the names they suggest or propose as 'the greatest ever ornithologist'. The writer says that these names are 'strong contenders' – are all good candidates for that title.

in the sentence after the gap, the writer follows a sentence about the colleagues' choices by saying who Birkhead chose. 'Birkhead's own choice' emphasizes that the sentence is about who Birkhead, not his colleagues, chose.

15   B   The sentence that fits into the gap starts a new paragraph. The sentence after the gap describes something that happens in the book concerning a man mentioned in the previous paragraph. Later in the paragraph, we are told that this is a 'fitting ending' to the book (a suitable way of ending the book), so we know that the paragraph is describing something at the end of the book.

B refers to how the book 'concludes' (ends) and says that it ends with a 'striking (impressive, effective) image'. The sentence after the gap describes what this image is.

p.13–14 PAPER 1 Part 3

16   C   He says that 'engineers are absolutely essential in a crisis' (when there has been a disaster) and then gives examples of what engineers can do that make them extremely important in these situations.

17   A   She says that riders at the British Big Air Championships who used snowboards made by her company (and which she and her two colleagues created) achieved a 74 per cent medal rate' (most of the people who used them won medals). She says that this 'says something about how good they are' (shows how good the snowboards are).

18   D   She says that when she was at university, she was 'torn between studying astrophysics and laser physics'. This means that she found it difficult to decide which of the two subjects to choose.

19   B   She says 'I head up a team', which means she is the leader or boss of that team. She mentions what that team makes and what their present project is.

20   A   She is an engineer who started a company with two colleagues and she says that as a result of this she is now 'an engineer and an entrepreneur' (an engineer and a person who owns a business) at the same time.

21   D   She says that she went to 'an open day' (an event that is organized so that visitors can come and learn about what happens at a place) at an engineering company, and she says she learnt about 'the use of lasers and fibre optics' at this event. As a result of this experience, she decided to study lasers ('Lasers won') rather than astrophysics.

22   A   The information given about Lisa Brooks before her own words includes the fact that she 'is still studying for her engineering doctorate in advanced snowboard design', which means that she has not completed her studies for that qualification yet.

23   C   He says that 'Aid agencies really value engineers for their management skills in stressful situations, because we work as a team' and because they are 'taught how to break down problems into smaller pieces'. He is saying that organizations that provide help in countries that have serious problems have a high opinion of engineers for these reasons – they are good at working together in difficult situations and they solve problems by dealing with each part of the problem separately.

24   C   He says that it is 'vital we get young people into this sector' (it is extremely important that people in the field

of engineering attract young people to become engineers). Getting young people to become engineers is 'vital' because they 'can help save lives'.

25   B   She says that she decided that she wanted to work in space technology 'when I made my first telescope at the age of 15'. The experience of making the telescope caused her to choose a career related to it.

26   A   She says that she is 'experimenting to find new shapes to make the boards perform even better' (she is trying to produce snowboards with designs that are different from the ones they have already produced). She is doing this 'Right now' (currently, at this time).

27   B   She says 'I have been engineering instruments ever since' – she has been working on instruments for space technology from the time that she finished her studies (since she did a PhD in mechanical engineering) until now.

28   C   He says that workers 'who can contribute to disaster relief plans (who can be involved in helping after a disaster, which is what he does) are increasingly sought after' (are required, are looked for, more and more). The requirement for these people is growing all the time.

29   A   She says 'I get to go outside and play with the prototypes', meaning that she is pleased that she has the opportunity to use the snowboards that she designs, and enjoys using them (she is 'a keen snowboarder' she says at the beginning).

30   D   She says 'Knowing that what I do is useful really keeps me motivated', meaning that she remains enthusiastic about her work and continues to enjoy it very much because she knows that her work is useful for many people (her work 'will have far-reaching relevance, meaning we could all benefit in the long run' – it will affect a lot of people and it might be useful to everyone in the future).

p.15–17 PAPER 2 Part 1

Further practice and guidance (p.16–17)

1   A, C, F, H

TASK-SPECIFIC MARK SCHEME

Content

The letter must include all the points in the notes. You must:

- tell David that his visit was not a problem for you

- suggest that David stays for longer the next time he comes

- accept David's offer to send you photos

- accept and talk about David's invitation to you.

Organization and cohesion

You should organize each point in a logical order (probably the same as in David's letter) and in appropriate, probably short, paragraphs.

Range

You should use appropriate structures and vocabulary for responding to thanks, suggesting plans and accepting offers and invitations.

Appropriacy of register and format

Your letter should be informal and should open and close in an appropriate way for a letter to a friend.

Target reader

The reader should be clear about how you felt about the visit, what you are suggesting for the future and what you would like the reader to do.

ASSESSMENT OF SAMPLE ANSWER

Content

All the points from the notes are included. The first two points are in the first paragraph, the third point is in the second paragraph and the fourth point is in the third, short paragraph. The final paragraph is an additional point not mentioned in the notes, but it is relevant to the letter and a good use of the writer's own ideas.

Organization and cohesion

The letter is very well organized, covering each point in a logical order (the same as in David's letter). The short paragraphs (the third one is only one sentence) are appropriate for a letter of this kind. Ideas are well linked (for example, the use of 'By the way' in the second paragraph).

Range

Good and appropriate language is used for responding to thanks (first paragraph), asking questions (second paragraph), expressing interest (second paragraph), accepting an offer (second paragraph) and referring to the future (third paragraph). There is excellent use of a variety of verb tenses and verb forms (for example future, modal, present continuous and present perfect in the third and fourth paragraphs).

Accuracy

A lot of good language is used accurately, for example: *enjoy –ing, it was no problem at all, come over* (first paragraph), *Please say hello to, would like to, would love to* and second conditional *it would be .. if ...* (second paragraph), the linker *so* (third paragraph).

There are two mistakes but these are not serious mistakes: *My family and me* should be 'My family and I' and *definatly* should be 'definitely'.

Appropriacy of register and format

The letter is suitably informal and has the appropriate format for a letter of this kind ('All the best' is an appropriate ending for a letter to a friend).

Target reader

The reader would be completely clear about the writer's feelings and intentions , and what the writer wants the reader to do.

Mark

Band 5 (approximately 17–20 marks out of 20). This is an excellent letter which meets all the requirements with a high level of language and almost no mistakes.

p.18 PAPER 2 Part 2

QUESTION 2 STORY

TASK-SPECIFIC MARK SCHEME

Content

Your story should:

- continue logically from the opening sentence you have been given.
- describe a clear sequence of events/feelings/actions.

Organization and cohesion

Your story should be easy to follow, but may not have many paragraphs. The connections between events/feelings/actions should be clear. The story should make sense as a complete series of events/actions, with a beginning, a middle and an end.

Range

You will need to use appropriate past tenses. You may also need to use appropriate time linkers (when, after, while, as soon as, etc) and reported speech forms and/or direct speech. You will need to use a range of vocabulary appropriate for what you describe.

Appropriacy of register and format

Your story may be neutral or fairly informal (its aim is to entertain the reader).

Target reader

The reader would have no difficulty understanding what happens in the story and the events/feelings/actions you describe.

QUESTION 3 ESSAY

TASK-SPECIFIC MARK SCHEME

Content

You should:

- give your opinions agreeing or disagreeing with the statement or both agreeing and disagreeing
- end with a conclusion summarizing your views.

Organization and cohesion

The ideas should be organized into clear paragraphs in the essay, with an appropriate beginning and ending. Opinions should be supported with reasons and there should be a clear connection between the ideas expressed. Appropriate linking words and phrases should be used.

Range

A range of grammatical structures and vocabulary connected with the topic should be used.

Appropriacy of register and format

The essay should be neutral/fairly formal (it is a piece of work for a teacher).

Target reader

The reader should fully understand the writer's opinions on the statement and the topic.

QUESTION 4 REPORT

TASK-SPECIFIC MARK SCHEME

Content

You should:

- give the background to your report (the class discussion) and the purpose of your report
- give details of part-time jobs that people on your course are doing
- give information on other part-time jobs in the area
- give advice on how people can get part-time jobs locally.

Organization and cohesion

You should organize your report in separate sections, probably with a short and suitable heading for each section. Separate sections could deal with: background, jobs done by people on the course, other jobs, and advice on getting jobs. The report should have a logical progression within sections and from one section to another.

Range

You should use appropriate verb tenses and structures for past events (the discussion), for describing current work activities, and for making suggestions concerning other jobs and how to get jobs. A variety of verb tenses and modal verbs will be required, as well as other grammatical structures, for example for giving advice. You should also use a range of vocabulary connected with jobs and finding jobs.

Appropriacy of register and format

Your report should be neutral or fairly formal (it is a piece of work for a teacher).

Target reader

The reader should be clear about why you have written the report, and should get a lot of clear information and advice about part-time jobs in the area.

p.19–22 PAPER 3 Part 1

Further practice and guidance (p.21–22)

Question 1	Question 2
A unlike	A lost
B compared	B shortened
C opposite	C reduced
D different	D cut
Question 3	**Question 4**
A gaining	A creating
B rising	B causing
C lifting	C turning
D advancing	D resulting
Question 5	**Question 6**
A materials	A placed
B sources	B made
C means	C brought
D origins	D set
Question 7	**Question 8**
A Although	A properly
B Despite	B fully
C As	C really
D Even	D surely
Question 9	**Question 10**
A spread	A noticed
B extend	B known
C cover	C learnt
D pass	D experienced
Question 11	**Question 12**
A come	A reach
B happen	B land
C prove	C achieve
D end	D get

p.19–20 PAPER 3 Part 1 (Test)

1　C　'Unlike' is used before a noun or pronoun to compare things or people that are different from each other. The writer is saying that polar bears are different from other endangered animals – other animals are in danger because of hunters but climate change, not hunters, is the problem for polar bears.

2　B　If something 'reduces in size, number, etc', it gets smaller. The writer is saying that the ice cap is 30 per cent smaller than it was in 1979.

3　D　The verbs 'rise' and 'fall' go together with 'temperature' to talk about changes in temperature. The writer is saying that the temperature has been slowly going up in the Arctic over a period of time.

4　C　The structure *cause + object + 'to' infinitive* is used to talk about the result of something. The writer is saying that the ice is melting (becoming water) because the temperature has been getting higher.

5　A　A 'source' of something is where it comes from, what supplies it. The polar bears' food mostly comes from different types of seal, their food supplies are mostly seals – they eat seals.

6　D　If you 'make a hole in something' you do something that causes it to have a hole in it. The seals create holes in the ice so that they can breathe air and polar bears wait next to these holes so that they can catch the seals (the seals will come out of the water through these holes).

7　B　'Although' is used at the beginning of a sentence to contrast two facts, or to say that a possible result of one fact is not actually true. The sentence means 'Polar bears are very good swimmers but it is impossible for them to catch seals in the water'. The polar bears are good swimmers but the seals are faster swimmers than they are.

8　A　The word 'really' is used here with the positive auxiliary 'do' for emphasis. The writer is emphasizing the point about how much the bears depend on the ice for food – without it they can't catch seals to eat.

9   C   If someone 'covers' an area or distance, they travel around the whole of that area or travel that distance. The polar bears travel through 'a huge territory' (a very large area), using the ice as well as swimming.

10   C   If someone 'has been known to do something', they have done it in the past, but not often because it is something unusual. The writer is saying that it has happened that polar bears have swum 100km, but this is the maximum for them and not a common thing.

11   A   If something 'proves fatal to someone', it causes them to die. The maximum the polar bears can swim is 100km, but because there is less ice they may have to swim a longer distance than that. They can't do this, so they drown (die in the water).

12   D   If you 'reach a place' you arrive at a place you are trying to arrive at. The writer is saying that the polar bears want to swim as far as more ice but they are unable to do this. There is less ice and they can't swim far enough to find more sea ice.

p.23 PAPER 3 Part 2

13   when/if

This clause explains the circumstances or situation in which certain areas of the brain are 'far more active in younger people'. The writer is saying that younger people get more excited than adults when they are given a prize as a reward (something given to someone because they have done something good).

14   it

This completes the structure *find + it + possible/impossible/easy/difficult + 'to' infinitive*. This structure describes something that is possible/impossible, etc for someone to do. The writer is talking about something that children cannot do.

15   their

The plural possessive is required here, meaning 'children's excitement'. The writer is saying that children cannot control their excitement when they have a birthday.

16   A

The indefinite article is required here because the writer is talking about something that has not been mentioned before. In this case, 'team' means 'group of researchers working together'.

17   which/what

This part of the sentence means 'the parts of the brain which were stimulated' (became excited). The determiner 'which' (or 'what') is required with the noun 'parts' to talk about particular parts.

18   were

This is required to complete the past simple passive. The verbs 'used' and 'were stimulated' in the sentence show that the past simple is required. The plural noun 'rewards' is the subject of the verb. This part of the sentence means 'when the team presented rewards to the participants'. The verb must be passive because its subject is 'rewards'.

19   and/or

This links two actions – they viewed a game, they received money. If both things happened, 'and' is correct. If one of the two things happened, 'or' is correct. Both are suitable here

– it is possible that their brains showed more activity when both of these things happened, and it is also possible that their brains showed more activity when one of these things happened.

20   to

The passive structure *subject + be believed/thought/known, etc + 'to' infinitive* describes something that people believe/think/know, etc. The writer is saying that people (scientists in this case) believe that the chemical dopamine has a certain function in the brain's rewarding processes.

21   why

This explains the reason for something and links the reason with the result. The writer is saying that people get less excited about receiving presents because the system in the brain that makes them excited 'declines' (becomes weaker or less effective) 'with age' (when they are older).

22   get/become/grow

The phrase 'as people get/become/grow older' describes the process of becoming an older person.

23   of

The 'development of something' is the process of developing, producing or creating it. The writer is saying that focusing on the system in the brain involving dopamine may help scientists to develop ways of treating certain problems.

24   such

The phrase 'such as' means 'for example' and is used for introducing examples of something previously mentioned. The writer is giving examples of the 'various disorders' (in this case psychological problems).

p.24 PAPER 3 Part 3

25   lifetime

The compound noun 'lifetime' means 'all of someone's life'. The phrase *the ... of a lifetime* means 'the best ... in all of your life' or 'the best .... you will ever do'. The writer is saying that the event is the best or biggest adventure in the lives of the people who take part in it.

26   selection

The noun 'selection' completes the phrase *selection process*, meaning the process of choosing (in this case choosing people to take part in the event).

27   successful

You must form the adjective here, to go with the noun 'applicants'. The 'successful applicants' are the people who apply and are then chosen to be the British team.

28   demanding

You must form the adjective here, to describe the event. The writer is saying that the event, which lasts for three weeks, is very difficult and requires a lot of effort and energy.

29   populated

The adjective 'populated' describes how many people live in a certain place. The phrase *sparsely populated* means 'with only a few people living there'. The writer is saying that not many people live in Mongolia, compared with other countries.

30   variety

You must form the noun here, after the indefinite article 'A'. The phrase *a variety of + plural noun* describes different kinds of something. The writer is saying that the race takes place in different kinds of 'terrain' (landscape) and lists the different kinds – steppes, mountains and deserts.

31   spectacular

You must form the adjective here, to describe the noun 'country'. If a place is 'spectacular', it is wonderful to see, it is exciting and beautiful to look at.

32   extraordinary

You must use a prefix here to form the adjective that means the opposite of 'ordinary'. John Edwards is talking about how wonderful and how unusual the event is. The adjective 'extraordinary' means 'extremely unusual' or 'totally different from others' and is the opposite of 'ordinary', 'common' or 'typical'.

33   competitors

The plural noun describing people is required here. John Edwards is talking about the people taking part in the event and trying to win it, and saying that the event will 'push them to their limits' – it will be so difficult that it will require them to use the maximum amount of energy and effort that they are able to use.

34   adventurous

You must form the adjective here, to go with the noun 'person'. An 'adventurous' person is someone who likes to try to do new and exciting things, and who likes challenges.

p.25 PAPER 3 Part 4

35   never heard][such a

The word 'ever' (in all of my life) becomes 'never' (at no time in my life). The structure *such + a/an + adjective + singular noun* must be used (such a ridiculous thing = a thing that is equally ridiculous).

36   have thought][more carefully

The structure *should + have + past participle* must be used to talk about an opinion about the past. The phrase 'carefully enough' must be change to the comparative adverb 'more carefully'.

37   heard][from Gill

The past simple tense must be used in the structure *subject + last + past simple*, which refers to the last time something happened in the past. If you 'hear from someone', that person contacts you.

38   without making][any

The structure *without + -ing* refers to something not happening in a situation when it might be expected to happen. This structure is grammatically negative and so the structure *any + plural noun* must be used (not 'some').

39   be able to][give you

The structure *be able to do something* is required and the infinitive without 'to' follows the modal ('might'). The phrase *give someone a lift* means 'take someone in your car to a place'.

40   for][an explanation of

The structure *ask + object + for + noun* must be used because 'explanation' is a noun and it replaces the infinitive 'to explain'. The preposition 'of' is used in the phrase *an explanation of something*.

41   we set][off/out

The linking word 'unless' means 'if ... not' and is used in the first conditional structure *unless + positive present simple* (not 'will'). The phrasal verbs *set off* and *set out* both mean 'start a journey'.

42   be given][my money

'I' is the subject of the verb and so the verb must be passive, because 'me' is the object in the first sentence. The passive structure *modal + be + past participle* is required instead of the infinitive form 'to get'. If you get a refund, you *get/are given your money back* (the money you have paid is returned to you).

p.26–28 PAPER 4 Part 1

Further practice and guidance (p.27–28)

Question 1 A, B, E and F

Question 2 A, B, C, D and F

Question 3 A, C, E and F

Question 4 A, E and F

Question 5 A, C, D and F

Question 6 E

Question 7 A, B, C and D

Question 8 A, C, D and E.

p.26 PAPER 4 Part 1 (Test)

1   B   The speaker says that all politicians are 'the same' and they 'just say what they think people want to hear'. She thinks this politician is the same as all the others. Although she agreed with 'a lot of what he was saying' in the speech she heard, she thinks 'He'll probably be saying something different in a few weeks'. She thinks he'll change his mind 'if that seems like the right thing to do' because 'he seems to have a different opinion every time he makes a speech' - he changes his mind all the time.

2   A   She says that 'most people associate him with' the song because it was 'a big hit' – he is most well-known for performing this song because it was very popular and successful. She also says that he has 'written lots of great songs', which other performers have sung. These songs, which he wrote, are 'just as good, if not better' (possibly better) than this song, which he is very famous for. However, he didn't write this song, the one she is talking about – it's 'not one of his own'– and most people don't know this fact.

3   B   They mention a journey and delays on the journey but the journey was in the past. They both mention the hotel that they have 'been in for the past fortnight' but that was in the past also – the man says that the fact they didn't have to cook their own meals 'was great'. The man says that 'it's nice to be back', meaning that they have returned from the journey and from the hotel. He says that he likes being 'back surrounded by all the familiar things', meaning that he is now back at home. At the end the woman says that they are now 'Back to reality' – normal life – and that they are going to 'get the bags sorted out' – deal with their luggage, unpack, etc – after arriving home.

4   B   The speaker says that when he reads a review of his work, 'I tend to see if there's anything I can learn from it' – meaning that he usually reads it carefully and thinks about what the reviewer is saying about his work. He says that he thinks about 'whether the reviewer's got a point about something I've written that I haven't noticed' – whether the reviewer is saying something true about his work that he hadn't realized before. So he usually pays attention to criticism and reads it carefully to see if he can learn something from it. He thinks about negative criticism but 'I never let it get me down' – he doesn't allow it to make him depressed or unhappy.

5   C   She mentions several times that she is sad that she can't play an instrument and that she would feel good if she could play one. She feels a lot of 'envy' (the desire to do or have something that other people do or have) when she sees other people playing well. The fact that she made no progress when she tried to learn to play both the piano and the guitar is 'a shame' (something to feel sad about, an unfortunate thing). The fact that she can't play an instrument is 'a real regret' (something she feels bad about), and when she looks at people who can play an instrument, she thinks 'If only I'd kept having those lessons' (I really wish that I had continued with the lessons).

6   A   The woman says that 'there are just so many programmes like that' and that she 'can't be bothered to watch another one' (she isn't interested in watching another one). The man says 'I suppose you have a point', meaning 'I agree with you, you are right about that'. He is agreeing that there are 'an awful lot of them' (a very large number of programmes like that). Although he likes the programmes, he agrees that there are too many of them and says that he doesn't 'feel like watching them all the time' (doesn't always want to watch them). However, he thinks this particular programme will be 'fascinating' and intends to watch it. The woman doesn't think the same and will be 'giving it a miss' (she isn't going to watch it).

7   C   The speaker talks about going to 'the original one' – the stadium that existed before this one was built. He says that it was 'practically falling down' – in very bad condition. He says that people 'have to travel further to get there' – the distance to the new stadium is longer than the distance to the old stadium was – but the parking arrangements mean that it is 'more appealing to people' – people like it more than the old stadium. So he is saying that the old stadium no longer exists or is no longer used and that there is now a new stadium instead of it.

8   B   The manager agrees with the woman that Mr Butler 'can be very difficult' and says 'I appreciate how hard it is to deal with him' (I realize that he is not a nice person – he is 'horrible' – and that the experience of dealing with him is unpleasant). The manager says 'Yes, I know' when the woman says that she has always 'done my best to help him' – she has tried very hard to help him. Because the manager realizes that the problem with Mr Butler is not the woman's fault, and because he understands that it is an unpleasant situation for her, he offers to speak to Mr Butler 'next time he rings'.

p.29 PAPER 4 Part 2

9   to/To all/All

When Mildred Hill first 'composed' the song and her sister 'added words' to the song, the two sisters called it 'Good Morning to All'. It began with the words 'Good Morning to You' twice, but that was not its title.

10   the/a teacher/teachers

The song was 'initially' (at first, originally) 'intended, and used, as a welcoming song to be sung by the teacher to the class each morning'. The original idea was that teachers would sing the song to their class at the beginning of the day's lessons.

11   to/To you/You

After the song was published in a book of songs, it became 'popular in reverse' – instead of teachers singing it to children, children sang it to teachers. As a result, its title had to change because 'Good Morning to All' would not make sense any more (children were singing it to a single person – their teacher – and it was no longer sung for a group of people ('All') – children). So the song's title 'gently morphed' (slowly changed) and the first two lines became the title.

12   at parties

We are told that the 'slow development from 'Good Morning' to 'Happy Birthday' seems to have come from children themselves' when they 'liked it enough to sing it at parties'. Patty Hill encouraged this change and 'helped create the new lyric' (words). So children began to sing the song with the words 'Happy Birthday' when they were at parties.

13   show

In 1924, the song was published again. This time it was still called 'Good Morning to All' – its original title – but it had 'Happy Birthday to You' as 'an optional second verse' – the 'Happy Birthday' words could be sung after the original words if people wanted to do that. As time went on, the 'Happy Birthday' words 'replaced the earlier version' ('Good Morning to All'). The 'Happy Birthday' song appeared in a show called *Band Wagon* in 1931 and in another show, called *As Thousands Cheer*, in 1934.

14   until 2030

In 1934, Jessica Hill 'was able to establish legal copyright' of the song for her sisters (it was officially accepted that the sisters had written the song and therefore owned it). This meant that the sisters could get money ('some profit') for the song. After two legal changes to the system, this situation will continue to be the case 'until 2030' (the sisters will continue to own the song until that year).

15   3/three

According to the Guinness Book of Records (a book listing world records for many things), the song is 'one of the three most sung songs in the English language'.

16   profit(-)making enterprise

The 'copyright can be enforced' (the legal situation means that people have to pay) if the song is used 'in a public place', if a group of people larger than a family are singing it, for example at a sports event. The speaker says that 'Royalties (money for a song or book) must be paid if the song is ever part of a profit-making enterprise'. The speaker then gives examples of profit-making enterprises – these include a TV show, a 'commercial stage performance or movie, 'toys' and several other goods that people buy (two of these are listed in the question).

17   a foundation

To collect the money paid for using the song, the sisters 'established a foundation through which royalties were paid until their death.' This 'foundation' (a type of organization) received the money and the sisters could get this money from it. It continues to receive 'several millions of dollars of income a year'.

18   (short) musical phrases

The speaker says that the song 'has only four short musical phrases' and only one line of repeated words, but it 'has become a part of the musical landscape' – it is a very famous piece of music and almost everyone is familiar with it.

p.30 PAPER 4 Part 3

19   F   The speaker says that when the customer complained, 'I felt that she had a point' – I felt that she was right to complain, that she had a good reason to complain. He says that he 'didn't blame her for being so angry' – he could understand why she was angry, he felt that she had a good reason to be angry. He says that he 'would have felt the same in her position' and that his company 'really had treated her badly' – the speaker would have felt the same as the woman – angry – if he had received the bad treatment that the woman received.

20   C   The speaker says that her friend accused her of 'saying terrible things about her' but that she 'really didn't know where she got that idea from' – she couldn't understand why her friend thought that she had done this. She says that 'Nothing she was saying made any sense' – there was no logic or reason for what the friend was saying. She 'didn't get any clear answers' when she asked her friend about this, and she didn't know what to say to her friend because she 'didn't have a clue' (had no idea, didn't understand or know) what her friend was talking about.

21   D   The speaker says that the fact that the family party has been cancelled and so won't happen is 'a pity' (a sad thing). He 'was really looking forward to' the party (he was excited about it and thought it would be very enjoyable). So the speaker wanted the party to happen and is disappointed that it isn't going to happen on the agreed date.

22   B   The speaker says that, after their 'huge argument', she thought that the person in her class at college, 'was going to be really angry' with her. She 'assumed' (believed that it was certain to be true) that the person had 'fallen out with' her (stopped being friends with her). But this was not true. The other person apologized and the speaker was 'really pleased because I didn't want to lose her as a friend'. So the speaker expected something bad to happen but in fact it did not happen.

23   A   The colleague phoned the speaker at a time that was not 'convenient' and the speaker didn't want to talk about work. The speaker was therefore 'fed up' (annoyed, angry) that the person had phoned. The speaker hopes that he 'wasn't too rude' (that he wasn't very impolite because he was annoyed), but because he felt annoyed, he 'wanted to get rid of him' (he wanted to end the call, to make the person go away).

p.31 PAPER 4 Part 4

24   C   The interviewer says that Emma's character thought it would be 'rainy and cold' in England, and it was rainy. However, Emma says 'I don't mind the rain' (I don't dislike it) and she got clothes for rain. She says that in LA, where she comes from, 'it's never really rainy' and that's why she didn't mind the rain in England – it was different from the weather she was used to. She adds 'I love the weather' in England. So she liked the rain because it was a change for her.

25   A   When asked about her relationship with the actors 'when the cameras were turned off' (in real life, not when they were acting), Emma says that they 'became really good friends and really close'. She says that 'that' (the fact that they really were friends) 'shows on screen a lot' and that you can't 'fake' it (you can't pretend to have a feeling that you don't really have). She says they 'had so much fun together' and that they still 'hang out' (spend time together) a year after they finished making the film. So they were close friends in the film and close friends in real life too.

26   B   She says that she can 'do' (copy, talk in) an English accent, but gets embarrassed when she's doing it. She can talk in a London accent but she 'can't do any other accent' because other accents are 'so difficult'. The accent in Wales is 'the hardest' one to copy and she can't do the accent of one of the other actors, who she sees a lot and whose accent she likes. She also can't do a Scottish accent. So she can do one accent – London – but not other English accents and not other British accents (Welsh, Scottish).

27   B   She says that, when they were making the film, the 'cast and crew' (the actors and the technical people working on the film) 'made fun of' (made jokes about, laughed at) her accent, which is American. She then says 'I guess I have an accent' (I suppose it's true that I have an accent) and asks 'Do I have an accent?' The interviewer says that she certainly sounds American (has an American accent). Emma than asks 'I do?', meaning 'Do I really have an accent?' She says that everyone tells her she has an American accent. The interviewer says 'But you are American', meaning, 'You are American so of course you have an American accent'. Emma agrees, saying 'I am' (American), 'so I should sound like one' (an American). So Emma is asking whether she has an American accent and is not certain that she has one. When she speaks, she clearly isn't aware that she has the accent and doesn't think she really has one.

28   C   When asked how she would 'cope' (deal with a difficult situation, adapt) if she became a pupil at a boarding school (a school that the pupils also live in), she says that she thinks it 'would be such fun' and she 'would love to' go to one. She says that she has always wanted to be a pupil at one because she has always wanted to find out 'if the books and the movies are right about it'. So she has read about boarding schools in books, and seen films that involve boarding schools. These books and films make boarding schools seem attractive to her and have given her the idea that they are 'fun'. She hasn't been a pupil at a boarding school herself, so the books and films are her only experience of them and she wants to know if they show boarding schools accurately.

29   A   The dancing scene was 'embarrassing' and 'intimidating' (a difficult thing that she was nervous about) at the time when she filmed it, although she also 'had fun' doing it. She says that they 'did a lot of takes' – they filmed the scene a lot of times – so she 'had to keep doing it' – had to repeat it many times. She thinks it 'turned out OK' – the final product is fine – and that they 'edited it well' (the film makers used the best bits to make it look good).

30   B   Emma says that being a movie star is 'hard work' and you have to have 'tough skin' (not be sensitive), so that you aren't 'knocked down by criticism'. She says that you 'have to understand that not everyone is going to like you' – you won't be popular with everyone. If people don't like you, you 'can't let it wreck' (destroy) 'your life'. She thinks movie stars aren't liked by everyone and shouldn't get upset about that.

p.32–33 PAPER 5 Part 1

Further practice and guidance (p.33)

Personal history

A correct

B I've always lived in <u>the</u> same place.

C correct

D <u>I've lived/I've been living</u> there <u>for</u> five years.

E I've been studying at college <u>for</u> six months.

F I was <u>a</u> waiter in a restaurant during the college holidays.

G correct

H I don't like this place because <u>there are</u> <u>too many</u> people here.

I correct

J I'm only planning to stay here for a short time because <u>I'm going/I'm going to go</u> back to my own country.

Reading

A I don't read <u>much/(very) often</u>.

B correct

C correct

D I don't read a newspaper regularly because I'm not very <u>interested</u> in them.

E I like reading music magazines because <u>listening</u> to <u>music</u> is my favourite thing.

F I like reading celebrity magazines because I like reading <u>gossip</u> about famous people.

G correct

H correct

I I <u>really enjoyed</u> this book because it made me laugh a lot.

J I thought that <u>this book was</u> very good because of the characters.

TEST TWO

p.35–36 PAPER 1 Part 1

1   B   Three trips are mentioned. After the trip to the Natural History Museum, the child remembered an accident, when she hit her head on a banister (the structure at the side of some stairs, which you can put your hand on), not the museum's exhibits (such as dinosaurs), which they had gone to see. After the trip to the Tate Modern, some children remembered the escalators (moving stairs), not the art that they had gone to see. After the trip to the zoo, the child remembered a caterpillar that he found at the zoo, not the more interesting animals that were part of the zoo.

2   C   The writer says that her children are 'blank-faced' when important events are mentioned, meaning that they don't remember these events at all. They remember the 'minutiae' (small details, unimportant things), but they don't have any memories of important things.

3   B   The food examples given are examples of the writer's point that 'Food features large in other children's memories' (food is something that children in general remember). One example is a memory of a journey, the others are memories of places visited. In all cases, what the children remembered was food they had. The food was the main or only thing they remembered.

4   A   Suzie Hayman thinks that food is an important part of what everyone remembers – it 'figures high in everybody's memories'. However, she thinks that adults are usually 'less direct' about this – they don't mention it, they don't tell other people that food is something they remember about an event. This is because adults 'try hard to come up to other people's expectations' – they know that other people want them to remember more important things about past events than food. Her point is that adults remember food as much as children do, but children say that they remember it, whereas adults usually don't say this.

5   A   Suzie Hayman says that, when parents take their children to a place, they can 'convey' (indicate or communicate) their 'appreciation for something' – they can show or tell the children that they really like something – but they should not expect the children to 'share it' – they should not expect their children to like the same thing. Parents should provide 'the buffet' – they should show their children a variety of things – and allow them to 'pick' – choose the things they like. What children 'pick' (like or enjoy) may not be the same as what the parents like or enjoy, and parents should realize this.

6   B   The writer's child's memories of holidays focus on the beds the child slept in on holiday. The child associates uncomfortable beds with good holidays. The writer intends to 'nurture' (encourage) this memory because it means that she doesn't have to pay for expensive holidays. Places that have comfortable beds with soft pillows and mattresses cost more than places with uncomfortable beds. So the way her child's memory works is good for her concerning paying for holidays.

7   C   The whole article is about what the writer calls 'odd-memory syndrome', a term the writer has invented, meaning a habit of remembering strange things, a tendency to remember things that you would not expect someone to remember and not to remember things that you would expect someone to remember. Throughout the article, the writer gives examples of this – on trips to museums, zoos, etc and on a number of different holidays. She also gives an expert's opinions on it. One of her main points is that this 'syndrome' is very common among children.

8 D The writer's main point about children's memories is that 'their treasured recollections (the things they really like remembering) don't match parental expectations' (aren't the same as what their parents would like them to remember). She makes this point in the first paragraph. Her aim in the article in general is to make the point that adults take children to places and want them to remember important things about the places, which are the things that adults remember. However, children don't remember these things, they remember other things. She gives many examples to illustrate this point and quotes an expert in support of this point.

p.37–40 PAPER 1 Part 2

Further practice and guidance (p.39–40)

Question 9

1 A   2 C

Question 10	C	Question 13	C
Question 11	A	Question 14	B
Question 12	C	Question 15	B

p.37–38 PAPER 1 Part 2 (Test)

9 D This sentence continues John Gibbons' description of the sport of climbing in general.

Before the gap, he compares it to other sports, saying it is 'one of the few sports where you compete against yourself'.

In D he makes another comparison with other sports and gives another example of a good thing about this sport.

10 G This sentence continues John's description of easy climbs.

In G, 'them' refers back to 'Big holds, spaced comfortably apart'. In G, John says that these holds make it possible to climb to the top 'without any difficulty'.

In the sentence after the gap, 'That kind of climb' refers to the kind of climb with big holds that make it possible for you to climb easily, and the sentence then tells you the name given to this kind of climb.

11 B This sentence continues the description of 'trickier' (more difficult) climbs.

In B, 'one of those' means 'one of the trickier climbs'. B then mentions something connected with doing trickier climbs.

The sentence after the gap contains the word 'also' because it mentions another thing connected with doing trickier climbs, in addition to the thing mentioned in B.

12 H This sentence continues the subject of whether or not the idea is to climb to the top as quickly as possible. Before the gap, Graeme Alderson says that people are not necessarily trying to get to the top as quickly as they can – they are simply trying to get there. After the gap, we are told that the aim may be to climb as high as you can 'without falling off', meaning that you are not necessarily trying to climb to the top.

H links these two points about getting to the top, because it is about people who don't climb to the top.

13 F The whole paragraph is about falling and safety and what happens if you make a mistake. In the sentence before the gap, the phrase 'in case you slip' means 'because

it is possible that you might slip'. The sentence after the gap begins with 'Instead', which must refer to something previously mentioned that does not happen.

'If that happens' in F means 'if you slip' and so refers back to 'in case you slip'. In F 'you don't plunge (fall quickly) to the ground' refers to what does not happen.

In the sentence after the gap, 'you dangle (hang) safely in your harness' describes what does happen if you slip (fall).

14 E The sentence before the gap describes one attitude towards climbing on indoor walls. The sentence after the gap and the rest of the paragraph are about climbing in different places and outdoor climbing that people can do and that people have done.

E connects these things because it refers to beginning with indoor climbing and then moving to outdoor climbing. In E, 'it' refers to 'climbing on indoor walls' in the sentence before the gap and E says that you can use your experience of indoor climbing to decide the difficulty of outdoor climbing you would be able to do. The rest of the paragraph is about climbing 'outside', as mentioned at the end of E.

15 A The paragraph is about information on climbing that is available on the website. The sentence after the gap begins 'Well, you can find out' and this must refer back to something about finding information.

A is about people who want to try climbing but don't know what to do in order to try climbing. The sentence after the gap tells these people 'where to start' – how they can get the information they need if they want 'a go at climbing' (if they want to do or try to do some climbing).

p.41–42 PAPER 1 Part 3

16 B The writer says that people who write about fashion in magazines ('Fashion editors') 'can make or break a brand (can cause a company's clothes to succeed or fail) with a favourable or cruel review'. If a review or comment is cruel, it is negative and unpleasant.

17 E The writer says 'An early indicator of a show's success is who turns up (attends) – or pointedly fails to'. If you do something 'pointedly', you do it in order to make a point or show what you think about something. The writer is saying that some people show their dislike for a company's clothes by not going to that company's show. The success of a show can be judged by which people go to it and which people decide not to go to it (if important people go, it's a success, if they don't, it isn't.)

18 D The writer says that the 'ranges (the sets of clothes a company produces at a particular time) are only mass-produced once the orders come in after Fashion Week'. This means that the company doesn't produce the clothes in large quantities until customers have ordered them after Fashion Week.

19 E The writer says that the company 'does not disclose the event's budget, but it is clearly huge', meaning that it does not tell people or reveal how much money it spends on the event, but it clearly spends a lot of money on it. If you 'disclose' something, you give private or secret information to someone.

20 F On the morning after the show, the company 'opens its showroom above its store in Milan' and this is where 'store buyers place their orders'. People who work for shops and who buy the clothes that are sold in their shops go to this building (the company's store) and order clothes that appeared in the show from the company – they will then sell these clothes in their shops.

21   D   According to Christopher Bailey, 'Standing out from the crowd is the name of the game' – the most important thing is to be different from everyone else. He says that they are 'up against some of the biggest names in fashion' – competing with some of the biggest and most important fashion companies, and they 'have to make an impression' – impress people by being different from the other companies and showing clothes that are different from those of the other companies.

22   A   The tent where the show happens 'gradually fills with' people (fills slowly as more and more people go in) and these people are all 'clutching invites as thick as slices of bread' – they all have very thick invitation cards, which they show in order to enter the tent.

23   A   The writer says that when the lights 'rise' – when all the lights are switched on – at the end of the show, the 'crowd (the audience invited to the show) dashes (hurries, goes very quickly) to the next event' – they leave very quickly and go immediately to the next fashion show that they are attending (the people who 'rush backstage' at the end of the show in F are media people reporting the event, not the audience).

24   C   In the UK, Burberry is known as a 'retailer' (a shop company), so in the UK it sells its clothes in its own shops. In other parts of the world, it sells its clothes in 'other people's shops', and 40 per cent of the clothes it sells are sold in these shops, outside the UK.

25   A   The writer says that the show 'has taken more than six months to plan' but it 'is over (finished) in 18 minutes' – it takes a very long time to plan it but it only lasts for a very short time.

26   F   The writer says that as soon as Christopher Bailey 'takes his bow at the end of the show, (goes in front of the audience at the end to thank them and receive their applause) dozens of fashion journalists and TV crews rush backstage to grab a word with him' – hurry to speak to him as soon as he leaves the stage, because he organized the show and was responsible for it.

27   E   The writer says that 'The seating arrangement has a strict hierarchy' – a fixed system concerning where different kinds of people sit. There are different blocks of seats for important fashion editors, the company's management, retail buyers, emerging markets (people from places that are beginning to buy and sell the company's clothes) and other categories of people.

28   B   The writer says that 'To the outside world' (people not involved in the fashion industry), events like this 'appear to be little more than a love-in for the luxury goods sector' (appear to be only events in which people involved in producing and selling expensive goods are extremely nice to each other). 'However', the writer says, 'beneath the glitzy exterior, there is serious business going on' – the events look glamorous and attractive, but really they are serious because of the commercial importance of them. The writer is saying that these events are more serious and important than people who aren't involved in them may think.

29   F   After the show, 'Clips, quotes and reviews are online and on newswires within minutes' – bits of film of the event, things said by people at the event and reviews appear in the media only minutes after the end of the show.

30   B   The writer says that 'Designers' entire careers can hang on one collection', meaning that their whole careers can depend on whether a particular set of clothes they designed, and which appears in a show, is popular and successful or not.

p.43 PAPER 2 Part 1

TASK-SPECIFIC MARK SCHEME

Content

The email must include all the points in the notes. You must:

- respond very positively to the news that Richard got the job
- ask Richard what his new job involves
- tell Richard that he shouldn't worry about what will happen
- ask Richard to describe his first day in the new job.

Organization and cohesion

You should organize each point in a logical order (probably the same as in Richard's email) and in appropriate, probably short, paragraphs (a paragraph might contain only one sentence).

Range

You should use appropriate structures and vocabulary for expressing happiness for someone else, asking for details about a job, telling someone to be confident and to stop worrying and asking for a future action.

Appropriacy of register and format

Your email should be informal and should open and close in an appropriate way for an email to a friend. It should be lively and enthusiastic in tone. Grammar and spelling should be accurate and standard (the same as for a letter).

Target reader

The reader should understand fully your reaction to his news, what you want him to do and the advice you are giving him about how he should feel.

p.44–49 PAPER 2 Part 2

Further practice and guidance (p.45–49)

QUESTION 2 LETTER

1   A, C, D, G, H

TASK-SPECIFIC MARK SCHEME

Content

You should:

- say what you like about the magazine and why
- say what, if anything, you dislike about the magazine
- suggest something new to include in the magazine.

Organization and cohesion

The letter should be organized into clear paragraphs, which follow a logical order, with clear linking between the points made in each paragraph. It should start with an introductory paragraph, explaining why you are writing and making general comments on the magazine. Other paragraphs should deal with good things about the magazine and why you like them, possible negative comments and a suggestion for something new to include. The letter should end in an appropriate way.

Range

You should use a range of appropriate structures and vocabulary for describing the content of a magazine, making positive (and perhaps negative) comments, giving reasons and making a suggestion.

Appropriacy of register and format

The letter should be neutral or fairly formal (it is to a magazine editor). It should begin and end with suitable phrases for opening and closing a letter in this context.

Target reader

The editor should be completely clear about what you like about the magazine and why, and should understand fully what you are suggesting as an additional thing for the magazine.

ASSESSMENT OF SAMPLE ANSWER

Content

The letter contains everything that it should contain. The writer gives details of aspects of the magazine she likes and why she likes them, makes general comments about the magazine and suggests a new section that could be included.

Organization and cohesion

The letter is organized in clear, mainly short, paragraphs, each dealing with a separate point. Separate paragraphs deal with general comments, particular aspects of the magazine and the suggestion for something new. Good linking is used (for example *Firstly* and *Finally*) and there is good linking between comments and reasons for making those comments.

Range

A good range of structures and vocabulary is used for describing aspects of the magazine and for giving opinions on them. The structures and vocabulary used are not simple but are used in more complex sentences. A wide variety of effective and appropriate phrases is used, for example, *make comments, of all, comes as a surprise, jump with joy, make me realize, just like us, without + -ing, would like to, as well as*. The present simple is appropriately used most of the time, and there is also correct use of the present continuous (*are still having doubts, am really looking forward to*).

Accuracy

The structures and vocabulary are almost all used correctly. There are no mistakes with verb tenses and there is a lot of good vocabulary used correctly, for example *honoured, fears, anxieties and boredom, obviously, invaluable, attempting, covers, hints, issue*.

There are a few mistakes but these are not serious ones and do not affect understanding. In the third paragraph, *celebrities real life* should be 'celebrities' real lives' or 'the real lives of celebrities'; in the fifth paragraph, *reading* is an uncountable noun and so the article *a* should not be included in the phrase; in the sixth paragraph, *extreme* should be 'extremely', *everyone who are* should be 'everyone who is' because 'everyone' is singular, and *prospectives* should be 'prospects'.

Appropriacy of register and format

The register is appropriately neutral/fairly formal and the letter opens with an appropriate introduction

and closes with an appropriate conclusion. The writer expresses enthusiasm for the magazine very effectively.

Target reader

The reader would be completely clear about the writer's views on the magazine and fully understand what the writer suggests for inclusion.

Mark

Band 5 (approximately 17–20 marks out of 20). This is a very effective letter, which does everything required in the instructions and uses a wide range of more than simple grammar and vocabulary. The mistakes are not basic ones and there are not many of them. A lot of language of a high level is used correctly.

QUESTION 3 ESSAY

TASK-SPECIFIC MARK SCHEME

Content

You should:

- give your opinions agreeing or disagreeing with the statement or both agreeing and disagreeing

- end with a conclusion summarizing your views.

Organization and cohesion

The ideas should be organized into clear paragraphs in the essay, with an appropriate beginning and ending. Opinions should be supported with reasons and there should be a clear connection between the ideas expressed. Appropriate linking words and phrases should be used.

Range

A range of grammatical structures and vocabulary connected with the topic should be used.

Appropriacy of register and format

The essay should be neutral/fairly formal (it is a piece of work for a teacher).

Target reader

The reader should understand the writer's opinions on the statement and the topic completely.

ASSESSMENT OF SAMPLE ANSWER

Content

The essay fully addresses the task. It deals with the statement in a completely relevant and direct way and everything in it is related to the topic. The writer agrees with the statement and supports this agreement with reasons.

Organization and cohesion

The essay is very well organized. The opening paragraph states the writer's general view, the second and third paragraphs discuss aspects of the topic and give opinions on these aspects, and the final paragraph presents a conclusion that does not simply repeat what has been said before. There is particularly effective use of linking (*However, In addition, Furthermore, In conclusion*).

Range

The essay contains a good range of grammatical structures, for example the relative clause in the first paragraph (*which money ...*), the use of the *–ing* form as a subject (*Having*) in the second paragraph, the use of comparative structures in the third paragraph (*more + noun phrase + than* in the first sentence, *being healthy is undoubtedly more important than being rich*), and again the use of the *–ing* form as a subject (*Feeling*) in the last paragraph. There is also a good range of vocabulary connected with the topic of money and wealth.

Accuracy

Many structures of a high level are used correctly to create effective sentences that are not only short and simple. A lot of vocabulary connected to the topic is used accurately, for example *shape our dreams, show respect, prosperity, materialistic, affection*.

There are a few mistakes. The first paragraph should be one sentence (the sentence beginning *Because* is not a complete sentence). In the second paragraph, the first sentence should be 'Everyone wants to have a high standard of living', the phrase *all these such things* should be 'all these things' or 'all such things' and *but up to a point* should be 'but only up to a point'. In the third paragraph, *the happiness* should be 'happiness' (without 'the'), *most of people* should be 'most people', and *money only able* should be 'money is only able'. In the last paragraph, the use of *despite* is incorrect grammatically and it should be 'although money is described' or 'despite the fact that money is described', *things that impossible* should be 'things that are impossible', and *as being* should be 'by being' or 'because of being'.

Appropriacy of register and format

The register is appropriately neutral/fairly formal and the essay has an appropriate introduction and conclusion.

Target reader

Although there are a number of mistakes, the reader would be completely clear about the writer's opinion on this topic.

Mark

Band 4 (approximately 13–16 marks out of 20). This is a good essay, which expresses clear and relevant opinions and fully addresses the statement. It has a good range of grammar and vocabulary that is not only basic or simple. However, it contains a significant number of mistakes, which prevent it from being in the highest band. Some of these mistakes are serious grammatical mistakes, but they do not make it impossible to understand what the writer is saying.

QUESTION 4 REVIEW

1 A, B, C, E, G

2

A had	F didn't become
B gave	G made
C found	H didn't pay
D didn't get	I didn't do
E came	J didn't catch

TASK-SPECIFIC MARK SCHEME

Content

You should:

- name what you are reviewing and describe it
- say why you think it is so good
- discuss its lack of general success and popularity
- say why it should be more successful/popular.

Organization and cohesion

Your review should be organized into clear paragraphs, each paragraph dealing with different topics (a description of the book/music, why you like it so much, its lack of success, why it should be more popular). The points you make should follow a logical order and be linked appropriately.

Range

You should use a range of grammatical structures and vocabulary for describing a book/music, giving opinions, describing your feelings and reactions and talking about a situation that you believe should be different.

Appropriacy of register and format

Your review should be neutral or fairly formal (it is for a magazine and it is about something that most people don't know).

Target reader

The reader should have a clear idea of why you like the book/music so much and why you are recommending it and suggesting that it should be more well-known.

ASSESSMENT OF SAMPLE ANSWER

Content

The review contains a detailed description of the book and why the writer likes it so much. However, it does not refer to the book's lack of success/popularity or give reasons why it should be more well-known/popular.

Organization and cohesion

The review is well organized in clear paragraphs. The opening and closing paragraphs are effective and not repetitive and the second and third paragraphs explain very clearly what happens in the book and why the writer of the review enjoyed it so much. There is some good linking within sentences, for example the use of a dash (–) to link points in the first sentence/paragraph and the first sentence of the third paragraph, the use of *–ing* forms to continue a description in the first two sentences of the second paragraph and *As* in the final sentence of that paragraph, and *However* in the third paragraph.

Range

A good range of grammatical structures is used, for example appropriate use of the past simple for the experience of reading the book and the present simple for describing the plot of the book, many uses of the *–ing* form to create longer and more fluent sentences (*living in a small town, being an overweight ..., telling part of the story*), and the use of *What* as the subject of a sentence (third paragraph). A very good range of vocabulary is used for describing the book.

Accuracy

There are no real grammatical mistakes and high-level grammatical structures are used accurately. The use of vocabulary is also very good, for example *I found myself really enjoying, struggling, unwinds, unravel, twists, narrative structure, narrator, taking turns with.* There are no errors with vocabulary.

Appropriacy of register and format

The review is appropriately neutral/fairly formal and it begins and ends appropriately.

Target reader

The reader would be completely clear about what the book is about and why the writer likes it. However, the reader would not be informed about the book's lack of popularity/success or the writer's views on that – these things are not mentioned in the review.

Mark

Band 3 (approximately 8–12 marks out of 20). The writer has written an excellent review of a book but not addressed all of the required content points. The review is only about the book and why it is good, it does not mention the book's lack of popularity or give reasons why it should be more popular. Therefore, very important requirements in the instructions have not been covered. This means that a significant number of marks are lost. The level of language in the review is extremely high – if the review included all the content points at this level, it would be a Band 5 answer.

p.50–51 PAPER 3 Part 1

1 A If something is 'long gone', it stopped existing a long time ago. The words 'over', 'done' and 'finished' can all be used to talk about something that no longer exists, but only 'gone' forms a phrase with 'long'. The writer is saying that the idea that people could have the same job for the whole of their working lives ended a long time ago and it doesn't exist now because it doesn't happen any more.

2 D A 'period of time' is a continuous amount of time when something happens or is true. The writer is saying that people today often don't 'stay loyal to' (continue to work for because they feel that they should do this) companies for even a short amount of time, and therefore certainly not a long time.

3 B If something is 'particularly true in a place', it happens more in that place than in some others. The writer is saying that it is more common for people in London to change from one company to another than for people in other places to do this.

4 C If you 'keep an/one eye on something', you look at it while you are doing something else. The writer is saying that, while people are working in one job, they are always looking for another job and paying attention to the possibility of opportunities to get another job.

5 D In this context 'even if' means 'although it may be true that …'. The writer is saying that the fact that they are happy in their existing jobs does not stop people from looking for other jobs. They may be happy doing the job they have, but they look for other jobs.

6 A If you are 'on the lookout (for something)', you are looking for something because you want to find it or you want to know if it exists. The writer is saying a lot of London workers say that they like their current jobs but are always looking for other jobs.

7 C If something 'provides someone with something', it gives someone something that they want or need. The writer is saying that people who are looking for a job get

information about job opportunities quickly and easily from the internet. The internet gives them the information they need.

8 B If you 'register with' an organization, you put your name and other personal details on a list kept by that organization for a particular purpose. In this case, the writer is saying that 53 per cent of the people asked in the survey had contacted an employment agency and put their names on those agencies' lists of people who are looking for jobs. An employment agency is a company that finds jobs for people who have registered with it.

9 B An 'approach' is the way that you do something, the way that you try to deal with a task successfully. The writer is saying that people who register with an employment agency while they have a job are being 'proactive' – they are taking action in advance, before it becomes necessary or before a problem happens (in this case, before they really need to find a new job).

10 D If you do something 'with the minimum of' something, you do it with as little as possible of that thing. The writer is saying that by registering with an employment agency, people can find a job that suits them perfectly ('a perfect job match') without having to try hard – they can do the smallest possible amount of trying in order to find this job.

11 B The phrasal verb 'end up' describes the result of something or what happens at the end of a process or series of events. The writer is saying that employers might have a big problem in the future because more and more people want to leave companies after only working there for a short time.

12 A A 'factor' is one of the reasons for something. In this context 'biggest' means 'most important' or 'main'. The adjective 'big' is the only one of the choices that can be used with words like 'problem,' 'reason', 'influence', etc. The writer is saying that the main reason why people are more attracted to a job is because it is 'challenging and interesting', not because of the salary.

p.52–53 PAPER 3 Part 2

Further practice and guidance (p.53)

Question 13	B	Question 19	A
Question 14	B	Question 20	B
Question 15	A	Question 21	A
Question 16	A	Question 22	B
Question 17	B	Question 23	A
Question 18	B	Question 24	B

p.52 PAPER 3 Part 2 (Test)

13 there

This sentence tells us how many kite surfers existed in the UK five years ago. The structure *there + be + noun* is required to talk about something existing.

14 is

The present simple of 'be' is required here to talk about the present number. The writer is saying that the number is now closer to 10 000 than to a few hundred.

15 to

If something is 'attached to something', the two things are physically connected by something. The writer is saying that there is a harness (a group of strong leather bands) round the middle of the rider which is fixed firmly to the kite.

16 more

The structure *even + comparative adjective* is used for emphasis when comparing things. The writer is saying that watching kite surfers is 'thrilling' (very exciting) but actually doing it is more exciting (it's extremely exciting).

17 much

The phrase 'so much' emphasizes that there is a very large number of things and 'There's so much' here means 'There is such a large number of things'. Aaron Hadlow is talking about the large number of things you can do when you are kite surfing and he then lists them.

18 age

The phrase *at the age of + number* is used for talking about how old someone is/was when they do/did something. The writer is saying that Hadlow was 12 years old when he started taking part in kite surfing competitions.

19 later

The writer is talking about a point in time in the past after a previously mentioned point in time. The writer is talking about something that happened three years after Hadlow started competing in kite surfing competitions. The word 'later' means 'after that time' and is used alone after a period of time. The word 'after' must be followed by what happened before – 'after that' or 'after he started competing' would be correct.

20 for

This completes the structure *present perfect + for + period of time*, to talk about how long something has been happening or has been true. The writer is saying that Hadlow continues to be world champion and has won that title every year for four years.

21 because/as/since

The writer is reporting the reason for something, and 'because' is required to link a result with a cause. The linking words 'as' and 'since' can also be used with the meaning 'because'.

22 takes

This completes the structure *it + take + period of time + 'to' infinitive*, which is used to talk about the amount of time required to do something. Richard Gowers is saying that you can learn the basics of kite surfing in two or three days.

23 One

This completes the structure *one of + superlative adjective + noun*, which is used to talk about one thing from a number of things. The writer is saying that the fact that you don't need a lot of equipment is a very good thing about kite surfing.

24 it

The pronoun 'it' is required here to refer to the 'equipment' previously mentioned. The phrase 'it all' means the same as 'all of it'. Here it means 'all of the equipment'.

p.54 PAPER 3 Part 3

25 wooden

You must form the adjective here to describe the noun 'houses'. The houses are simple and they are made of wood.

26 unemployed

You must use a negative prefix here to form a negative adjective. If someone is 'unemployed', they don't have a job. The writer is talking here about the problems of the Lakota people and how difficult their lives are – 'times are tough' means 'life is difficult'.

27 difficulties

The plural noun is required here – 'many' must be followed by a plural noun. The writer is saying that the Lakota people have many problems in the place where they live but they don't want to leave that place and prefer to stay there.

28 visitors

The plural noun describing people is required here. The writer is saying that some Native Americans want people to come and visit the places where they live and are trying to attract them to these places.

29 jewellery/jewelry

The noun is required here to describe the group of objects that people wear for decoration (eg, rings, bracelets, necklaces, etc). The writer is talking about goods made by Native Americans which they sell in their shops to people visiting the places where they live.

30 wisdom

You must form the noun here after the definite article 'the'. The noun 'wisdom' means 'knowledge developed as a result of long experience of life'. The writer is saying that the 'elders' (the old and important members of the tribe) have this knowledge and experience and they use it to teach the children.

31 Traditional

You must form the adjective here, to go with the noun 'stories' and to describe the kind of stories that Native Americans tell (stories that have existed for a very long time and been passed from one generation to another).

32 grandchildren

The 'children' of the elders have already been mentioned, so you must form a plural noun meaning 'the children of the children'. The writer is describing the process of stories being told to each generation.

33 forgotten

You must form the adjective/past participle here, with the meaning 'not remembered by people in general'. The writer is saying that the stories will disappear and nobody will remember them if the tradition of telling them to young people stops.

34 forever

You must use a prefix here to form an adverb meaning 'for all time'. The writer is saying that there is a possibility that the stories will disappear and never return, people will forget them and they will never be told again at any time it the future.

p.55 PAPER 3 Part 4

35 as/so good][at cooking as

The comparative structure *not as + adjective + as* is required here to compare two people in a certain way ('so' can be used instead of 'as' when this comparative structure is negative, but this is not very common). The phrase *good at + -ing/noun* is also required for someone's ability to do something.

36 she hadn't][made me

You must form the third conditional structure here – *if + subject + past perfect + subject + would have + past participle*. This describes the result of something in the past not happening or being different from what happened. The structure *make + object + adjective describing a feeling* is also required with the meaning 'cause someone to have a particular feeling'. The verb 'annoy' means 'make angry'.

37 don't we][have something

The structure *Why don't we/you, etc + verb* is used for suggesting something that the speaker believes is a good idea. 'Let's' = 'Why don't we?' The phrase *have something to eat* means 'eat something'.

38 too cold][for us to

You must form the structure *too + adjective + for + object + 'to' infinitive* here. This structure explains why something is/was impossible.

39 what][that sentence means

The pronoun 'what' is required here in the structure *what + noun + verb*. This structure is often used after the verbs know/understand etc, to talk about things that people know, understand, etc. The word order in this structure is the same as a statement, not a question ('what' is followed by a subject, not by a verb).

40 wasn't keen][to talk

The phrase *be keen to do something* means 'really want to do something' or 'be very interested in doing something'. The phrase *talk about* means 'discuss'.

41 not used to][eating

If you *are used to doing something*, it is not strange for you because you have done it many times, you are accustomed to it and it is not a new experience any more. The negative form must be used here, because the experience is strange.

42 politics][always interested

The first word 'Has' is singular and so the subject of that verb must be 'politics' (which is grammatically singular). If you *are interested in something*, you take an interest in it, it interests you.

p.56 PAPER 4 Part 1

1   A   At the moment, they are 'not speaking to each other' but the woman says that she is 'sure we could reach an agreement if we both calmed down' – she thinks they can solve the problem if they discuss it again but this time without getting angry with each other. She says at the end that she is 'sure we'll sort it out' – she believes they will talk about the problem again and reach an agreement. She thinks her opinion was right but she hasn't 'fallen out with' (stopped being friends with the other person because of being angry with that person) Nick, and thinks that they can discuss the matter again in a pleasant way.

2   C   He says that the player 'does try hard' and that he does 'put the maximum effort in' – he tries as hard as he can. However, he thinks that he has never 'had what it takes at this level' – he has never had the necessary skills, never been good enough, to play at this high level of football. When the club first bought the player, he was 'really rubbish' (very bad) and 'things haven't got any better since then' (he continues to be really bad). The speaker keeps thinking that he will improve, but he never improves.

3   B   The teacher is ill and they 'haven't been able to find a replacement', and a teacher who taught on the course previously is 'not available'. They are going to 'arrange for that lesson to be in the final week of the course', so they will have two lessons that week instead of one. Therefore they will have 'the full number of lessons' that they have paid for and they will not get 'money back for this one' (the lesson that should happen tomorrow). The extra lesson in the final week will 'make up for' (replace, take the place of) the one they cannot have this week.

4   C   The speaker says that some of the managers 'started at the bottom here and worked their way up' to become managers, and that he is hoping to do the same thing. He says that the place 'has got a really good culture' and that it is 'made clear to all of us (all of the people who work there) that it's possible to do that here' (that they can rise to become managers). He says that he has been in places where managers haven't 'got a clue what to do' (don't know how to run things, are poor managers) but 'that's not the case here' (that's not true of this place). So the speaker works for a successful company that has appeared a lot in the media and would like to become a manager there.

5   B   The woman doesn't like the place where they have arranged to meet because it's very 'noisy' and they won't be able to have 'any sort of conversation' (she says the reason for getting together is to have conversation). She is not saying that she won't come, she is saying that she would prefer to 'meet up somewhere else' and wants them to think of a better place to meet. So she wants to change the place where they are going to meet.

6   A   The speaker says that people 'don't know what to put into the various containers they now have at home' and are 'getting confused about what gets collected from their homes at different times'. They also don't know what kind of things can and cannot be recycled in the places where they live. So the speaker is talking about problems people have about recycling where they live – they are confused about what the system is, and the speaker says that this must become clear quickly. The increase in recycling and its connection with the environment are things that the speaker doesn't intend to 'go into' (discuss, deal with) now.

7   B   The woman says that she believes they will 'settle in' – get used to living in a different place, become happy in a new place – quickly. The man says that it will be a 'fresh start' – the beginning of something completely new, the start of a new way of life. The woman says that they will be in 'new surroundings' – living in a different place. Both of them are going to start new jobs in this place – he is 'looking forward to starting work' and she mentions going into 'the office'.

8   A   The man says that 'there wasn't a great deal to say' (it wasn't necessary to have a long conversation) because the problem at work wasn't an important one. However, his friend always 'gets very worked up' (becomes very worried, angry or upset) about unimportant things and 'goes on and on about them' (talks about them for a long time, much longer than is necessary or desirable). During the phone call, the friend 'wouldn't listen' when the man told him not to worry about the problem, so they repeated the same things 'over and over again' (many, many times). The man is therefore saying that the conversation lasted for a much longer time than was necessary.

p.57–58 PAPER 4 Part 2

```
┌─────────────────────────────────────────────────────┐
│ Further practice and guidance (p.58)                │
│                                                     │
│ Question 9    B        Question 14    B             │
│ Question 10   A        Question 15    A             │
│ Question 11   A        Question 16    A             │
│ Question 12   A        Question 17    A             │
│ Question 13   A        Question 18    A             │
└─────────────────────────────────────────────────────┘
```

p.57 PAPER 4 Part 2 (Test)

9   1942

Petrie 'lived from 1835 to 1942'. He studied 'ancient Egypt'. We are told when he died but we are not told where he died.

10   ordinary things

Petrie 'was more interested in looking at the ordinary things that people used every day'. He was more interested in collecting ordinary (typical, common, usual) things used in daily life in ancient Egypt than in 'raiding their treasure houses' – taking things that were very valuable in ancient Egypt from the places where they were kept.

11   pottery bowl

The curator says that his favourite object 'is a pottery bowl which was found in a tomb' (a place, often a structure made of stone, where a dead person or a group of dead people are buried). The bowl is his favourite object in the museum, and someone wrote letters on the bowl to his dead parents.

12   packed

The curator says that Petrie 'packed the objects properly' (wrapped them and protected them in strong containers in the necessary way) before sending them from Egypt to his museum in London. Because he did this, the objects 'survived the journey' – were not damaged or destroyed as they travelled from Egypt to London.

13   72 000/seventy-two thousand

There are a total of 80 000 objects. 6000 of them are 'on display' in the museum and you can also see 2000 more objects in the museum – these are 'in drawers that you can look in easily'. So visitors to the museum can see a total of 8000 objects. The other objects, a total of 72 000, are 'all in cupboards' and 'we can't let people see them' – the museum cannot show them to people.

14   glass cupboards

They are 'going to move the collection to a much better building' and, in this new building, 'all the objects will be in glass cupboards where they can be seen'. The present museum 'was converted from stables' (used to be a place where horses were kept) and is 'very small and cramped' (there is not much space in it) – the new museum will be big enough for all the objects to be shown.

15   his work

In the new museum, they intend to show Egypt 'both thousands of years ago and in the present day' and they will show objects that are 'in store at the moment' (not shown in the museum but kept in another place where people cannot see them). In addition to showing all these objects, they will also have 'a small section for Petrie himself and his work' – a small section that deals with the man and what he did.

16   (information) labels

The curator says that he doesn't like information labels because people read them but don't look at the objects. He prefers to use 'big graphic panels (boards with pictures and designs on them) showing timelines (illustrations showing different points in time when things happened) and how the objects appeared in life'. So the new museum will not have information labels that people simply read, it will have 'graphic panels' for people to look at while they look at the objects.

17   (big) (graphic) panels

The curator says that it is 'important to talk to lots of different people about what should be on the panels' – and they 'are talking to as many people as possible' about their plans for the new museum. So they are asking people for their opinions on what the panels should contain.

18   useless for display

The inverted commas here indicate that the gap must be filled by actual words used by Petrie. The curator quotes Petrie's words – Petrie said this about his collection (he believed it was useful for 'students and researchers' but not suitable for display to the public). The curator says that Petrie believed this because the objects are not 'big' or 'flashy' (impressive and exciting).

p.59 PAPER 4 Part 3

19   C   The speaker says that they saw 'just about every animal in the place' and were shown 'all sorts of things' but 'after a while' (a period of time), they 'all got very tired and lost interest'. They were at the zoo 'from early morning until late afternoon' and they had 'all had enough (they didn't want to stay or do any more) after a couple of hours'. So their time at the zoo was too long for them and they didn't enjoy it after a certain amount of time.

20   F   The speaker says that after getting his 'name tag' (identification label worn so that people can see the person's name), 'the whole event was chaotic' (disorganized). People were given the wrong information about rooms and times for events, everyone was 'confused' and didn't know where to go. The whole thing was 'a mess' (a disorganized thing).

21   B   The speaker 'was really impressed' by the place and what she saw there. It was 'great' to see things she had only seen in books. She 'could have stayed there for ages' (would have been happy to stay there for a very long time) and didn't want to leave. She 'was running around looking at one fantastic picture after another' (was going in an excited way from one picture she really liked to another).

22   A   The speaker was right to think he would be 'scared' (frightened) because 'the very first thing' he did was frightening. He says that the experience of that first activity was 'enough to put me off (make me not want to continue) straight away' (immediately). He didn't feel better at any time in the day after that, and 'spent the whole of the day errified' (very frightened). So the first thing he did during he day was a terrible experience for him and he 'never ecovered from that' all day.

!3   **D**   The speaker says that before the trip she 'wasn't ooking forward to it at all' (didn't think it would be good, vasn't enthusiastic about going) because she thought it was hot going to be well organized. But in fact, she was wrong about this and the trip was 'fine'. It wasn't 'the most thrilling lay' (the most exciting day in her life), but it was 'worth loing' (fairly enjoyable, not a waste of time). So she had hought the trip would be terrible (she 'was dreading it') but n fact it wasn't so bad.

p.60 PAPER 4 Part 4

!4   **B**   Sébastien says that free running is 'part of my life' and that for him it's the same as walking, which people do simply because they can'. So he does it simply because he is able to do it, it is a natural thing for him to do.

!5   **A**   Sébastien says that people who have 'done some sport' (people who are fit) 'often want to do something too impressive too soon' (often want to do something difficult before they are ready and able to do it). He prefers beginners who 'start with not such a healthy body' because they are willing to learn more slowly and 'start at a low level'. Fit people want to do difficult things as soon as they start free unning.

!6   **C**   Sébastien says that 'there is risk' in free running (it s dangerous) 'but there is risk everywhere'. He says that driving a car and flying in a plane can also be dangerous but people don't think much about the dangers of those hings and try to make them as safe as possible. He says hat 'It's the same with free running' (the same is true of free unning) – it can be dangerous but the people who do it try o make it as safe as possible.

!7   **B**   Sébastien says that he isn't 'a risk-taker' because everything he does is 'calculated' (he has prepared it and hought about it before he does it). He then says that not everything he does is '100 per cent safe' but that he is always thinking of the safest way to do what I'm doing'. So he makes sure that everything he does is as safe as possible and involves the smallest amount of risk possible. This might involve using various pieces of equipment.

!8   **A**   Sébastien says that he wasn't nervous about the ump because he only had to jump a distance of three to four metres, and he had jumped much longer distances when ne was competing in athletics and doing the long jump (his longest jump in that was over seven metres). So he was sure that he could jump the required distance easily and 'had no stress'.

!9   **B**   Sébastien says that people think he has 'no fear' but in fact he suffers from 'vertigo' (a bad feeling when n a high place) and he is 'afraid of heights'. This is a problem he always has to deal with, and he uses 'focus and concentration' – he thinks about 'something else' (not the fact of being in a high place).

30   **C**   Sébastien says that people believe that 'free running is only about the city' (can only be done in cities), but that this idea isn't true. He thinks you can do it in the countryside (with trees and rocks) and in water. He thinks people should not have such a narrow view of free running and where it can be done.

p.61–63 PAPER 5 Part 2

Further practice and guidance (p.62–63)

Photographs 1A and 1B

Describing

traffic B   bars A   crowded A/B   lanes B   holding A

queue B   stationary B   carriage A   busy A/B

congested B

Comparing

1   correct

2   That journey isn't as easy <u>as</u> this one.

3   This person is getting <u>more exercise</u> than those people.

4   correct

5   The person on the bike might get to work more quickly <u>than</u> the people in the cars.

6   The person on the bike <u>looks happier</u> than the people on the train.

7   correct

8   Whereas that person <u>is</u> relaxed, those people are not.

Personal response – preference

1 to go   2 go   3 to be   4 cycling   5 to go

Photographs 2A and 2B

Describing

team A/B   coach B   furious A   encouraging B

yelling A/B   crowd B   meeting A   pointing A

fist B   argument A

Guessing and suggesting

1 B   2 D   3 B   4 A   5 B   6 A   7 C   8 C

Personal response – your life and experience

1   I try <u>not to</u> lose my temper very often.

2   I get angry when people are rude <u>to</u> me.

3   I only shout at people if they have done <u>something</u> really bad.

4   My friends <u>tell</u> me that I shout when I'm using my phone.

5   I shout <u>a lot</u> when I'm supporting my team at a football match.

TEST THREE

p.65–66 PAPER 1 Part 1

1   **B**   When Brunetti went into the room full of postmen dealing with mail for delivery, he asked someone to tell him where he could find a certain postman. This person, a woman, 'looked at him with open curiosity' – she looked at him in a way that made it clear that she wanted to know why he wanted to speak to this postman (Mario).

2   **C**   Mario was sorting letters (putting them into the correct places so that they could then be delivered to the correct addresses). He looked at each letter, 'merely glancing at the names and addresses' (only looking at the names and addresses on each one for a moment), and then he put them quickly into the 'slots' (sections or compartments) in front of him. He therefore did the job of organizing the letters for delivery very quickly and without having to spend time looking at each address. This indicates that he was very familiar with the addresses and with the sorting process, because he had done this many times before.

3   D   Mario said that he had to climb a lot of steps to deliver registered mail to the old woman. Brunetti immediately decided that the old woman had not 'tipped' Mario (given him extra money) for doing this and he 'anticipated his anger' about this – expected Mario to say that he was angry about this. He waited for Mario to 'give voice to it' – express his anger. But Mario didn't do this, he said that he didn't expect to be tipped. So Brunetti formed the opinion that Mario was angry about not being tipped but he was wrong about this.

4   C   Mario mentions a Swiss watch in connection with how often the registered mail arrived for the old woman. He said that the envelopes arrived once a month and that this pattern was 'As regular as a Swiss watch' – it was always the same, the letters always arrived once a month. Mario is saying that Swiss watches are very exact and reliable, and he is comparing them with the arrival of the letters, which always followed an exact pattern.

5   A   Mario said that he could remember something about some of the addresses the registered envelopes had come from, but when Brunetti asked him if he could remember any of the addresses 'exactly', he said that he delivered mail to 'almost four hundred people'. His point here is that he delivers a lot of mail to a lot of people, and so he could not be expected to remember the exact addresses that particular mail had come from. (In addition, Mario focuses on the addresses he has to deliver mail to, not addresses of where they came from that may appear on the envelopes.)

6   A   Mario knew that the other registered letters came from 'people in the neighbourhood' because the local people who had sent these letters told him that they had sent them. He says that they told him about the letters because they wanted him to confirm for them that he had delivered these letters.

7   B   Mario says that the noise made by the old woman's television was a problem for other people ('Everyone heard it') but that 'there was nothing they could do' about it. The people affected by the noise couldn't stop the noise because 'the police wouldn't do anything'. Mario says that the police are 'useless' because they didn't take any action about the noise. This is a criticism of the police. Mario immediately remembers that he is talking to a policeman, and he says 'Excuse me' to make it clear that he is criticizing the police officers who did nothing about the noise, not the particular policeman he is talking to.

8   A   Brunetti explains the system for dealing with complaints about noise. A certain department (not the police) deals with the complaints, but they don't go to places at night to measure how loud the noise is because they don't work at night. Complaints are about noise at night, but when the department people go in the morning to measure the noise, it is no longer as loud as it was the previous night, when the complaint was made. He is clearly suggesting that this situation is stupid and that the system doesn't work, because it means that complaints about noise are not correctly dealt with.

p.67–68 PAPER 1 Part 2

9   B   In the sentence before the gap, the writer says that she is 'intimidated' (nervous, lacks confidence) if she draws at home and so is very nervous about drawing in public.

In B, 'But' means despite this fact (although she is nervous about drawing in public), she is at a drawing workshop and drawing in front of people she doesn't know and professional artists.

In the sentence after the gap, she says that she has come to the event with her daughter who is 'just as daunted' (nervous, intimidated) as her.

10   F   In the sentence before the gap, Sue Grayson Ford talks about the aims of The Big Draw. She says that it aims to get people to realize that drawing is 'a way of engaging with the world'.

In F, Sue Grayson Ford continues with this point and explains why drawing is a way of engaging with the world. This is because 'Virtually every discipline' (almost everything you can study) 'uses drawing as a basic form of communication'.

In the sentence after the gap, she adds to what she has said in F – because it is a basic form of communication in so many things, drawing is a 'universal language'. In 'It's our universal language', 'It' refers to 'drawing' in F.

11   H   Before the gap, the writer describes something that all the participants do during one of the workshops – 'drawing pictures inspired by words listed on a card'. While she is doing this, she looks around the room.

H describes what she sees when she looks round the room. Everyone is 'engrossed in' (concentrating fully on) 'what they are doing'.

The sentence after the gap describes what happens when they have finished the task previously described.

12   A   The two sentences before the gap describe another workshop, which involves learning how to create animated cartoons.

In A, the writer moves on to talk about another workshop, after the one about cartoons. In A she describes what this workshop involves.

After the gap, the writer mentions a change in the way she is thinking as a result of doing the workshop mentioned in A.

13   D   Before the gap, the writer mentions an elderly woman, who says that before going to the workshops, she hadn't drawn 'for years'.

D continues what this woman says. In D, she says that as a result of attending the workshops, she feels like 'taking it up again' (she now wants to start drawing as a hobby again). In D, 'it' means drawing, which is mentioned in the previous sentence.

After the gap, the woman says that she is going to 'do that', meaning take up drawing again, as mentioned in D, 'straight away' (immediately).

14   G   In the sentence before the gap, the writer says that children become 'self-conscious' (embarrassed) about drawing and stop doing it.

In G, Sue Grayson Ford comments on the situation mentioned in the sentence before the gap. She regrets it, saying that 'It's a shame' that it happens. In G, the second 'that' means the fact that children become self-conscious and give up drawing.

After the gap, she says why it's 'a shame' (as mentioned in G) that people give up drawing and explains that the purpose of The Big Draw is to get them to start drawing again.

15 E In the whole of the paragraph before the gap, the writer describes the history and development of The Big Draw. Before the gap, she mentions that it includes 1000 events in Britain, and events in other countries.

In E, the writer says that these previously mentioned events are on a variety of topics and gives details of the topics and locations of two of them.

p.69–72 PAPER 1 Part 3

Further practice and guidance (p.71–72)

Question 16   A

Question 17

A number   B age

C number   D age

Question 18   A and B

Question 19   A and B

Question 20   A, B and C

Question 21

1 D   2 A

Question 22

1 A and C

2 A: (more than) six months   C: ten weeks

Question 23   B and C

Question 24   A, B, C

Question 25   A and D

Question 26   A and C

Question 27   B and D

Question 28   A and D

Question 29   A and C

Question 30   A and B

p.69–70 PAPER 1 Part 3 (Test)

16 C She describes an occasion when 'children burst into tears' (started crying very much) at an audition. An audition is part of the process of choosing performers for a show or play; people who want to perform in the show or play go to a place and do a small performance in front of the people who are choosing performers for it. At the auditions for children 'the vast majority of the children (most of the children) get rejected' (are not chosen). At these particular auditions, the children who were not chosen were crying because they were 'devastated' (extremely unhappy and upset) that they had not been chosen.

17 A He says that he usually chooses 'three teams of children' for each show and these three teams perform in the show 'according to a rota system'. This means that there are three different groups of children who perform in the show at different times, and there is a timetable of performances for each group.

18 B She says that in the show she is performing in at the moment, the older children 'are good to me'. They tell her what she has to do next so that she doesn't forget and they 'encourage' her 'a lot' (they say nice things to her to give her confidence).

19 A He says that it's 'essential' (absolutely required) that child performers are able to 'grab the audience's attention' (make the audience look at them and be interested in what they are doing). For this reason, he only chooses children with 'lively personalities and a lot of confidence', because they are able to do this.

20 B She says that she wants to 'keep on performing in musicals for the next few years at least'. She isn't sure if she wants to make it her career but she is sure that she wants to continue doing it for a few years.

21 D He says that people 'in the business (working in the entertainment industry) tend to think' (generally, usually think) that child performers 'aren't capable of developing into good adult performers'. For this reason, child performers 'aren't taken seriously' (people don't think they are good enough to employ) when they are older.

22 A He says: 'No child is in a show for more than six months.' This means that six months is the maximum period of time for any child to be in any show.

23 C She gives two examples of things that Tom and his family are or were unable to do because of Tom's involvement in the show – they can't go on holiday and they couldn't go to a family wedding. These are both examples of Tom's involvement stopping them from doing something they want to do.

24 B She mentions various feelings that she has during a show – she feels 'nervous' and 'worried' because she might make a mistake but she also feels 'excited' and 'proud' when she is on stage.

25 A He says that the children 'learn an enormous amount about discipline, teamwork and concentration, as well as special skills such as choreography and singing'. This means that their abilities at all these things increase enormously as a result of performing in a show.

26 C She says that when her son got chosen to be in the show, they 'were given the schedule (timetable) for the ten weeks of rehearsals' – the period of practising. She says that she 'hadn't realized how much time would be taken up' and that it's 'all rather exhausting – for the parents as much as the children'. This means that after Tom was chosen, they discovered that there would be a period of rehearsals lasting ten weeks and that both the children and their parents were now involved in something that required a lot of their time and energy. They had not known this before and only found out after he was chosen.

27 D He was a very successful performer when he was a child, but when he started secondary school he stopped performing because 'I developed other interests and lost my enthusiasm for it' – he was no longer interested in doing it. Instead, he wanted to do the same things as his friends. He stopped wanting to perform and became keen on other things.

28 D He doesn't want his children to be child performers because he thinks that performing 'can be very stressful for children' and because he thinks it is 'much better for children to concentrate on getting a good education'. He thinks that if they want to perform, they can train to do this when they are older, but he is against the idea of children being performers.

29 C   She says that, in addition to the performances on the timetable that her son has, he 'also has to be available at short notice to replace a child who is ill'. This means that he may be told only a short time before a performance that is not on his timetable that he is required for that performance because he has to replace a child who is ill.

30 B   She says that because of her involvement in the show, she doesn't have time 'to be in any of the sports teams at school' and that this is 'a shame' (an unfortunate or sad fact) because she would like to be in the school sports teams.

p.73 PAPER 2 Part 1

TASK-SPECIFIC MARK SCHEME

Content

The letter must include all the points in the notes. You must:

- ask for information about what has been happening since Clare moved
- ask Clare to describe her new home
- ask Clare what things and which people she misses
- suggest an arrangement for going to stay with Clare.

Organization and cohesion

You should organize each point in a logical order (probably the same as in Clare's letter) and in appropriate paragraphs. In each paragraph you should link what you say with what Clare says in her letter.

Range

You should use appropriate structures and vocabulary for asking for information and details and for suggesting a future plan.

Appropriacy of register and format

Your letter should be informal and should open and close in an appropriate way for a letter to a friend.

Target reader

The reader should understand fully what you are asking for and suggesting and should know what to include in a letter replying to your letter.

p.74–77 PAPER 2 Part 2

Further practice and guidance (p.75–77)

QUESTION 2 REPORT

1 A, C, E, F

TASK-SPECIFIC MARK SCHEME

Content

You should:

- give the background to your report (the class discussion) and the purpose of your report
- describe more than one possible place to visit
- give reasons for choosing these places
- make recommendations on the planning of the trip.

Organization and cohesion

You should organize your report in separate sections, probably with a short and suitable heading for each section. You should link your suggestions with reasons why you are making them.

Range

You should use appropriate verb tenses and structures for past events (the discussion), for making suggestions for the future (for example modals such as 'could', 'would' and 'may/might'), for expressing opinions and for recommending/advising (for example, 'should', 'I suggest that ...', etc). You should also use a range of vocabulary connected with trips and the places you suggest.

Appropriacy of register and format

Your report should be neutral or fairly formal (it is a piece of work for a teacher). It should begin with the purpose of the report and end with a conclusion/recommendation.

Target reader

The reader should be clear about why you have written the report, what you are suggesting and your reasons for suggesting this.

ASSESSMENT OF SAMPLE ANSWER

Content

Everything that should be included is included. The report begins with the background and purpose, with three requirements of the trip to be chosen. A place is recommended, and different things to do and see in that place are described and discussed. The planning of the trip is included (transport) and there is a clear conclusion, justifying the writer's choice.

Organization and cohesion

The report is very well organized in sections with clear headings. Each section and heading covers an aspect of the report or a place being recommended. The order of the sections is logical and the report is easy to follow – it progresses from the introductory section to sections on places and then to sections for organization and conclusion.

Range

A good range of structures and vocabulary is used. Appropriate verb tenses and verb forms are used for the background to the report, for example present perfect for the discussion, *has to* and *should* for requirements (first section), and for describing the present situation and future possibilities (the other sections). A good range of vocabulary is used for talking about trips, places and experiences.

Accuracy

Good structures are used accurately, for example *The aim of this report is to ...*, *Firstly, Secondly, Thirdly* and *Bearing these aspects in mind* (first section), *as well as* (second section), *is said to have* (third section) and *seems ideal* (last section). Some very good and appropriate vocabulary is used, for example *angles, elements, costly* (first section), *charm, leafy tranquillity, picturesquely scattered* (third section), *cost-effective, option* (fifth section).

There are some mistakes: *discussed about* should be 'discussed' (without 'about'), *Windsor area* should be 'the

Windsor area' (first section); *We are planning* is not correct because it means that the decision has been made and the trip has been planned, which is not true in this situation – it would be better to say 'We could/can visit ....', and *the English history* should be 'English history' without 'the' (second section); *fetching* is not the appropriate adjective – 'attractive' would be better, and again the present continuous is used incorrectly – *We are having* means that the plan is fixed, which is not true, and 'We could/can have' would be better (third section).

Appropriacy of register and format

The report is appropriately neutral and very well-presented in an appropriate format for a report of this kind.

Target reader

The reader would be completely clear about why the report was written, what the writer is suggesting and why the writer is suggesting these things.

Mark

Band 4 (approximately 13–16 marks out of 20). This is a very good report, which is very well organized, covers all the necessary points and is very easy to follow. There are a number of mistakes – these do not make it hard to understand what the writer is saying but the verb tense mistakes are serious ones, so the report is not in the highest band.

QUESTION 3 STORY

2 happy feelings: pleased, glad, thrilled, delighted, enthusiastic, relieved, satisfied

   unhappy feelings: disappointed, upset, miserable, awful, concerned, depressed, devastated, disturbed, dreadful, fed up, tearful, shocked, sad

TASK-SPECIFIC MARK SCHEME

Content

Your story should:

- continue logically from the opening sentence you have been given.
- describe a clear sequence of events/feelings/actions.

Organization and cohesion

Your story should be easy to follow, but may not have many paragraphs. The connections between events/feelings/actions should be clear.

Range

You will need to use appropriate past tenses. You may also need to use appropriate time linkers (when, after, while, as soon as, etc) and reported speech forms and/or direct speech. You will need to use a range of vocabulary appropriate for what you describe, including vocabulary for feelings.

Appropriacy of register and format

Your story may be neutral or fairly informal (its aim is to entertain the reader).

Target reader

The reader would have no difficulty understanding what happens in the story and the events/feelings/actions you describe.

ASSESSMENT OF SAMPLE ANSWER

Content

The story continues logically from the opening sentence and establishes the situation immediately. It then describes feelings and thoughts connected with the main point of the story (the letter and opening it). It then describes her reaction after opening it and has a very clear ending, which explains finally what the letter was about and her reaction to it.

Organization and cohesion

The story has a coherent beginning, middle and end, with excellent linking of events, actions and feelings. It is very easy to follow and the paragraphing is very good – the first establishes the context, the second describes the opening of the letter and the last describes reading the letter and reacting to it.

Range

A wide range of past tenses is used appropriately – past simple, past perfect continuous (*had been waiting*), past continuous (*were sweating, were rolling*), past perfect (*had finished*). Modals are also used appropriately (*could change, would make*). A range of vocabulary for describing feelings and reactions is also used.

Accuracy

As well as accurate use of verb tenses and modals, the level of grammatical use is high, for example the linkers *After all* and *as*, and *anything else* (first paragraph), the use of *What* as a subject, the structure *want + object + 'to' infinitive* and *nothing else* (second paragraph) and the relative clause (*who was ...*) and the adverbs *finally* and *excitedly* (last paragraph). Appropriate vocabulary that is more than simple is used throughout, for example *shaking, her palms were sweating, held it very close to her, Tears were rolling down her cheeks, right next to her*.

There is only one small mistake – *on this world* should be 'in this world'.

Appropriacy of register and format

The story is appropriately neutral. It is also lively in tone and interesting for the reader.

Target reader

The reader would understand everything in the story and find it entertaining. The reader is likely to want to find out about the letter while reading the story. At the end, the reader will feel that a whole story has been told.

Mark

Band 5 (approximately 17–20 marks out of 20). This is an excellent story which meets all the requirements with a high level of language and only one very small mistake. It shows a high level of grammar and vocabulary.

QUESTION 4 ARTICLE

TASK-SPECIFIC MARK SCHEME

Content

You should:

- specify clearly the thing that annoys you the most
- explain why it makes you so angry.

Remember that you can write about more than one thing.

Organization and cohesion

The article should be divided appropriately into paragraphs. One paragraph could describe the thing that annoys you and another could describe why it annoys you. Or each paragraph could be about different annoying things. Appropriate linking should be used to connect what annoys you with why it annoys you.

Range

You should use appropriate verb tenses (probably present tenses) and appropriate structures for talking about the causes of something (for example the causes of angry feelings). You should also use a range of vocabulary appropriate to the behaviour/situation that makes you angry and appropriate vocabulary for describing angry feelings.

Appropriacy of register and format

The article can be informal, neutral or formal, but the register should be the same throughout the whole article.

Target reader

The reader should be completely clear about what makes you angry and why it makes you angry. The reader should also find the article interesting/entertaining.

ASSESSMENT OF SAMPLE ANSWER

Content

The article explains exactly what annoys the writer, describing in detail the behaviour of the neighbour. The article also explains clearly why the neighbour's behaviour is so annoying for the writer. It concludes with a general paragraph about annoying behaviour, which is not mentioned in the instructions but which is a good and relevant use of the writer's own ideas.

Organization and cohesion

The article is well organized – the opening paragraph outlines the problem caused by the neighbour, the second paragraph gives more details and explains why it annoys the writer and the final paragraph is an effective generalized conclusion. Facts and opinions are linked well in sentences that are not all short and simple, and effective linking phrases (for example, *such as, Instead of -ing, Only because, it does not mean ..., The worst of all, In addition*) are used throughout.

Range

The present simple is used appropriately through the article, because the article is about a present habit and regular and repeated actions, behaviour and feelings. There is also good use of the structure *find + object + adjective* (*I find this behaviour selfish*), possessive pronouns (*ours*), the *-ing* form for a result (*making the place ...*) and passive verb forms (*will not be picked up, could be left, are finally removed*). A range of appropriate vocabulary for the

topic of the article is used, describing household items, feelings, places and actions.

Accuracy

Verb tenses and verb forms are all used correctly, and a wide range of grammatical structures is used correctly. A very wide range of appropriate vocabulary is used accurately, for example, *unwanted, items, selfish, unacceptable, in such a state, muddy patches, worn-out lawn, has the right to, unsightly, come along, picked up, irritate, show no respect, make other people's life a misery.*

There are two mistakes. In the first sentence of the second paragraph *of which* should be 'which' (without 'of'). In the second paragraph, the words *stuff* and *rubbish* are both uncountable nouns and they should be singular grammatically – *she puts them* should be 'she puts it', *collect them* should be 'collect it' and *they could be left* and *they are finally removed* should be 'it could be left' and 'it is finally removed'.

Appropriacy of register and format

The register is appropriately neutral/informal and the writer expresses anger in a lively and entertaining way. Strong opinions are expressed in a very effective way.

Target reader

The reader would be completely clear about what annoys the writer, how annoyed the writer is and why the writer is so annoyed. The reader would also be clear about the writer's general opinion of people who behave in the way the neighbour behaves.

Mark

Band 5 (approximately 17–20 marks out of 20). Despite the errors in the second paragraph, which do not affect understanding, this is an excellent and lively article, which uses a very wide range of grammatical structures and appropriate vocabulary and does everything specified in the instructions.

p.78–79 PAPER 3 Part 1

1 A   The linking word 'therefore' means 'because of this, because of what has previously been said' and links a cause and a result. It can come at the beginning of a sentence or it can come in a clause. The writer is saying that because life is full of 'man-made sounds', it is not surprising that camping remains popular – it is popular because people want to get away from all these man-made sounds. The linking word 'so' has the same meaning (it links a cause and a result) but it only comes at the beginning of a sentence or clause – it would be correct here if it was the first word of the sentence.

2 B   If something 'grows in something', it gets more of it. If something 'grows in popularity', it becomes more popular. The writer is saying that camping is becoming more popular and is explaining why this is happening.

3 D   If something 'helps to do something', it is a reason why it is possible to do it, it makes it easier to do it. The writer is saying that camping teaches people to stop focusing on 'distractions' (things that take their attention away from what is important) and makes it possible for people to 'enrich' (make more enjoyable) their lives.

4 D   The preposition 'in' is used for giving certain statistics in the phrase *one in + number*. The writer is saying that of every eight holidays in Europe, one is a camping holiday (this means 12.5 per cent of holidays that people take in Europe are camping holidays).

C If 'money is tight', there is not much money, you have little money for a period of time. The writer says that some people 'would still have you believe' (continue to tell you that you should think) that camping is 'an alternative holiday' (something chosen instead of the holiday you really want) that you are 'driven towards' (forced to choose) because you don't have enough money for a better holiday. The writer is saying that some people believe that camping is only for people who don't have much money but this is really untrue ('Nonsense').

C If something 'allows someone something', it makes it possible for someone to have something. The writer is saying that camping gives people the chance to explore.

7 B If you do something 'at your own speed', you do it as quickly or slowly as you want to. The preposition 'at' goes with 'speed' to form a phrase. The writer is saying that if you are camping, you can explore a place as quickly or slowly as you want, you are not forced to do anything.

8 A If you 'mix one thing with another thing', you do two things at the same time, you combine the two things. The writer is saying that you can do some form of 'recreational activity' (something done for enjoyment during free time) while you are camping and gives examples of the large number of places where you can do this.

9 A If you 'escape something', you get away from something that you don't like. The writer is giving reasons why you might choose a certain kind of activity and one reason is that you might want to do something alone or without being surrounded by a lot of people.

10 C If something 'disturbs' something, it causes it not to continue. The writer is saying that the only things that 'disturb the peace' (the only sounds in a quiet place) are the quiet sounds of dragonflies and a cooker.

11 B The linking phrase 'as long as' means 'if' and comes before something that must be true in order for the other part of the sentence to be true. The writer is talking about what is possible for you if you are enjoying camping.

12 B The 'rest of something' is the part or parts of it not previously mentioned. The writer is talking about the parts of life that are not camping and saying that, if you are camping, you don't have to be involved in your normal life.

p.80 PAPER 3 Part 2

13 have

This completes the present perfect tense with a plural subject ('scientists'). The present perfect is used earlier in the sentence ('have suggested') and it is used because the writer is talking about something that happened in the past but is important now and has a result now.

14 make

This completes the structure *make + object + adjective*, which describes the result of something. In this context 'make' means 'cause to be'. The writer is saying that studies prove that people can become more 'quick-witted' (intelligent, able to think clearly quickly) as a result of doing mental exercise.

15 to

This completes the 'to' infinitive in order to explain the purpose of something. The writer is saying that the purpose of using computer-based exercises was that people's problem-solving ability would improve as a result of doing these exercises.

16 The

The definite article must be used here, because this particular team has already been mentioned in the previous sentence, so we know which team the writer is talking about.

17 of

A 'type of something' is one example of something that exists in different forms. The writer is saying that people taking part in the experiment had to look at squares that were different from each other.

18 one

The pronoun 'one' must be used here with the meaning 'a square'. The people had to decide if a square they were shown was the same as a square they had seen before.

19 whether/if

This completes the structure *decide + whether/if*, which is used for talking about deciding 'yes' or 'no'. The people had to decide 'yes, that square is the same as a square I saw earlier' or 'no, that square is not the same as a square I saw earlier'.

20 it

The pronoun 'it' must be used here, with the meaning 'the task'. The writer is describing the system that was used when people were doing the task.

21 and

This completes the phrase *between ... and ...* , which is used for giving the range of something, from the lowest to the highest. The writer is saying that the smallest number of days was eight and the biggest number of days was nineteen. People repeated the exercises for eight or more days but not for more than nineteen days.

22 had

This completes the past perfect tense. One group did the exercises and another group didn't do them. Then the problem-solving ability of the two groups was compared. This happened after the people did or didn't do the exercises, so the past perfect is required.

23 in

This completes the phrase *take part in something*, meaning 'be involved in something' or 'participate in something'. The writer is saying that the people who did the exercises were a lot better at solving problems than the people who didn't do the exercises.

24 they

This pronoun means 'the participants' mentioned earlier in the sentence. The writer is saying the number of problems they could solve increased if they did more training.

p.81–82 PAPER 3 Part 3

Further practice and guidance (p.82)

1

Question 25	H	Question 29	E
Question 26	G	Question 30	D
Question 27	D	Question 31	A
Question 28	I	Question 32	G

Question 33   D   Question 34   E

2

prefixes: un-, in-

suffixes/endings: -ful, -ment, -ly, -ing, -n, -ies, -ive, -ison, -th

---

p.81 PAPER 3 Part 3 (Test)

25   elderly

You must form an adjective that is used as a noun here with the definite article 'the' to describe a group or category of people. The writer is saying that not only 'the elderly' (old people) suffer from problems with their knees and shoulders – young people now have the same problems.

26   painful

You must form an adjective here to go with the noun 'knees'. If something is 'painful' it causes pain, it hurts. The writer is talking about the number of young people who have problems with their knees.

27   comparison

The noun is required here to complete the phrase *in comparison with*, which links things that are being compared. The writer is comparing the number of young people who have knee problems with the number of older people who had knee problems when they were young (this suggests that a lot more young people have knee problems than in the past).

28   youth

The noun is required to complete the phrase *in + possessive + youth*, which describes the period of time when someone is young. The writer is talking about how many people aged 55 had knee problems when they were young.

29   inactive

You must form an adjective with a negative prefix that means the opposite of 'active'. The writer is talking about the causes of the physical problems previously described.

30   pavement

You must form the noun here to go with the definite article 'the'. The writer is saying that people only walk in streets on hard surfaces and don't have the opportunity to walk on the softer surfaces in the countryside.

31   injuries

The plural noun is required here, to talk about something in general. The writer is listing problems caused by walking on hard surfaces and referring to ankle problems in general, not a specific ankle problem.

32   worrying

The '–ing' adjective is required here, meaning 'causing someone to worry'. The writer is saying that the physical problems of young people cause him/her to worry (to feel that something is a serious problem).

33   treatment

The noun is required here to complete the phrase *have treatment for something*, which means 'receive medical help to solve/cure a problem'. The writer is asking whether teenagers will have to receive medical care because they have problems with their hips (hip = a joint at the side and top of the leg).

34   unknown

The negative prefix is required here to form an adjective that means 'never happening' or 'not known to exist'. The writer is saying that only 10 years ago, no teenagers had hip problems.

p.83 PAPER 3 Part 4

35   visit to London][was great

The first word is a possessive ('Our'), meaning that you must form a noun from the verb 'visiting'. The phrase *be great fun* means 'be very enjoyable'. If something 'was great fun', you enjoyed it very much.

36   there are][six of us

The structure *there + be + number + of + object pronoun* must be used to talk about the number of people in a group of people.

37   came up with][the idea

The structure *who + verb* must be used here. The phrasal verb *come up with* is used with the nouns 'idea', 'plan' 'suggestion' etc, with the meaning 'think of' or 'suggest'. The noun 'idea' is used in the phrase *the idea of doing something*. This is a subject question, meaning that the answer to the question is the subject of the verb after 'who' (eg, I/Paul, etc came up with the idea of ....).

38   time][she's/she has ever had

The structure the *first, second, etc time + subject + present perfect* with *'ever'* is required here, to talk about something that has not happened before the present time.

39   although he knew][what

The structure *although + subject + verb, etc* is required here, instead of the structure 'despite + -ing'. The pronoun 'what' is required after 'know' in the structure *what + subject + verb*.

40   him][not to give up

You must form the reported speech structure *advise + object + not + 'to' infinitive* here to describe negative advice (I don't think you should = I think you shouldn't).

41   don't mind][changing

The structure *not mind + -ing* is required here. If you 'don't mind doing something', you are not unhappy about doing it, it is not a problem for you.

42   compared with][the other

The phrase *compared with* is required here, to link things that are being compared. You must also complete the pronoun phrase *the other ones*, meaning 'the other hotels' or 'the others' (the other ones = the others). This pronoun phrase refers to things not previously mentioned (a particular hotel is mentioned at the beginning of the sentence).

p.84 PAPER 4 Part 1

1   B   The speaker says that on one of the days it rained a lot and it was very windy. People were very cold ('shivering') and very wet ('soaked') but they all 'kept their spirits up' (remained happy, despite the problems caused by the weather) and 'enjoyed the music'. There was a 'great' atmosphere all the time and the speaker enjoyed all the bands.

2   C   The woman says that the teacher has not 'taken a course' before and the man says that this 'doesn't show'

- the fact that the teacher is inexperienced is not noticed by the people she is teaching. This is because she seems to 'know what she's doing', and because she prepares everything before teaching. She also has 'a clear idea of how to structure the course' – she knows the best way to organize the lessons and what she teaches in each lesson. She is 'serious' about teaching and doesn't want people to 'mess about' (waste time, not concentrate). The man likes this, and the fact that she wants to 'get on with the lesson' – teach what she has prepared for each lesson.

B The speaker reports a phone call with an assistant and then a second phone call with another assistant, saying that she did not get the result she wanted during these two calls. She says that she then spoke to a manager ('someone senior') but also with no good result ('that hasn't got me anywhere either'). She then says to the person she is talking to that she is 'sorry to bore' this person (make the person bored) by telling him/her about the problems she has had and the phone calls she has made. She says 'you know me', meaning 'you know me well, you know what my personality is like' – she is going to continue trying to 'get a satisfactory response' from the people who are causing her the problem. So the speaker is describing to a friend a problem she has and phone calls she has made in order to solve this problem.

B When the woman asks him if he would like to be extremely rich, the man says that he 'can't imagine there's much chance of that' (he thinks it is very unlikely that this will happen, it's almost impossible). However, if it did happen, he doesn't think he would change, and unlike the woman, he wouldn't buy lots of things.

C The speaker says that she didn't take school 'as seriously as I should have done' – she had the wrong attitude, she wasn't serious enough about school and education. She says that she had fun and remembers it as a good time in her life, but she 'messed up' (did badly in) most of her exams and she didn't do 'as well as I could have done'. If she had 'worked a bit harder', her results would have been 'much better' and her life would have been different. So she is saying that she now feels that she had a bad attitude when she was at school – she didn't work hard enough and so she did not do as well as it was possible for her to do, because she 'preferred to have fun'.

A The speaker is explaining her 'point of view' and describing her situation in her opinion. A problem has happened, and she is saying that it is not her responsibility and there is nothing that she 'can do about it'. She says that the problem has happened because another person 'hasn't done their job properly'. So she is telling the person she is speaking to what her situation is and why she cannot take any action in this situation.

B The speaker talks about 'changes in attitude'. The speaker says that 'expectations of life' have changed, and the way that people 'think about the world around them, the way they interact with others' have changed. At the end, the speaker talks about research into 'what we have become'. So the main topic is how people think and behave in the modern world, and their relationships with other people, in comparison with the past. Technology may have an influence on that, but it is not the main subject.

A The man says that the food was 'of the very highest quality' but he was surprised that it was also 'quite reasonably priced' (not very expensive). He says that the place is becoming popular and advises the woman to book a table in advance because it might be full sometimes. When he was there, 'just about every table was full' (almost every table was full), probably because of publicity, but he doesn't say that it was hard for him to get a table.

p.85 PAPER 4 Part 2

9 keeper

We are told that her father was a 'lighthouse keeper'. This means that he looked after the lighthouse (a tall tower next to the sea with a big light that goes on and off all the time to show ships where to go and to keep them away from danger) and made sure that its light was always working properly.

10 oil lamps

We are told that 'The oil lamps needed checking and topping up' (it was necessary to keep them filled with oil – when some oil had been used, it needed to be replaced so that they were always full). The speaker says that 'all the children helped their father' to do this. The lantern, the windows and the reflectors all needed to be kept clean.

11 rocks; currents

We are told that 'The rocks and currents around the island were treacherous' (extremely dangerous, particularly something that people might not see or be aware of).

12 boilers

On that night in September 1838, 'there was a problem with the ship's boilers'. A boiler is a machine that heats water and provides hot water for something. In those days, the boilers on a ship provided hot water for the steam that powered steam engines.

13 lifeboat

The ship 'had a lifeboat' (a boat that people can use to get away from the ship if it sinks or has a problem) 'but in the confusion only nine people got aboard' (because people didn't know what to do, only nine people got into this boat and got away from the ship).

14 too dark

In the morning, Grace and her father 'spotted (managed to see in the distance) the wreck' (the broken and damaged ship) but it was 'too dark for them to see the people clinging to the rocks' (they couldn't see the people who were holding onto the rocks because there was not enough daylight).

15 (wooden) rowing boat

Grace and her father got into 'a small wooden rowing boat' and 'battled (fought against, had to try very hard because of) wind and tide' in order to 'reach' the people who were in the water.

16 five people/5 people

While Grace 'took charge of the boat', making sure that it did not hit the 'jagged' (sharp) rocks, her father 'helped five people into their little craft' (boat). Their little boat was now full, so they returned to the land. Then her father went back with two other people (not Grace) and saved 'the other four', meaning that a total of nine people were saved. Grace took part in saving the five people.

17 her portrait

Grace and her father 'became world famous' and 'Her portrait was painted several times' – several artists painted pictures of her face. She was also given 'presents, honours and medals'. Someone's portrait is a painting showing that person's face.

18 her hair

We are told that 'People clamoured for (really wanted and tried very hard to get) locks of her hair' (pieces of her hair) as 'souvenirs' (they wanted to possess things directly connected with this famous person).

p.86–87 PAPER 4 Part 3

Further practice and guidance (p.87)

Question 19	Question 20	Question 21
1 yes	1 no	1 yes
2 yes	2 no	2 yes
3 no	3 no	3 no
4 no	4 yes	4 no

Question 22	Question 23
1 no	1 yes
2 yes	2 no
3 no	3 yes
4 yes	4 no

p.86 PAPER 4 Part 3 (Test)

19 E   The speaker has already got 'all the information' about charges and they have 'fixed up' (arranged) a time for the person to come for the repair. But the speaker is 'still not sure' about the system for paying for the repair – he needs to know if he will pay 'at the time' (when the person is with him) or whether he will be sent 'an invoice' (a bill). He also wants to 'find out' what the situation will be if his computer is taken away. So he is phoning to check details about two things – payment and what happens if his computer has to be taken away for repair.

20 D   The speaker has paid for a course but the course has been 'cancelled' (it will not take place). The letter telling the speaker about this does not explain why this has happened and the speaker does not have enough time to find another course. The speaker thinks this is 'a terrible way to treat people' and wants to 'register my dissatisfaction' (make a formal complaint, report officially that she thinks the college has behaved very badly).

21 A   The speaker has 'a new postal address and a new email address' and wants to 'update my details with you' – wants to provide the new information for the company, changing the two addresses. He has tried to do this online but was unable to do so (he is not sure why he couldn't do it online). So he is now trying to change those personal details by phone.

22 F   The speaker has received a letter about a new type of bank account and wants to know if it is 'a good thing' for her. She wants someone to tell her 'if it suits someone in my position'. She has all the details of the account and understands them – what she doesn't know is whether she should 'switch' (change) to this account. She is phoning to ask for someone at the bank to give her advice about this, and to advise her in simple terms about whether this new account is suitable for her.

23 C   The speaker wants to inform the appropriate person that he thinks 'there's a slight smell of gas' in the street (although he is not sure). He has tried phoning several times but has not been able to tell anyone about this. He is phoning to report that there may be a problem concerning gas and to ask for someone to come and check whether there is a problem. He is reporting the problem because if he is right about it, the situation may be 'dangerous'.

p.88 PAPER 4 Part 4

24 C   Laura was shocked at first because the water was so cold but she 'got over that' (got used to it). Then a whale was 'right there' (suddenly close to her) and she thought 'Oh my word, I am in the middle of something so much bigger than me' – she focused on the situation that she was in. What was happening to her had a powerful effect on her and she paid attention to her situation.

25 C   Laura says that when she is in the pool with a whale, she is 'in the middle of a miracle' because whales are 'the top predator' (the biggest and most important species that hunts and kills other creatures), but the whales choose not to 'cause you harm' – they don't try to hurt or kill you. Instead, they 'choose to love you', 'to enquire' and 'to follow you'. So the 'miracle' – the wonderful and extraordinary thing – is that these powerful creatures that can be very aggressive choose to be friendly to the people in the pool with them. She does say that each whale is 'different', meaning that they all have different personalities, but she says this later and not in connection with what is a 'miracle'.

26 A   Laura says that the relationship an animal trainer has with a whale is like the relationship between people. She says that when you have just met someone, you don't invite yourself to that person's house because that would be impolite – you don't know the person well enough to do that. Instead, you 'take small steps' – you get to know the person slowly over a period of time. So, when a trainer begins to train a whale, they should behave in the same way that people behave with people they don't know well – the trainer shouldn't try to form a close relationship with the whale too soon, but develop the relationship over a period of time.

27 B   The first part of training whales involves seeing what they do 'naturally' (without any training). Jumping out of the water is an example of a 'natural action' for a whale. The trainer then combines that natural action with a 'signal' which tells the whale something about that natural action. An example of a signal is blowing a whistle, and the signal might tell the whale that it did the natural action well and that it should 'come back' to the trainer. These signals are called 'secondary reinforcers' and they happen after the whale has done a natural action.

28 A   Laura says that food 'isn't the best' kind of reinforcer – it isn't the best way of giving a signal to a whale or showing a whale what you think. Food is 'not as good as a hug' (putting your arms around the whale to show love or friendship). The trainers use 'touch' a lot because whales love it. So the whales like physical contact with the trainer much more than being given food.

29 A   Laura says that the relationship between the whale and the trainer is 'the most important part of training', and more important than 'the show or the learning sessions'. She says that whales 'can tell if you're sincere' (know if the feelings you are showing them are real feelings or not) and 'can tell if you love them'. She is saying that whales are intelligent and know the difference between real feelings and pretended ones. Whales know if a trainer really likes them and a successful relationship will only develop if the whale and the trainer both really like each other.

30 B   Laura says that you have to think about what you are going to do when you are in front of a creature that is very very big and heavy, has a very large number of teeth and has eyes that are far apart from each other. She is saying that whales look frightening to a human being but you have to deal with that fact if you are an animal trainer and decide what you are going to do with the whale.

).90–92 PAPER 5 Parts 3 and 4

Further practice and guidance (p.91–92)

Discussing the visuals

tidy up 4   refreshments 2   publicity 5/7   promote 5/7
take round 1   tour (noun) 1   display 6   leaflet 5
change/coins 2   stall (noun) 2   guide (noun) 1/3
clear up 4   sign (noun) 3/6   print (verb) 5/7
bin (noun) 4   spaces 3   hand out 5   direct (verb) 1/3

Making suggestions

1	we offer/offering	4	not do
2	we choose	5	to look
3	discuss	6	to choose

Asking for opinions and suggestions

1	What	4	Tell
2	like	5	of
3	How/What	6	have

Agreeing and disagreeing

1	you're	4	the same
2	agreed	5	against
3	of	6	in

Topic vocabulary

1	in	4	from
2	of	5	about
3	on	6	for

Giving reasons

1	because	4	so that
2	for	5	why
3	to	6	because of

TEST FOUR

p.93–94 PAPER 1 Part 1

1 **B** The events described in the first paragraph happen while they are 'pushing' (not riding) their bicycles by the side of a road. People going very fast on motorbikes see a very big lorry coming towards them and they 'swerve within inches of us' – change direction and go very close to the writer and his family, while still moving very fast. Then another big lorry comes along and this causes them to move completely off the road. They think they will go into a 'ditch' – a long hole often found at the side of roads for water to go into – but in fact there is no ditch, so they have to stand at the edge of the tarmac' (at the side of the road) while the lorry goes loudly past them. So the motorbikes and the lorry come very close to them and these events frighten them a lot because the vehicles almost hit them. They have to take action to make sure that they don't hit them.

2 **B** The writer says that after the events on the first day of the holiday, 'it was doubtful they (his wife and son) would ever get back on a bike again'. He is saying that he was worried that the cycling holiday would end after only one day because his wife and son would not be willing to do any more cycling.

3 **B** The writer says that he found 'the best route for beginners' – this was therefore suitable for his family, who had not been on a cycling holiday before. He emphasizes throughout the paragraph the ways in which it seemed suitable – most of it was on paths for cyclists only, and these paths were fairly flat and away from traffic; and it included bikes, maps, transport of luggage and a team of people supporting the cyclists. He ends by saying that the holiday 'sounded perfect for cycle-tour newcomers' – people like his family, who had not done this before.

4 **C** The writer says that they had been told the first day's ride was 19 miles but in fact the distance was longer. Therefore, it took them longer to complete the ride and this meant that they were too late for the ferry they had to catch at the end of the ride. To get to their hotel, they had to follow the map they had been given and this meant going on the road where they had the unpleasant experience described in the first paragraph. He says about all this that 'Grim first impressions are difficult to wipe out' – if your first experience of something is a very unpleasant one, it is very hard to change your opinion about that thing in the future. He is therefore saying that their attitude to the whole holiday was badly affected by what happened to them on the first day.

5 **D** The writer says that he mostly blames himself for the problems (he thinks they were mainly his fault). He knew that the total distance they had to cycle was 'a bit ambitious' (quite hard to achieve) but he also thought it was 'not impossible', so he did not think this would be a serious problem. He says that cycling 22 miles in one day is 'fine' but he had not realized how difficult it would be to do that every day for several days. He blames himself for not realizing what problems this would cause, and lists those problems at the end of the paragraph.

6 **B** The writer says that every morning they had to make sure that all their luggage was ready to be taken to the next place. He says that his family has 'a totally disorganized approach to packing'. It was therefore very difficult for them to pack by 8.30 every morning, because they are not good at this. They managed to do it, however, because their luggage was taken to the next hotel every morning. So it was a big achievement for people who are not good at packing to get all their luggage packed by 8.30 in the morning every day.

7 **A** The writer agrees that the 'rigid' (fixed, never changing) schedule was necessary in the circumstances, but he thought that it wasn't suitable for a cycling holiday, because cycling should involve 'freedom' and 'spontaneity' (doing things without planning them first, doing something because it seems like a good idea at that moment).

8 **C** In this paragraph, the writer is talking about the good aspects of the holiday. The Wachau district is an example of these. It was 'the real discovery' of the trip (the best thing they found on the trip). He describes the place and what was good about it and says that it is 'best savoured from the saddle of a bicycle' (the best way to enjoy the place is by bicycle).

p.95–96 PAPER 1 Part 2

9 **E** In the sentences before the gap, the writer describes a ceremony for students receiving their qualifications and says that these students were 'no usual students' (they were very different from most students).

In E, the writer describes the reason why they were different from other students getting degree qualifications – their degree course had lasted for only five months, not three years.

After the gap, the writer explains more about the students and the course mentioned in E.

10 A In the sentence before the gap, the person who runs the course explains that its aim is to give training in 'enjoyable, manageable and sustainable (that can be continued for a long period) selling'.

In A, the writer explains the theory of how this aim can be achieved. In A, 'this' means all of the things listed at the end of the sentence before the gap. In A, the writer says that the belief of the course is that these three things can all be achieved if the people selling develop 'a good relationship with customers'.

After the gap, the writer explains that the ceremony came at the end of the first course, the first time that the theory mentioned in A had been tried, in a 'pilot scheme' (a practical attempt to see whether something works or not).

11 G The sentence before the gap gives details of what the course involves – some teaching in class ('tutorial') and a lot of individual learning by people at their desks.

In G, the writer gives more details on the course – the fact that each 'module' (part of the course) involves one day of formal training.

In the sentence after the gap, the writer gives more details of the course, following from G. In this sentence, he talks about the 'remainder' of the course – everything in the course that is not the 'formal training' mentioned in G.

12 D In the sentence before the gap, the writer says that the company involved in the first course (Chelsea Building Society) is pleased with the results and has decided to give the course to all of its employees.

In D, the writer continues to talk about how successful the course was when employees of the Chelsea Building Society did it – only one of the people who started the course didn't finish it.

After the gap, the writer says that 'The rest' (the other 10 people who took the course from the 11 who started it, as mentioned in D) 'did so' (completed the course, again referring back to what is stated in D) and thought that it was very useful.

13 C Before the gap, someone who did the course talks about what he learnt from doing it. He says that one particular thing he learnt was to 'compliment people' (say nice things to people, tell them you think they are good in some way) when talking to them on the phone. He says that people 'appreciate' this (notice it and like it when people compliment them).

In C, he continues his point about complimenting people. He says that it's easy to do it and it produces great results for the person who does it. At the end of C, 'it' means 'complimenting people', as mentioned before the gap.

14 H In the sentence before the gap, someone who did the course says that before he took the course he thought he was good at selling to customers on the phone.

In H, the same person says that in fact there was a problem with his telephone skills – something was 'missing' (there was something important that he was not doing).

After the gap, the same person talks about what he learnt from doing the course with regard to what was 'missing' – the fact that he didn't ask people for their thoughts and feelings about what he was presenting to them. He now does the thing that was 'missing'. The fact that this was 'missing' is the 'failing on my part' at the beginning of the sentence after the gap.

15 B Before the gap, the training manager of the company that used the course says that the subject of the course is something that appears to be very simple.

In B, he says that this subject is more complicated than it appears to be. The phrase 'there's an awful lot more to it than meets the eye' means 'it's a lot more complicated than it appears to be'. In B, 'it' means 'making telephone calls and engaging customers' in the sentence before the gap.

After the gap, the same person says that he had not expected to discover so much about the subject and had not realized how complicated the subject of telephone conversations really was.

p.97–98 PAPER 1 Part 3

16 B The writer says that her children were 'horrified' (very shocked) when they saw her 'transform (completely change) into a wild person on a drum kit' at the 'school summer fete' (an event for schoolchildren and their families).

17 D Ralf, the drumming teacher, 'left a job in electronics' and became a drumming teacher in schools. So, before becoming a teacher, he worked in the field of electronics.

18 A Researchers discovered that one drummer in a rock band 'burned off up to 600 calories per hour' – used up a large number of units of energy from food, the maximum being 600.

19 D Ralf says that 'Virtually any child – or adult – can get some sense of achievement from drumming', meaning that almost every child and adult can feel the satisfaction of achieving something if they learn drumming.

20 D The writer says that during their first lesson, 'it is not long before we all get the hang of the beat' – it does not take a long time for all of them to be able to hit the drums with the same rhythm as the loud rock music that is playing and that they are trying to accompany. They were pleased to find that they were 'actually doing it right' after a short time.

21 A The writer says that the researchers are planning to 'develop rock-drumming programmes in schools as an ingenious (very clever) way to get non-sporty, computer-obsessed children to burn off calories'. This means that they want to attract children who don't do sport and children who spend all their time on computers to drumming, so that they can get some exercise and use their energy.

22 B The writer mentions various ways in which it is believed that drumming makes people feel better – it 'activates the brain's pleasure centres, tackles stress, takes you out of your self-obsessed rut (causes people to stop being in the undesirable situation of always focusing on themselves and their own feelings) and promotes a sense of community' (encourages people to feel that they are part of a wide group of people).

23 B The writer says that drumming is 'enormous fun' for people of 'all ages' and that she 'first discovered this' ('this' = the fact that drumming is very enjoyable for people of all ages) when she was at the school summer fete, where Ralf had organized a drumming competition. The competition was for children, but she 'elbowed my offspring out of the way' (pushed her children aside) and played the drums herself. The experience of doing this caused her to become 'hooked' (very attracted to drumming, wanting to do it as often as possible).

4 C Ralf compares the basic 'four-beat rock rhythm' with 'rubbing your tummy and patting your head at the same time while introducing yourself to a group' (moving one hand on your stomach in a circular way, hitting yourself gently on the head with an up and down movement of the other hand, and talking to some people you don't know). The drumming pattern involves three separate things (hands, foot and brain) and he compares it with doing these three other things all at the same time to show how complicated it is.

5 C The other subject is maths – their first lesson begins with maths'. This is because drumming 'is all about recognizing multiples of four so you can go at different speeds'. Being able to do some simple maths, involving counting in blocks of four, is a basic part of drumming, according to Ralf.

6 E One of the mothers who formed a band after attending one of Ralf's weekly rock schools says that she thought 'if they (the children) can have fun, why can't we?' (their mothers). She thought that the enjoyment of drumming should not only be for the children but for the adults too.

7 B Ralf says that drumming 'is seen as cool' and that 'no child thinks of it as exercise' – children in general think that it is a good thing to do, that is fashionable and impressive and it is something that other children admire them for if they do it.

8 E The writer says that she is not the only mother who has 'a yearning' (a strong desire) to do drumming – lots of other mothers are keen on it too. However, according to Ralf, fathers are often 'more reticent' – more shy, less willing to take it up – because they 'don't want to look as if they don't know what they're doing'. They don't want to start drumming because they don't want to look stupid in front of their families.

9 C The writer says that when you are using electronic drum sets you can control the volume (amount of noise) and you can 'plug in headphones to avoid upsetting the neighbours' – you can make sure that you do not disturb the neighbours by making a lot of noise.

10 C The writer says that when they were told at the beginning of the first lesson that it would begin with maths, they had 'horrified faces' – they looked shocked because they had heard some unpleasant news. The children were very unhappy to hear that they would be doing maths.

p.99 PAPER 2 Part 1

TASK-SPECIFIC MARK SCHEME

Content

The email must include all the points in the notes. You must:

- respond appropriately to Judy's news
- confirm that you will go to the wedding
- ask what you should buy as a wedding present
- ask Judy to choose and organize your accommodation.

Organization and cohesion

You should organize each point in a logical order (probably the same as in Judy's email) and in appropriate paragraphs. You should link what you say in your email with what Judy said in her email to you.

Range

You should use appropriate structures and vocabulary for congratulating someone, confirming a future plan, asking for information and requesting action.

Appropriacy of register and format

Your email should be informal and should open and close in an appropriate way for an email to a friend. It should be lively and enthusiastic in tone. Grammar and spelling should be accurate and standard (the same as for a letter).

Target reader

The reader should be clear about how you feel about the news, your intention to attend the wedding, the information you require and what you want the reader to do for you.

p.100–102 PAPER 2 Part 2

QUESTION 2 REVIEW

TASK-SPECIFIC MARK SCHEME

Content

You should:

- describe the film and its message
- explain how the film changed your opinion
- say what you felt and learnt when you saw the film
- talk about your reaction after seeing the film.

Organization and cohesion

You should deal with each point in a logical order in clear paragraphs with appropriate linking, for example linking causes (aspects of the film) with results (how you felt, what you thought).

Range

You should use appropriate structures for describing the film (for example correct past or present tenses) and appropriate vocabulary for describing the film and its effect on you (for example your feelings, how it changed your opinion, etc.).

Appropriacy of register and format

The review should be neutral or fairly formal – it is for a magazine.

Target reader

The reader should understand from the review what the film's message was and the effects that it had on you.

QUESTION 3 LETTER

TASK-SPECIFIC MARK SCHEME

Content

You should:

- specify the course and say why you have applied for it, giving more than one reason
- explain why you think you would do well on the course and why you should be given a place.

Organization and cohesion

The letter should be organized in clear paragraphs, each covering different areas (reasons for applying, reasons why you should get a place on the course). You should use appropriate linking words and phrases for linking statements with reasons why they are true.

Range

You should use a range of verb tenses for talking about your past, your present situation and beliefs and your future intentions. You should also use appropriate modal verbs for talking about a possible future (particularly 'would'). You should use appropriate vocabulary for talking about your personal qualities and your beliefs and intentions.

Appropriacy of register and format

The letter should be formal (it is to a college Principal about a serious matter). It should begin and end with appropriate phrases for introducing the topic of the letter and for ending a formal letter.

Target reader

The Principal should fully understand why you have applied for the course and why you think you should be given a place on that course. The letter should persuade the reader to give you a place.

QUESTION 4 ARTICLE

TASK-SPECIFIC MARK SCHEME

Content

Your article should:

* present a sequence of events/actions for your perfect day
* explain why you would enjoy these events/actions so much.

Organization and cohesion

The article should describe the events in a logical order (probably from the beginning to the end of the day), with suitable paragraphing for each part of the day. Appropriate linking should be used to link events/ actions with why you have chosen them.

Range

You should use appropriate verb tenses and verb forms for talking about the future and possible actions (for example 'would'), and for describing choices and preferences (for example 'would like/love'). You should also use a range of vocabulary for describing the events/ actions that you choose, as well as vocabulary for expressing enjoyment.

Appropriacy of register and format

The article can be informal, neutral or formal, but the register should be the same throughout the whole article.

Target reader

The reader should understand exactly what would happen during every part of the day and why these things would give you so much pleasure.

p.103–104 PAPER 3 Part 1

1   D   If you are 'interested in doing something' you want to do it, you like the idea. If you are 'willing to do something', you are happy to do it, you don't mind doing it. If you are 'eager to do something', you really want to do it. If you are 'attracted to something', you want to do it or have it. The writer is saying that the people organizing the trip advertised for young people to become members of the crew on the boat for the trip.

2   B   If you 'hear about' something, you know that it exists or you are aware of it because someone tells you or you read about it. Amie discovered that the project existed when she was at school.

3   C   If you are 'excited about the prospect of doing something', the idea of doing that thing in the future makes you feel very excited and happy because you really want to do it. Because Amie had enjoyed her experience at the Sailing Academy, she really wanted to take part in this boat trip.

4   C   The linking word 'so' links a cause and a result, and introduces the result of something. Amie applied to join the crew because she was excited about the idea of going on the trip.

5   A   If you do something 'properly', you do it in the correct and appropriate way and you do it completely. Before the boat trip started, Amie had to do all the preparation for it that was necessary. If you are 'properly prepared' for something, you have prepared for it completely and fully.

6   D   The phrase 'of course' is used before something that it is not really necessary to say because it is already known or expected. The writer lists what Amie's training included and is saying that one of these things was 'the ins and outs' (the details of something complicated) of sailing a yacht, which is a basic requirement of being a crew member.

7   B   If you 'keep someone company', you spend time with that person because it is helpful and because that person does not want to be alone or should not be alone. During the journey, Amie wasn't frightened because another member of the crew stayed with her all the time and she did not have to do anything alone.

8   B   The phrase 'soon after' means 'a short time after' ('soon' can mean 'a short time in the future' or a 'short time in the past' – here it is in the past). The writer is talking about something that happened a short time after the voyage ended.

9   C   If you 'are awarded something', you are given something good by an official authority or organization. The United Kingdom Sailing Academy gave Amie a scholarship (money to study or train on a particular course at a particular place), and she is training to teach watersports as a career.

10   A   If you are 'proud of something', you are very happy about something that you have done and feel that it was a very good thing. The adjectives 'satisfied', 'delighted' and 'pleased' can all have this meaning but they are all followed by the preposition 'with'. Amie is saying that she feels good about the things she has achieved.

11   A   If something 'comes your way', it appears in your life or happens to you, perhaps by chance. Amie thinks that people should act if they get a chance to do things that are difficult and require them to try hard – they should use these opportunities for experiences.

2 D The word 'otherwise' means 'if not' – it introduces result if something previously mentioned doesn't happen. Amie is saying that people should take any opportunity for challenging experiences in a very enthusiastic way – if they don't do this, they will regret the fact.

p.105 PAPER 3 Part 2

3 been

This completes the present perfect form of 'be able to'. The writer is saying that other creatures in addition to the dodo were 'wiped out' (became extinct) but until now scientists only knew about the dodo and didn't know that these other creatures had existed. Now they have been able to reconstruct these other creatures that lived in the same place as the dodo and became extinct a long time ago.

4 where

This completes a relative clause connected with a place. This part of the sentence means 'dozens of extinct birds and animals used to live on certain tropical islands and the dodo also used to live on these tropical islands'.

5 there

In this context, 'there' refers to a place previously mentioned and means 'in/to this/that place'. The phrase 'before humans set foot there' means 'before humans arrived on the islands of Mauritius, Reunion and Rodrigues in the Indian Ocean'.

6 at

The phrase *at least* describes the smallest possible or minimum number or amount of something. It often means 'not less than this number but probably more than this number'. The writer is talking about the number of species that have become extinct in a period of approximately 150 years.

7 as

The phrase *as a result of* comes before the cause of something and links a cause and a result. The writer is saying that a minimum of 45 species became extinct because of hunting and the introduction of other species.

8 What

The pronoun 'what' is used as the subject of the verb 'happened', with the meaning 'the thing or things which happened'. The scientist is saying that the events on the islands that caused the creatures to become extinct are sad – bad things happened.

9 like

What someone or something 'looks like' is the physical appearance of someone/something. The writer is saying that researchers have created copies of these creatures, and the writer explains what they have used in order to produce these.

20 how

In this context 'how' means 'the way'. The writer is saying that the researchers now know the physical appearance and behaviour of these creatures.

21 nowhere

The word 'else' is used to form a phrase after something/nobody/everywhere/anything, etc, with the meaning 'another thing/person/place'. In this case 'nowhere' must be used because the writer is talking about places. The

meaning of the sentence is '31 species of birds which lived on the islands but became extinct were not found in any other places'. The negative 'nowhere' must be used with the meaning 'in no other places' – the birds only existed on these islands.

22 and

The phrase *a combination of .... and ....* describes two things that join together in a way. The writer is describing the result of two things that happened together (hunting and the arrival of certain creatures on the islands).

23 which

This completes a relative clause, giving more information about the nouns mentioned before it (rats, cats and monkeys). The writer is talking about what these creatures did to the birds. This is a non-defining relative clause (it gives extra information, it doesn't explain what something is) and so 'which' is the only word that can go into the gap – 'that' is incorrect in this type of relative clause.

24 to

This completes the structure *cause + object + 'to' infinitive*, which describes the result of something. The writer is saying that many birds became extinct because they lived on the ground and rats, cats and monkeys destroyed their nests.

p.106 PAPER 3 Part 3

25 strengthen

You must form the verb here, to go with the modal 'may'. The verb 'strengthen' means 'make strong or make stronger'. The writer is saying that some people believe that laughing causes the immune system to be stronger (this helps to protect people against illnesses and diseases).

26 circulation

The noun is required here to form the phrase *blood circulation*, which means the flow of blood around the body. Good blood circulation is a sign of health and the writer is talking about the ways in which people think that laughing improves people's health.

27 happiness

The noun is required here to go with the verb 'increase' and to match the noun used in the phrase 'reduce pain'. The writer is talking about the good effects of chemicals in the body called endorphins.

28 encourages

A prefix is required here to form the verb. The subject of the verb is singular (Enda, a person) so the third person form must be used. The present simple tense is required because the writer is talking about something that this person does in the present in general. If you 'encourage someone to do something', you tell them that it is a good thing to do.

29 psychological

The adjective is required here, to go with the noun 'problems'. The adjective 'psychological' means 'connected with the mind and how it works'. The writer is talking about the idea that laughing can 'heal' (cure, solve medically) problems of this kind.

30 greatly

You must form the adverb here to go with the past participle 'rewarded', with the meaning 'very much'. The writer is saying that laughter therapists get a lot of satisfaction from teaching people to deal with their problems by laughing.

31   management

The noun is required here, with the meaning 'the process of dealing with or controlling something'. The phrase 'stress management' means 'controlling stress so that it is not a problem' and in this context a 'tool' means 'a technique or method that helps to achieve something'. The writer is saying that laughter is both a natural and a good thing that people can use for controlling stress.

32   equipment

You must form the noun here, to go with the adjective 'special'. The writer is saying that if you use laughter, you don't require particular objects to use with it or to make it possible to use it.

33   gifted

You must form the adjective here, to follow the adverb 'naturally' and to complete the phrase 'be gifted at something/at doing something', which means 'having a special ability to do something impressive'. The writer is asking whether the reader has a special ability to make people laugh, an ability that is natural for them, not one that requires them to try hard.

34   professional

The adjective is required here, to go with the noun 'training'. The writer is talking about being trained by someone who has the paid job of training people.

p.107–108 PAPER 3 Part 4

Further practice and guidance (p.108)

Question 35	D	Question 39	A
Question 36	D	Question 40	B
Question 37	B	Question 41	E
Question 38	E	Question 42	C

---

p.107 PAPER 3 Part 4 (Test)

35   everyone/everybody][except (for) me

You need to use the structure *everything/everyone/everywhere + except (for) + object pronoun* here. This structure describes the only thing/person/place that something is not true of, the only exception. The subject of the verb 'enjoyed' is the people who enjoyed it, not the person who didn't enjoy it. The subject 'I' becomes the object pronoun 'me'.

36   don't/do not][agree with

You must form the phrase *I don't agree with* to express disagreement with someone or something. The negative form is 'don't/doesn't agree' (not 'I am not agree').

37   was taken][by one of

A passive structure is required here, because 'This photograph' is the object of the verb in the first sentence but it is the subject of the second sentence. The verb 'took' is in the past simple tense, so the past simple passive structure *was/were + past participle* must be used. The agent 'by' must be used after the passive verb to say what the subject of the verb is (who 'did' the action). The structure *one of + possessive adjective + plural noun* is also required instead of the structure

a + singular noun + of + possessive pronoun in the first sentence (a friend of mine = one of my friends).

38   to cause][(any) problems for

The structure *want + 'to' infinitive* is required here and the phrase *cause something for someone* is also required, with the meaning 'be the cause of something unpleasant that happens to someone'.

39   out][how to solve

The phrasal verb *work out* is required here with the meaning 'find a way to do something by thinking carefully about it and trying to deal with it'. The structure *how + 'to' infinitive* means 'the way of doing something, the action required in order to do something'.

40   to stop][being so

The reported speech structure *tell + object pronoun + 'to' infinitive* is required here to report an order. The structure *stop + -ing* is also required and the verb 'be' must be used to go with the adjective 'noisy'. The structure *so + adjective* must be used instead of the structure *so much + uncountable noun* in the first sentence.

41   had][a long discussion

The phrase *have a discussion* must be formed with the meaning 'discuss'. The past simple form of 'have' is required. The adjective 'long' must be used before the noun 'discussion' instead of the phrase 'for a long time'.

42   was over(,)][all of

The phrase *be over* means 'end' or 'finish', and the past simple form of 'be' must be used. The quantifier 'all' must be used in the structure *all + of + object pronoun + verb*, which means the same as *subject pronoun + all + verb* (all of us helped = we all helped).

p.109 PAPER 4 Part 1

1   C   The speaker says that he hasn't 'written anything in it for quite a while', meaning that he hasn't written anything in his diary for a fairly long time. This is a common thing to happen with his diary – he says that, like most people, he doesn't have time to 'write down every little thing that happens every day'. So his diary is not up to date at the moment and this is not unusual – 'there are quite a lot of gaps in it' (periods of time when he didn't write anything in it). But he intends to continue writing 'memorable' (interesting, important) things in it when they happen.

2   C   The announcer says that this series of programmes will show 'the workings of a major international company from the inside' – it will show what happens in the company, how it is organized and what it does. The programme on Friday, the second in the series, will be about the lives at work and outside work of 'the top people' (the senior managers). So it is a factual programme, showing real life and real people, including interviews with some of those people.

3   A   The man says that he 'hadn't run into' (met by chance) the woman 'on my way out in the morning' (while he was leaving the place where he lives). He says that he misses their 'little chats on the way to the bus stop', meaning that they used to talk to each other while they were walking together to the bus stop. So the situation is that they live close to each other and they used to meet when they were both going out in the morning, but now this doesn't happen because the woman's working hours have changed and she eaves her home at a different time in the morning. The man as now left his job and become a student, but they both still ive near to each other.

B The reviews said that the film was 'nothing like the book' (completely different from it) and the woman agrees with that, but she says that the comments made in the 'bad reviews' (negative ones) that the film has received have not been 'fair' (true, justified). She says that the film was 'really entertaining'. And although it was long, it held her attention all the time. So her opinion is that the negative comments made about it by critics are wrong.

B The speaker has already phoned twice and left two messages. She needs the 'arrangements for the weekend' to be 'sorted out' (she wants to organize, deal with these arrangements with George). She needs to make a booking but she must speak to George about this first. George has not contacted her. It is now very important that he contacts her because it will be hard for her to make the booking if he doesn't do this. So she is insisting that George phones her back, and she is telling him that he really must do this.

C She says that this person 'keeps on smiling' (he always looks happy) 'no matter what happens'. He's had a lot of problems but 'he never seems to get miserable at all' (he never seems to be unhappy or sad). He 'never worries' and always thinks that things will be fine – he has a very positive attitude'. So the person is always in a good mood, and always seems to be happy. The speaker says that she thinks he's a bit 'strange' because of this.

B The speaker says that he did 'a stupid thing' and had done the same thing in an 'efficient' way many times before. He was 'really cross' (angry) with himself and at the time he was 'furious' (extremely angry) with himself. He is not angry with himself now, he's 'got over it' (he's recovered from it, he feels calm about it now) but when he made the mistake ('at the time') he was very annoyed with himself.

B The speaker says that the subject of economics is very 'complicated' and always involves a lot of 'jargon' (special words and phrases, technical language connected with a specific subject). Because of that he didn't learn a lot from reading the article, even though the article began by saying that it would 'explain the basics' to people who were not experts on the subject. After the beginning of the article, he found it 'confusing', he got 'completely lost' (he couldn't understand what it was saying) and he 'couldn't follow it at all' (understand anything in it). Although he tried hard to understand it, he couldn't 'work out (understand after thinking) what the writer was saying'. So the speaker mentions several times that he could not understand the article and that is his main point.

p.110 PAPER 4 Part 2

9   (their) friends

Suzy says that on this site, 'you can see where your friends are' – you can find out where they are at any time, and therefore 'it's really good for keeping in touch with them'. This is one advantage of the fact that the site 'allows members to find and meet people from anywhere in the world'.

10   celebrity gossip

Suzy says that 'If celebrity gossip is your thing, then this is the one for you', meaning if you're very interested in celebrity gossip, this is the best site for you to look at. So in her opinion, it's the best site for celebrity gossip and she describes what kind of celebrity gossip it contains (stories about meeting or seeing famous people while travelling).

11   hotel rooms

The site also includes 'photographs and videos of hotel rooms' that people have stayed in, as well as those people's opinions and advice on various things. So people send their photos and videos to the site.

12   most expensive dessert

Suzy says that on this site 'you can learn what you can expect to pay for the world's most expensive dessert'. The site contains information 'for the rich' – although you can enjoy looking at it 'even if you aren't rich' – and this is part of its information on restaurants.

13   clear maps

Suzy says that this site has got 'striking' (impressive and attractive) 'photography and clear maps'. The photography and maps are examples of the ways in which it is 'beautifully designed'.

14   travel agency

Suzy says that this site 'was started by someone who needed a place to express his anger and frustration following a dispute with a travel agency' – he started the site because he wanted to say how angry he was after a disagreement with a travel agency.

15   interactive

Suzy says that this blog 'is one of the most interactive blogs around' – it is more interactive than most of the travel blogs that exist. She also says that it solves travel problems and gives objective advice, but she doesn't compare the number of problems it solves or the quality of its advice with other blogs.

16   by train/by rail

Suzy says that this site 'helps keep the romance of rail travel alive with regularly updated blogs on travelling around the world by train' – it helps to continue the idea that travelling by train/rail is romantic by providing blogs by someone who is travelling by train/rail in different parts of the world.

17   paperback

Suzy says that 'a paperback version' of the site has just been published. So the blogs written by this man have been produced as a paperback book and Suzy gives the title of this book.

18   hotel owners

When talking about this site, Suzy says 'One word of caution about this site, though', meaning that when you look at it and read the reviews, there is something negative that you should know. She says 'Watch out for fake reviews that hotel owners have written, pretending to be enthusiastic guests'. This means that you should realize that some of the reviews are not really written by people who have stayed in certain hotels and liked them very much, they are in fact written by the owners of those hotels.

p.111 PAPER 4 Part 3

19   D The speaker says that she thinks that 'pretty soon the media will get bored with him and move on to someone else' – fairly soon he will stop appearing in the media. She thinks that 'everyone will forget all about him' – he won't be famous any more. She adds that 'teenagers move on quickly' (change to the next thing quickly) and they will 'soon have another hero' to replace this person.

20 F   The speaker asks if there is 'anyone who says they actually like' this person, meaning that she has not met anyone who says they like him. Everyone the speaker has spoken to about this person says that 'they can't stand him' (they really dislike him). This is because 'he's … an awful person' (a very bad person) who is 'like a particularly horrible child'. The speaker is saying that a lot of people really dislike this person.

21 C   The speaker says that this person 'stands out' (is different from other people) and is 'quite unique' (is totally unlike anyone else). He says 'controversial things' (things that cause disagreement) but he has thought about these things and a lot of his opinions 'make sense' (are right). The person has 'a different point of view' (unusual opinions). So the speaker is saying that this person has opinions that are not the same as other people's and the speaker finds these opinions interesting.

22 A   The speaker 'can't see what all the fuss is about' (can't understand why the person is so famous and gets so much publicity). He only presents TV programmes and the speaker doesn't think this is a 'big thing' (an important or difficult thing to do). He says that 'anyone could do what he does' – it doesn't require any special skill. So the speaker is saying that this person is not famous because he has any particular ability.

23 B   The speaker says that this person has had 'a hard life' (a life full of problems) and had a terrible childhood. When she read about this, she found it 'moving' (she felt emotional about it, she felt sympathetic towards him). She doesn't like his behaviour but she 'can't help feeling sorry for' him (she finds it impossible not to feel sympathy for him) because of what has happened to him in his life. She 'can see why' (understands why) he 'acts like a fool' (behaves stupidly) in public.

p.112–114 PAPER 4 Part 4

Further practice and guidance (p.113–114)

Question 24	A, B and F
Question 25	A, B, C and F
Question 26	A, D and E
Question 27	A, C, E and F
Question 28	B, C, D and E
Question 29	A
Question 30	A, B and C

---

p.112 PAPER 4 Part 4 (Test)

24 C   The interviewer says that Jo's philosophy is 'not centred on just selling products' and Jo agrees. She says 'it is not just about doing a one-off deal' (selling something to a customer once), it is 'much broader than that'. She thinks her best deals 'have always been with people, not products' – the customer is more important than the product she is selling. Her company 'is all about people' – people are the main focus of it. As a result, it could be called The People Shop – because it is based on the idea that people are the most important thing, not the products that are sold in the shops.

25 B   The owner of a business in Minnesota developed the principles after he saw 'the enthusiasm' (the positive attitude and enjoyment of work) of some 'fishmongers' (people working in a shop selling fish) in another part of the US. Jo says the principles are 'based on the belief' that you don't need to be 'very serious' at work and a place of work doesn't have to be 'very formal'. The four principles include 'Have fun' and 'Play'. So the fishmongers showed that they enjoyed their work and enjoyment of work is one of the main parts of the principles.

26 B   When describing each of the four principles, Jo says that one of them, 'Choose your attitude' means 'being positive at work'. So this principle involves making a conscious decision to have a positive attitude to your work while you are doing it. Another principle involves listening to customers and giving them advice (not necessarily to buy something). She illustrates the principle of playing by talking about when staff suddenly decided to get together and dance during a company event.

27 A   Jo says that 'sometimes people really associate perfumes with a particular occasion like their wedding or with a particular person' – the smell of a perfume makes people remember an important time when they smelt it or makes them think of a certain person who wore it. For this reason, perfume is 'very emotional' – it causes people to have strong feelings. Jo agrees with the interviewer that perfume is an 'emotional product' because of these connections for people.

28 C   The girl had been using a perfume that her late (dead) grandmother used but she was 'worried because her supplies were running out' (that she had used almost all of the perfume that she had) and she didn't think it was possible to buy any more of it in the shops because it wasn't 'still available' (no longer sold). So she hadn't tried to find the perfume because she didn't think any shops had it.

29 A   Jo told the girl that she could get the perfume in The Perfume Shop. She told her this because she 'just didn't want her to think that she couldn't get it' – simply so that the girl would know that she could buy the perfume somewhere. She wasn't trying to get the girl to buy it from her shop, she simply wanted her to know that the perfume was available. The girl was very 'pleased' to hear this, and Jo's intention was that she would be pleased to hear the information.

30 B   The man was trying to find a perfume that 'had been discontinued' (was not made or produced any more). He 'could not get it anywhere' because it wasn't available in any shop. She sent him a bottle of this perfume that belonged to her personally, but she doesn't know how he felt about this and she doesn't know whether he returned to the shop again.

LISTENING SCRIPTS

TEST ONE Part 1

Extract one

Well, I read about that speech he gave yesterday about the state of the country and I thought he had a point. I was quite surprised to find that I agreed with a lot of what he was saying, because I haven't been very impressed by him in the past. But they're all the same really, aren't they? They just say what they think people want to hear. He'll probably be saying something different in a few weeks if that seems like the right thing to do. It's hard to know what he'd really do if people voted for him because he seems to have a different opinion every time he makes a speech.

Extract two

Oh I really like that song. I guess it's the one that most people associate him with, because it was such a big hit. I think he's written lots of great songs, but in fact that's not one of his own. Most people don't know that, because so many of his songs have been done by other people and he's considered to be a really good songwriter. It's a shame some of those songs aren't as well-known – they're just as good, if not better.

Extract three

Man: Wow, that was some journey!

Woman: Yeah, I thought we'd never get here. All those delays!

Man: Well, it's nice to be back. Travelling's great but I always like the bit when I'm back surrounded by all the familiar things.

Woman: Mmm, well, it's not quite as luxurious as the room we've been in for the past fortnight!

Man: No! And all that time not having to cook our own meals was great.

Woman: Yes, well, it's over now. Back to reality. Come on, let's get the bags sorted out.

Extract four

Criticism? Well, you certainly get plenty of it in my game! The key is not to be too sensitive to it. Even if I get a really negative review, I never let it get me down. That's not to say that I never read reviews of my work. Lots of people say they never do, but I don't believe them. No, I tend to see if there's anything I can learn from it, work out whether the reviewer's got a point about something I've written that I haven't noticed. If that's the case, I take it on board. If not, I dismiss it as a load of rubbish!

Extract five

Yes, when I see people playing really well, it fills me with envy. It must be fantastic to be able to do that. I had a few piano lessons years ago, but I couldn't get anywhere with it, so I just gave up. And I tried learning the guitar too, I thought that might be easier, but in fact the opposite was true and I was even worse at that. It's a shame. These days there are so many chances to learn, so many books on the market and so many teachers offering lessons, but I guess it's just not for me. It's a real regret though, because I look at other people and think 'If only I'd kept having those lessons, I might be able to play like that!'

Extract six

Man: I see there's another reality TV series starting tonight. About people who exchange jobs. It sounds good.

Woman: Yes, I've seen the adverts for that. I think I'll be giving it a miss, though.

Man: Really? Oh, I really like that kind of thing. I like watching ordinary people and how they react in different situations.

Woman: Yes I know you do. But there are just so many programmes like that. I can't be bothered to watch another one.

Man: Well, I suppose you have a point. There are an awful lot of them. Even *I* don't feel like watching them all the time. But this one sounds fascinating.

Woman: Well I hope you enjoy it.

Extract seven

I've only been there once, just after it opened. But I was very impressed. It's certainly a big improvement on the original one, which was practically falling down. I went there lots of times and it wasn't great. But this place has been a big success, I gather, with crowd numbers up all the time. In fact, it's quite a long way outside the town and people have to travel further to get there, but it's got lots of parking close by, and that's actually made it more appealing to people. Mind you, it's never full, so if you want to go to a game there, you shouldn't have much trouble.

Extract eight

Man: Ah, Jenny, could I just have a quick word with you?

Woman: Er, yes. No problem I hope.

Man: Well, actually there is. I've just had a complaint from a client. He says you were rude to him on the phone.

Woman: What? Me? Who said that?

Man: Well, I'm sure you won't be surprised to hear it was Mr Butler.

Woman: Oh, him. He's always really horrible.

Man: Yes, I know he can be very difficult and I appreciate how hard it is to deal with him.

Woman: And now he's complained about me! I've always done my best to help him.

Man: Yes, I know. Look, next time he rings, just put him straight on to me.

Woman: OK.

TEST ONE Part 2

Happy Birthday had its origins in 1893, when Mildred Hill, a kindergarten teacher in Louisville, Kentucky, put together a simple little tune. Whether she composed it entirely out of her own head, or was influenced by other 'folk song' fragments, is not clear. But when her younger sister Patty (also a teacher) added words, the groundwork was laid for a very pleasing song. They called it *Good Morning to All*:

Good morning to you,

Good morning to you,

Good morning dear children,

Good morning to all.

Good Morning to All was initially intended, and used, as a welcoming song to be sung by the teacher to the class each morning. But when it was published later in 1893, in a book of songs for kindergartens, it proved to be popular in reverse – children sang it to their teachers, rather than the other way round, and the word 'children' was popularly replaced by 'teacher'. So the song gently morphed into *Good Morning to You*.

In this form, young children across the United States began to sing the song. The slow development from 'Good Morning' to 'Happy Birthday' seems to have come from children themselves, with encouragement from Patty Hill, who helped create the new lyric when children liked the song enough to sing it at parties.

In 1924, *Good Morning to All*, with *Happy Birthday to You* printed as an optional second verse, was published. By then, radio was gaining attention and movies were beginning to take hold. The *Happy Birthday* words replaced the earlier version, and in 1931 the song appeared in the show *Band Wagon*, then became a 'singing telegram' for Western Union in 1933, and surfaced again in Irving Berlin's show *As Thousands Cheer* in 1934.

The third Hill sister, Jessica, believing that Patty and Mildred should have the credit for the now very popular song, and some profit from it, went into battle. Later in 1934, she was able to establish legal copyright to her sisters for their song, and it was officially published in 1935 as *Happy Birthday*. Since then, two legal changes in America's copyright system have made *Happy Birthday* copyright until 2030.

Fortunately this does not rule out its being sung privately, as it is at countless parties. It has been named in the *Guinness Book of Records* as one of the three most sung songs in the English language, along with *For He's a Jolly Good Fellow* and *Auld Lang Syne*.

But the copyright can be enforced when the song is used in a public place where a larger group than a family is gathered, such as a sports event. Royalties must be paid if the song is ever part of a profit-making enterprise, such as a television show, a commercial stage performance or movie, or is built into toys, music boxes, watches, mobile phones and 'singing' birthday cards.

In order to deal with their fully copyrighted property, the Hill sisters established a foundation through which royalties were paid until their death, and which still receives several millions of dollars of income a year. In 2002, the mayor of Louisville dedicated a 'Happy Birthday' parking lot near Main Street, with a commemorative plaque telling the story of the local sisters who composed the famous song.

Although *Happy Birthday* has only four short musical phrases, and a single repetitive line of words, it has become a part of the musical landscape. It is sung all over the world in many languages – by one estimate, several million times a year – often to children who are too young even to know what the song is about, but also to just about everyone else.

TEST ONE Part 3

Speaker 1

I had a phone call at work today from a customer who was very angry and wanted to make a complaint. She was going on and on at me about how bad the service from us was – she was really shouting. Well, I stayed calm and was as friendly as I could be, because I felt that she had a point. I didn't blame her for being so angry, I would have felt the same in her position. We really had treated her badly. It's a shame, because she's always been a good customer of ours.

Speaker 2

A friend of mine rang me last night and she was clearly very upset about something. She was accusing me of saying terrible things about her to other people, but I really didn't know where she got that idea from. Nothing she was saying made any sense to me – I kept asking her where she'd got that information from, but I didn't get any clear answers. I knew I hadn't said any of these things, so I didn't feel any need to defend myself. But I didn't know what to say because I didn't have a clue what she was talking about.

Speaker 3

My cousin phoned a couple of days ago to tell me that he'd had to cancel the family party he'd organized because a lot of people had said they couldn't make it. It's a pity because I was really looking forward to getting together with everyone, especially the ones I haven't seen for a while. I know some people don't like family events but I'm not one of those. Anyway, he says he'll try to organize it again at a later date so hopefully it'll take place at some point.

Speaker 4

I had a phone call last night from someone in my class at college. We had a huge argument yesterday about something that really didn't matter and I thought she was going to be really angry with me. I'd said some really horrible things to her and I assumed that she'd fallen out with me and would never speak to me again. But it turned out I was wrong about that. In fact, she'd phoned to apologize to me. She said the whole thing was her fault and she didn't want to fall out with me. I was really pleased because I didn't want to lose her as a friend.

Speaker 5

A colleague at work called me at home last night to talk about some problem in the office. He wanted to see if I had any ideas about how to solve the problem. It wasn't really convenient to talk at that time, I was just in the middle of eating, and anyway I don't want to discuss work when I'm at home. So I was pretty fed up that he'd phoned and I tried to make the call as short as possible. I told him I'd think about it and speak to him at work. I hope I wasn't too rude, and he's a nice person, but I just wanted to get rid of him really.

TEST ONE Part 4

Interviewer: I'm talking to Emma Roberts, who plays a spoilt, snobby brat from LA who gets dumped in an English boarding school in the film *Wild Child*, which has just opened here. Emma, what did you think Britain would be like before you came here? Did you think, like your character Poppy, that it'd be rainy and cold?

Actress: I was so excited. I love England! I don't mind the rain because I'm from LA and it's never really rainy. I got myself a really cute pair of rainboots and a rain jacket. I love the weather and I love the people!

Interviewer: You became great friends with your roommates in the movie. How did you all get on when the cameras were turned off?

Actress: We became really good friends and really close. I think that shows on screen a lot. You can't fake that. We had so much fun together. I loved making the movie. It's been a year since the movie finished filming and we still

hang out. I'm probably going to see a few of them while I'm here.

Interviewer: What did you do when you weren't filming?

Actress: We would go shopping together, they showed me around London a little bit. When we were on location, we would all be staying in the same hotel, it was just really good fun getting to know everyone, it was great.

Interviewer: Can you do an English accent?

Actress: Not really. Well, I can but I get embarrassed when people ask me to do it. I can do a London accent but I can't do any other accent, they're so difficult. I think Wales has the hardest accent to do. Juno Temple, who's in the film, comes to LA a lot so I see her a lot. I wish I could have her accent, it's so cute. I can't do a Scottish accent either.

Interviewer: How did you get on with the British cast and crew?

Actress: Really well. We all had so much fun together. They made fun of me because of my accent. I guess I have an accent. Do I have an accent?

Interviewer: You definitely sound American.

Actress: I do? That's what everyone says, that I really sound American.

Interviewer: But you are American!

Actress: I am, so I should sound like one! Anyway, we got on really well and hung out on the set.

Interviewer: How do you think you would cope if you were sent to a boarding school in another country?

Actress: I think that would be such fun! I've always wanted to go to boarding school just to see if the books and the movies are right about it. I would love to go to boarding school in England.

Interviewer: In one scene in the movie, you had to dance on your own in the middle of the room. How was that?

Actress: Embarrassing. It was really intimidating. I felt so dumb. I had fun with it but I was embarrassed because it's fun to dance but only with your friends. We did a lot of takes so I had to keep doing it too. It's not a popular thing among girls my age in LA. I think it turned out OK. They edited it well!

Interviewer: What advice would you give to young people who might want to be a movie star?

Actress: I would just say, know it's a lot of hard work. It's not just showing up and looking good. It's very difficult. You have to have tough skin so that you don't get knocked down by criticism. You have to understand that not everyone is going to like you. You just have to do your job and do your best and hope that people enjoy it but, if they don't, you can't let it wreck your life.

Interviewer: Emma, thanks for talking to me.

Actress: Pleasure.

TEST TWO Part 1

Extract one

Man: So, I gather you had an enormous argument with Nick.

Woman: Yes, he was really angry with me and he started shouting and I started shouting back at him.

Man: And now you're not speaking to each other?

Woman: Well, he's not speaking to me, but I'm sure we could reach an agreement if we both calmed down.

Man: So are you going to tell him he was right?

Woman: Certainly not, because I was right.

Man: But you haven't fallen out with him?

Woman: No, these things happen, don't they, even with the best of friends. I'm sure we'll sort it out.

Extract two

He's never been one of my favourite players, I must admit, but he does try hard. You certainly can't say that he doesn't put the maximum effort in. But I don't think he's ever had what it takes at this level. I mean, when we first bought him, everyone was expecting him to be a real star, but he was really rubbish at first, wasn't he? And things haven't got any better since then, have they? I keep expecting him to improve, but it just doesn't happen. To be honest, I can't understand why they keep putting him in the team.

Extract three

Yes, that's right, I'm afraid we've had to cancel tomorrow's lesson. Your teacher is ill and we haven't been able to find a replacement. We have got someone who's taught on the course before but unfortunately she's not available at such short notice. So what we're going to do is arrange for that lesson to be in the final week of the course. That's right, you'll have two lessons that week, to make up for missing this week's. So we're guaranteeing the full number of lessons, rather than offering money back for this one. You'll get everything you've paid for.

Extract four

Yes, the company's certainly been a success story and there's been quite a lot about it in the media recently – huge profits, enormous growth and all that. The fact is, it's all about good management. The place has got a really good culture, and that starts from the top down. I've been in places where you're taking orders from someone who hasn't got a clue what to do, and who clearly shouldn't be running anything. But that's not the case here. Some of the managers started at the bottom here and worked their way up and I'm hoping to do that myself. It's made clear to all of us that it's possible to do that here.

Extract five

Woman: Now this get-together we're having on Friday, it's at the Club Mango isn't it?

Man: Yes that's right. Why, have you got a problem with that?

Woman: It's not my favourite place. Couldn't we think of somewhere better?

Man: Well, the others seem to be happy enough with it.

Woman: Mmm, well, the trouble is, it's so noisy there you can't really have any sort of conversation. And surely that's the point of us all getting together.

Man: So, what, you don't want to come?

Woman: That's not what I said. I'd just rather meet up somewhere else. I'm sure we could come up with a better place if we give it some thought.

Extract six

Now we all know that recycling has become a major issue in recent times. Not that many years ago, nobody thought about recycling their household rubbish but now everyone's doing it. We all know the impact this has on the environment and I don't intend to go into all that now. The trouble is, people are getting confused. They don't know what to put into the various containers they now have at home and they're getting confused about what gets collected from their homes at different times. They're not sure what can be recycled where they live and what can't. We need to make all this clear, and fast.

Extract seven

Woman: So how are you feeling? Our flight will be called soon, and then we'll be off.

Man: Yeah, I'm really looking forward to it.

Woman: No second thoughts?

Man: Of course not. We've spent so long thinking about it but we know it's the right decision.

Woman: Yes, and it's not as if we don't know anything about the place. I'm sure we'll settle in really quickly.

Man: Yes. A fresh start. I can't wait. I'm even looking forward to starting work.

Woman: Yes, me too. And we've got time to relax a bit and have a good look round in our new surroundings before we have to go into the office.

Man: Oh look. Our flight's up on the screen.

Extract eight

Man: Yes, sorry about that. It was one of my friends. He had something he needed to discuss with me.

Woman: Anything serious?

Man: No, just a lot of gossip really. I thought he might call because there was a bit of a problem at work today and he wanted to see what I thought about it.

Woman: Ah huh.

Man: Well actually, there wasn't a great deal to say, nothing very important happened, but my friend always gets very worked up about these little things and goes on and on about them. I kept telling him not to worry about it but he just wouldn't listen. So we just said the same things over and over again.

TEST TWO Part 2

Interviewer: The Petrie Museum of Egyptian Archaeology in London may be small but it holds around 80 000 objects, most of them from sites excavated by the Egyptologist Sir William Petrie, who lived from 1835 to 1942. Petrie was one of the first people to study ancient Egypt scientifically, and he was more interested in looking at the ordinary things that people used every day than raiding their treasure houses. In 1913, he sold his large collection of Egyptian antiquities to University College, London, for students and researchers to study. And I'm talking now to Stephen Quirke, the curator of the Petrie Museum. Firstly, what is a curator, what does he or she do?

Curator: A curator has to know the collection well. I find the answers to people's questions about objects in the collection.

Interviewer: Do you have a favourite exhibit?

Curator: I like objects that connect me with the people that made them, so I feel that I get to know them. I think my favourite object is a pottery bowl which was found in a tomb from 4100 years ago. This bowl has two letters written on it, one on the inside and the other on the outside, from a son to his dead parents who were buried in the tomb.

Interviewer: What about looking after the artefacts?

Curator: Different objects need different conditions. The important thing is to ask expert conservators what needs to be done, never guess. As the curator, I know the importance of the objects, but not how best to conserve them. Good conservation is very expensive. Petrie packed the objects properly so that they survived the journey from Egypt to the museum. Not all archaeologists did that in those days!

Interviewer: What is the best thing about working at the Petrie Museum?

Curator: The best thing is the collection. There are about 80 000 objects, but at the moment only about 6000 of them are on display, with another 2000 in drawers that you can look in easily. The other 72 000 are all in cupboards, so we can't let people see them. At the moment the museum is very small and cramped – this building was converted from stables and the collection was only supposed to be here temporarily, but that was over 50 years ago! We are going to move the collection to a much better building and then all the objects will be in glass cupboards where they can be seen.

Interviewer: It must be a lot of work moving a whole museum!

Curator: At the moment we are trying to plan how to use the space we will have in the new building to show the collection to its best advantage. We want the way we display the objects to give an idea of where they came from and what Egypt is like, both thousands of years ago and in the present day. We will also have a small section for Petrie himself and his work. And you will be able to see all the objects that are just in store at the moment.

Interviewer: How will you explain everything to the museum visitors?

Curator: I don't like information labels. You see people going round museums or art galleries reading the labels and not looking at the objects. It's better to use big graphic panels showing timelines and how the objects appeared in life. It's very important to talk to lots of different people about what should be on the panels, and we are talking to as many people as possible about all our plans for the move.

Interviewer: Do you think Petrie would approve of moving his collection?

Curator: Petrie said that his collection was for students and researchers and was 'useless for display'. This is because there aren't big flashy objects in this collection. I disagree with him completely!

Interviewer: Thank you very much Stephen Quirke.

TEST TWO Part 3

Speaker 1

When I was at school we went on a trip to the zoo once. I remember that we were all looking forward to it and everyone was very excited on the coach on the way there. We went around in small groups, each group with a teacher, and we must have seen just about every animal in the place. The keepers showed us all sorts of things but what I remember is that after a while we all got very tired and lost interest. We were there from early morning until late afternoon and we'd all had enough after a couple of hours.

Speaker 2

I went on a business trip to a conference last month. I got to my hotel OK and I registered for the conference and got my name tag and all that and everything seemed fine. But the whole event was chaotic after that. A lot of the information we were given was wrong. Events weren't in the rooms that it said on the list and some of the times of events were different. So people were just wandering around in a confused state, not knowing where to go or what to do. And there was nobody to ask, so the whole thing was a mess.

Speaker 3

As part of my course, we went on a college trip to the Museum of Photography. We were all really keen on the subject and enthusiastic about going. We got there really early – they were only just opening the doors! And I must say I was really impressed by the place and the exhibits. It was great to see things that I'd only seen in books before and it made me really want to produce things as good as them. I could have stayed there for ages and it was disappointing when we had to leave. But they were closing then. I hadn't noticed the time because I was running around looking at one fantastic picture after another.

Speaker 4

A group of us from work went to an adventure centre for a day a few weeks ago. I hadn't been looking forward to it because I don't normally like things like adventure sports. I thought I'd be scared when I was doing some of the activities and I wasn't wrong about that! The very first thing involved climbing to a great height and swinging on a rope and that was enough to put me off straight away. I never recovered from that and spent the whole of the day terrified. I managed to do all the activities to some extent but I couldn't wait to leave.

Speaker 5

I went on a college trip to 'the big city' last week. I must say I wasn't looking forward to it at all, in fact I was dreading it. It didn't sound as if anyone knew what was going to happen or what we were going to do. But, in fact, when we set off in the coach that morning, we found out that there was a schedule and we were given maps and all sorts of information. We split up into small groups and did some sightseeing and some shopping and it was fine. Maybe it wasn't the most thrilling day I've ever had but it was worth doing.

TEST TWO Part 4

Interviewer: Sébastien Foucan is the co-founder and pioneer of free running, a physical discipline in which participants move through, across and over all sorts of obstacles and structures in a smooth and fluid way. People do free running in gyms, in the street and on buildings. He's appeared in movies and TV documentaries, performing spectacular movements. Sébastien, you routinely jump across rooftops to get from A to B. Why, exactly?

Sébastien: It's always been a real passion for me, but I think it's become more than that. It's a part of my life. It's like asking someone, 'Why are you walking?' They say it's simply because they can, and for me it's the same with free running. When we were young, my friend and I used to practise climbing around, just like any kids. We just kept moving, never stopped, until it turned into something special. First it turned into a lifestyle, and then into a real discipline.

Interviewer: Just watching you in action makes me tired! Do you have to be fit to be a free runner?

Sébastien: To start with, you don't have to be so fit. In fact, I often prefer beginners who start with not such a healthy body. If you can't do stuff because your body is not ready, you naturally start at a low level. When you get somebody who has done some sport, they often want to do something too impressive too soon.

Interviewer: Just one wrong step could see you fall and splatter on the floor, though. Surely it's just too dangerous?

Sébastien: Yeah, of course there is risk – but there is risk everywhere. When you're driving a car, you can have an accident. We fly on planes and just accept that there won't be an accident. We make it as safe as we can, but we know something can happen. It's the same with free running. There is danger, but we try to do it properly.

Interviewer: Would you say you're a risk-taker?

Sébastien: No, because everything I do is calculated. It's not like everything is 100 per cent safe, but I'm always thinking of the safest way to do what I'm doing. I'm not afraid of using wires in movies or putting crash mats down for big jumps. You have to be clever.

Interviewer: What went through your mind when you jumped across the Millennium Stadium roof?

Sébastien: I thought to myself, 'I know this jump, I know I can do it'. I used to do track and field, and my best for the long jump is 7.10m. This jump was between three and four metres, so I had a margin of safety. The weather was good and there was no one around, so I had no stress. We put a crash mat down below. You could always miss it, but it's better than nothing.

Interviewer: Are you basically just fearless?

Sébastien: People think I have no fear, but that is not true. I have vertigo, for example, but I know my body very well because I do everything step by step. It's about focus and concentration. Okay, I'm afraid of heights, but I just focus on something else and try not to think about it.

Interviewer: You've traditionally stuck to urban areas, but would you like to try further afield?

Sébastien: I would like to try Africa and the natural environment. People think free running is only about the city, but it's not. You can use trees and rocks, and even swim. You have to open your mind and not restrict yourself.

Interviewer: Well, Sébastien, good luck with everything, and thanks for talking to me.

Sébastien: Pleasure.

TEST THREE Part 1

Extract one

Well, I had a really good time, despite the weather! It absolutely poured with rain for a couple of hours on one of the days, and there was a really strong wind and everyone was shivering and getting soaked but that's all part of the experience, isn't it? Everyone kept their spirits up and enjoyed the music. The place was packed – it was completely sold out – and the atmosphere was great. There wasn't a single band I didn't enjoy – there were one or two I hadn't heard of but they were really good too. So all in all, a really memorable experience.

Extract two

Woman: What do you think of Olivia?

Man: Wow, yes, she's certainly different from the other ones we've had, isn't she?

Woman: Yes, and I think it's the first time she's taken a course.

Man: Really? Well, it doesn't show. She certainly seems to know what she's doing. She's got everything prepared and she seems to have a clear idea of how to structure the course.

Woman: Not much sense of humour, though. She's not exactly what you'd call friendly.

Man: True, but I think that's because she's serious about what she's doing. She doesn't want anyone to mess about, she just wants to get on with the lesson.

Woman: Well, I'm certainly learning a lot.

Man: Me too.

Extract three

Yes, that's what the first assistant told me when I called the first time, but she didn't seem to have any idea what she was talking about. And the next one was the same when I called again. Yes, it's become a really annoying problem and I can't seem to get anyone to take responsibility and sort it out. I demanded to speak to someone senior and finally I managed to speak to someone but that hasn't got me anywhere either. I'm sorry to bore you with all this, but I just can't seem to get anything done about it and, you know me, I won't rest until I get a satisfactory response.

Extract four

Woman: So, would you like to be really, really rich?

Man: I can't imagine there's much chance of that.

Woman: Yes, but if it did happen, wouldn't it be great?

Man: I don't know about that. I think it's all overrated. You know what they say, 'Money doesn't bring you happiness'.

Woman: I don't believe that! It would certainly make me happy.

Man: Yes, but you're different from me. You're always wanting to buy things. I don't really think that way. I'm much more cautious about spending. I don't think I'd change even if I could buy anything I wanted.

Extract five

I don't think I took it as seriously as I should have done. I mean, I had a lot of fun at school, and I've got some very fond memories of it, but I didn't exactly get a lot out of it. I messed up most of my exams and I don't think I did as well as I could have done. I'm sure that if I'd worked a bit harder I could have got much better results, and then everything would have been different. Some of the teachers were cross with me for not doing better – they said I was capable of doing quite well. But, well, I preferred to have fun.

Extract six

Well, as far as I'm concerned, it's got nothing to do with me. This problem has arisen because someone else hasn't done their job properly and it's really not my responsibility. I agree that it's a serious matter but there's nothing I can do about it. Actually, it shouldn't be hard to sort it out – I imagine there's a pretty simple solution. You can see my point of view, can't you? I'm sure you'd feel the same if you were in the same situation.

Extract seven

Well of course, when we talk about modern life we usually talk about modern technology and all the things it has made possible. What we may not notice so much is changes in attitude. People's expectations of life have changed, the way they think about the world around them, the way they interact with others, it's all very different now from how things were just a couple of decades ago. Now, technology may have something to do with that but it's not the only factor. There's been all sorts of research on this and some of the results make for interesting reading, telling us a lot about what we have become.

Extract eight

Woman: Have you been to that new place, The Rosette, yet?

Man: Yes, we tried it out last week.

Woman: What's it like?

Man: Well, it was certainly very busy when we were there. I think just about every table was full. I guess that's got something to do with all the publicity when it opened.

Woman: What was the food like?

Man: Excellent. We both had really good meals. The dishes were all of the very highest quality but, surprisingly enough, it was quite reasonably priced.

Woman: I think I'll try it myself.

Man: Well, I should book well in advance because it's already getting very popular. It might be hard to get a table.

TEST THREE Part 2

Grace Darling was an unlikely heroine. She was born on November 24th 1815 at Bamburgh, on the coast of Northumberland, in the far north-east of England. She had five brothers and three sisters. She lived on an island called Longstone, where her father was the lighthouse keeper. Longstone Lighthouse was perched on a bleak rock rising out of the sea, lashed by wind and waves. The lighthouse lantern needed constant attention because lives depended on its brightness. Its windows and shiny brass reflectors were kept spotlessly clean. The oil lamps needed checking and topping up and all the children helped their father. But one by one, as they grew up, Grace's brothers and sisters left the island, either to get jobs or get married. Her brother William still lived there, but there were only four people left to tend the lighthouse. It was very quiet after all the other children had gone. Grace was now 19 years old and her father relied on her to share the watches from the high tower. The rocks and currents around the island were treacherous and it was important to keep a lookout for ships in danger.

On the night of Wednesday 5th September 1838, a small passenger steamer, the *Forfarshire*, left the port of Hull. It was sailing to Dundee. It carried goods as well as over 60 people: passengers, children and the ship's crew. But there was a problem with the ship's boilers. By Thursday, her engines had stopped working and could not be restarted. Meanwhile, a terrible storm was brewing and the captain hoisted the ship's sails. The crew struggled for hours, but the *Forfarshire* was out of control, heading towards the rocks. Early on Friday morning, the ship smashed against the Big Harcar rock. The pounding waves soon broke the ship's back and over 40 people drowned. The *Forfarshire* had a lifeboat, but in the confusion only nine people got aboard. Another nine people clung desperately to the rocks, but they had little hope of rescue.

The Darling family, safe in their lighthouse, heard the fury of the storm that night as the wind howled and enormous waves battered their home. When morning came, Grace and her father spotted the wreck of the ship. It was too dark for them to see the people clinging to the rocks until a couple of hours later. The horrified Darlings realized the survivors wouldn't last long in such an angry sea. Grace's brother was away, and her father believed the storm was too fierce for the nearest lifeboat on the mainland to launch. Only Grace and her father could save them.

In a small wooden rowing boat, the Darlings battled wind and tide to reach the people. It seemed to take forever. As they reached the rock, Grace's father jumped out to help the survivors. This was a dangerous moment. Grace took charge of the boat, using all her strength, rowing hard to avoid the jagged rocks, as her father helped five people into their little craft. Their boat was full, so they returned to the lighthouse. Grace helped her mother care for the injured while her father and two rescued crewmen returned for the other four. All nine people were saved.

Grace was only 22 years old on the night which changed her life forever. The newspapers loved her amazing story. At a time when people believed 'a woman's place was in the home', her brave actions caused a media sensation. Grace and her father became world famous. She was showered with presents, honours and medals. Her portrait was painted several times. The famous poet William Wordsworth wrote a poem about her. People clamoured for locks of her hair for souvenirs. Even a circus wanted to exhibit her. But Grace still lived quietly with her parents, doing her usual chores. Sadly, she died in 1842 from tuberculosis at the very early age of 26. Today, there is a Grace Darling Museum, where you can see the original boat used by Grace and her father to rescue the survivors.

TEST THREE Part 3

Speaker 1

Oh yes, hello, I'm calling about the repair to my computer. I rang yesterday and arranged for one of your people to come round and deal with it tomorrow. You gave me all the information about charges and we fixed up a time but there are a couple of things I'm still not sure about. One is how you'd like me to pay – will you be sending me an invoice or do I have to pay at the time? And the other is what happens if my computer has to be taken away? As you said, it doesn't seem likely that it will have to be taken away but I just want to find out about that.

Speaker 2

Hello, yes, I came in a couple of weeks ago to register for the course in Film Studies. I paid the fee and I got all the dates and details for the different parts of the course. I was really looking forward to doing it. Then yesterday I got short letter from you saying that the course had been cancelled. There's no explanation for this in the letter, it just says 'Unfortunately this course has been cancelled'. It's very short notice and I can't find a course somewhere else so quickly. I think this is a terrible way to treat people and I'd like to register my dissatisfaction.

Speaker 3

Hello, I'm on your mailing list and I've been receiving the monthly newsletter and placing orders online since March. The thing is, I've got a new postal address and a new email address and I want to update my details with you, and I've tried doing that online but for some reason I can't get it to work. I don't know if I'm doing it wrong or if there's a fault there. Anyway, I thought it best to do it by phone instead.

Speaker 4

Hello, I've just had a letter from you concerning a new bank account you're introducing for existing customers. I'm not sure if it's a good thing for me or not so I was wondering whether someone could tell me if it suits someone in my position. I've got all the details in the brochure you sent and they're all clear. But what I need is someone who can explain to me in simple terms whether or not it's a good idea for me to switch to this new account. Do you think you could do that for me?

Speaker 5

Oh yes, hello. Good, I've tried phoning you several times today but I haven't been able to get through, the line's always busy. Anyway, I want to let you know that there's a slight smell of gas in the street here. At least I think there is, but I'm not totally sure. I think you should send someone out to check on it as soon as possible, because obviously if I'm right it could be dangerous. I can tell you exactly where it is or I could show the person you send when they get here.

TEST THREE Part 4

Interviewer: Ever wondered what it would be like to come face to face with the oceans' top predator? Laura Surovik does it every day! She is a killer whale trainer – one of only 200 in the world. I've met up with her to find out what it's like sharing her life with these beautiful beasts. Hi Laura! Tell us what it was like the first time you swam with a whale.

Animal trainer: I'll never forget it. I remember diving in and the rush of the cold water. That was shocking. It almost felt like I was diving into fire. But when I got over that, there was a whale right there, and I was like, 'Oh my word, I am in the middle of something so much bigger than me.'

Interviewer: Sounds amazing.

Animal trainer: Yes. Every time we get in the pool, we're right in the middle of a miracle, because they are the top predator, because they could cause you harm, and they choose to love you, they choose to enquire, they choose to follow you. We love these animals, we care for them, we teach them, we play with them, really, we're spending our lives together.

Interviewer: Does each whale have a different personality?

Animal trainer: Absolutely. Each one is different. Some are very quick to learn, some are slower to learn, some are very energetic, others are more low-key. We have eight killer whales, so it's like having eight brothers and sisters – each one is quite different.

Interviewer: Have the whales ever been aggressive towards you?

Animal trainer: One of the most important parts of being an animal trainer is being able to read and understand behaviour. So if a whale doesn't look like it's going to be responsive to you, you're not going to get in the pool. It's all about the relationship. It's like people. If you and I just met, I wouldn't say, 'Hi, can I come over to your house now?' We'd take small steps. We train using small steps. We call them 'successive approximations'. That's a big couple of words for small steps!

Interviewer: What are the steps towards teaching them a new behaviour?

Animal trainer: The first step is just observing what is going to naturally fit their bodies. Like the leaps out of the water, they do that naturally. So we would pair that natural action with a signal that we teach them gradually. Then you use secondary reinforcers, like blowing a whistle, that means 'good, come back, I'm going to show you that you did well'. Then you give it a back rub or a tongue rub.

Interviewer: How else do you encourage them? Do you give them fish?

Animal trainer: Food, of all our reinforcers, isn't the best. Like you and I eat bread, but it's not as good as a hug, or eye contact, or a toy, or a friend. One of the things that we apply the most is touch – they love it. We also play hide and seek with them – we'll hide and they'll look for us. Sometimes a group of us run around the pool – they're so inquisitive about what you do.

Interviewer: So do the whales feel like your friends?

Animal trainer: Absolutely. The most important part of training is the relationship you have. Just like you have favourite teachers. If you like your teacher, you're going to do as they say. So the most important part of training is not just the show or the learning sessions, it's all the things in between that build the relationship. They can tell if you're sincere. They can tell if you love them.

Interviewer: What special skills do you need to be a whale trainer?

Animal trainer: One of the most important things is to be a very good swimmer, to be very fit. Also to have no fear of speaking in a microphone in front of thousands of people. And you have to be very confident to step in front of a 5000-pound killer whale that has 52 conically shaped teeth, and an eye here and an eye there, and you think, 'OK, what do I do now?'

Interviewer: Laura, thanks for talking to me.

Animal trainer: You're welcome.

TEST FOUR Part 1

Extract one

Yes, I've kept a diary for many years. I don't really know why, I guess it's just a habit. But there are times when I can't be bothered to do it so there are quite a lot of gaps in it. I only really keep it going when lots of interesting things are happening. I don't put lots of boring everyday things in there. Actually, I haven't written anything in it for quite a while now. I mean, who's got time to write down every little thing that happens every day? But it's good to have a record of some of the more memorable things that have happened that I can look back on later.

Extract two

On Friday at 7.30, it's the second instalment of *Behind The Scenes*. In the first episode, we were introduced to some of the people that we'll be following in the rest of the series as the programme shows us the workings of a major international company from the inside. Friday's programme focuses on the working lives and the private lives of some of the top people there. How do they get on with each other? How does their work affect life at home? What kind of lifestyles do they have? They talk frankly about the pleasures and the pressures. That's Friday, 7.30.

Extract three

Man: Oh hi, I haven't seen you for a while. Have you been away?

Woman: No, I've been around. But my working hours have changed so I don't leave at the same time in the morning as you any more.

Man: I wondered why I hadn't run into you on my way out in the morning. I miss our little chats on the way to the bus stop.

Woman: Yes, me too. We should go for a coffee some time. Anyway, how's your job going?

Man: Well, I left that place I was at. I'm a full-time student now.

Woman: Really? I've been thinking about doing that myself.

Extract four

Interviewer: OK, I'm outside the cinema now and people are just coming out after the premiere. Ah, can I just ask you, what did you think?

Woman: Well, I've read the book and I loved it, so I was really looking forward to the film. And I wasn't disappointed. I know it's had really bad reviews, and people saying that it's nothing like the book. Well, that's true, it is quite different, but I don't think the comments have been fair at all. I think it was really entertaining. It's a very long film of course and that might put a lot of people off, but I didn't find my attention wandering at any point.

Extract five

Hi George, it's Louise. Again. Listen, I thought you were going to get back to me today about the arrangements for the weekend. I've been waiting for you to call and this is the third message I've left for you. I know you're probably very busy but it's important that we get this sorted out now so that I can make the booking. So, do you think you could phone me back straight away, please? It's going to be really difficult to get anything booked if you don't let me know. So call me back as soon as possible. OK?

Extract six

I find him a bit strange to be honest. Because no matter what happens, he keeps on smiling. He's had all sorts of problems in his life, but he never seems to get miserable at all. Most people wouldn't be like that. He seems to think that things are always going to be OK in the end, so he never worries. It must be great to have such a positive attitude. Maybe that's why he's so popular – it's good to be with people who have that kind of attitude.

Extract seven

I couldn't believe it when I realized what a stupid thing I'd done. I mean, I've done the same thing over and over again and I've never done it wrong before. I'm usually incredibly efficient and I never make that kind of mistake. So when it was pointed out to me, I was really cross with myself. How could I have done such a thing? Well, you can't go on blaming yourself for things, can you, so I've got over it now. But at the time I was really furious with myself.

Extract eight

Yes, economics is something I've never really understood so I thought I'd read that article because it said at the beginning that it was going to explain the basics. It was certainly aimed at the non-expert but the problem is, the subject is so complicated and there's such a lot of jargon you're expected to know, that I didn't actually learn all that much from it. I was OK at the beginning, but then it all got very confusing. About halfway through I was completely lost and I couldn't follow it at all. I tried, I eally did, but I couldn't work out what the writer was aying.

TEST FOUR Part 2

Interviewer: There are millions of travel-related blogs on the Internet, with hundreds more being launched each day. But with so many bloggers publishing boring blogs of the 'Today I went to a museum' kind, finding a good travel blog requires a lot of patience and effort. My guest today, travel writer Suzy Bennett, is going to save you all that effort by picking some of the best travel blogs. Suzy, welcome.

Suzy: Hi.

Interviewer: Which is the first one you've chosen?

Suzy: It's a site called wayn.com and it's got more than 14 million members in 193 countries. The really good thing about this one is that it allows members to find and meet people from anywhere in the world. On this site, you can see where your friends are, so it's really good for keeping in touch with them. You can also read travel information, guides, reviews and blogs and look at accompanying photographs.

Interviewer: Sounds good. What's next?

Suzy: Well, next I've chosen hotelchatter.com. If celebrity gossip is your thing, then this is the one for you. It contains descriptions and chat about what the rich and famous have been doing on their travels by people who've come across them in hotels. Travellers post their experiences, photographs and videos of hotel rooms, and their thoughts on services, costs and clever ways to find discounts.

Interviewer: I like a bit of luxury when I travel. Is there anything for me?

Suzy: Yes, there is, and it's called aluxurytravelblog.com. It's updated daily and covers destinations, tours, hotels, restaurants, travel gadgets and clothes for the rich, and it'll give you hours of escapist fun even if you aren't rich. For example, you can learn what you can expect to pay for the world's most expensive dessert.

Interviewer: OK, what about city breaks? Is there a site dedicated to those?

Suzy: Yes, quite a few actually. The best one for city breaks is gridskipper.com. It's updated five days a week and written by very knowledgeable writers and editors. It's a beautifully designed site and it's very easy to navigate your way around it. It tells you about the best hotels, restaurants and nightlife and it's got striking photography and clear maps.

Interviewer: Right, now one of the purposes of some of these blogs is to give people practical advice, isn't it? What are the best ones for that?

Suzy: Yes, that's right and I've chosen three of this kind.

First of all, travel-rants.com. This was started by someone who needed a place to express his anger and frustration following a dispute with a travel agency. He exposes travel industry secrets and tricks and offers advice on dealing with false information in holiday brochures. Then there's perrinpost.com, which is one of the most interactive blogs around. It solves readers' travel problems and offers objective advice. And then there's seat61.com, which helps keep the romance of rail travel alive with regularly updated blogs on travelling around the world by train. It is written by a former manager of stations in London and in fact a paperback version of his site called *The Man in Seat 61* has just been published.

Interviewer: Of course, one of the main reasons why people look at these sites is for research and information, isn't it? What's the best one for that?

Suzy: Well, I've chosen tripadvisor.com because it's an essential source of real reviews by real people. It has millions of reviews, along with photographs and videos of hotels, restaurants and tours, covering such topics as the room number of a hotel in Cairo with pyramid views or the location of a cash machine with the best exchange rate at Charles de Gaulle airport in Paris. One word of caution about this site, though. Watch out for fake reviews that hotel owners have written, pretending to be enthusiastic guests.

Interviewer: OK, now what about business travellers. What's the best blog for them?

Suzy: Well, there are quite a few and I've chosen…

TEST FOUR Part 3

Speaker 1

Yes, he's all over the papers and the magazines and on TV all the time, isn't he? Everyone seems to be talking about him. Mind you, it's more about all the problems in his private life than his acting career. In fact, I'm not sure I could name more than a couple of films he's been in. Well, I guess pretty soon the media will get bored with him and move on to someone else, and then everyone will forget all about him. And teenagers move on quickly too, don't they? – they'll soon have another hero.

Speaker 2

I suppose it's easy to mix up fame and popularity, isn't it? I mean, he's one of the most famous people around at the moment, but have you ever met anyone who says they actually like him? Everyone I've spoken to says that they can't stand him. OK, he might be a really good actor, although that's not what everyone thinks. But he's just such an awful person, it seems to me. He certainly seems to think he's somebody special, but he's like a particularly horrible child.

Speaker 3

I think he's really got something. I mean, you know, there are lots of so-called celebrities who are sort of famous for being famous but they can't actually do anything and then suddenly you never hear of them again. But I don't think he's one of those. I think he stands out as being something quite unique. I know he says some pretty controversial things in interviews, but he seems to have thought about them and a lot of them make sense. He's got a different point of view and I can see why young people think he's great.

Speaker 4

Perhaps I'm missing something but I can't see what all the fuss is about. This guy presents TV programmes and apparently he's one of the most famous people in the country. For what? What's the big thing about sitting in front of a camera and introducing things? I know that for young people he's a really big thing and they all copy the way he talks. But anyone could do what he does. There's nothing to it. And as for all his personal problems, which everyone seems to know about – who cares?

Speaker 5

I read something the other day about what a hard life he's had and how terrible his childhood was and it was quite moving actually. It makes you understand why he behaves the way he does now. I don't particularly like him and I can't see what the young see in him, but you can't help feeling sorry for someone who's experienced what he's experienced. So although he acts like a fool in public and gets a lot of publicity for the wrong reasons, I can see why he's like that.

TEST FOUR Part 4

Interviewer: Now Jo Walker has worked her way up from shop girl to chief operating officer of The Perfume Shop, the specialist perfume retailer, and she's my guest today. Now Jo, you've got a sales philosophy that's not centred on just selling products, haven't you?

Jo: That's right. The way I view sales is that it is not just about doing a one-off deal. It's about something much broader than that. My best deals have always been with people, not products. We sell products but this company is all about people. We are called The Perfume Shop but we might just as well be called The People Shop.

Interviewer: Now I understand that in your group, you've adopted what are called the 'Fish!' principles. I understand that these were developed by an entrepreneur from Minnesota after he was much impressed with the enthusiasm of some fishmongers at the Pike Place Fish Market in Seattle in the US.

Jo: Yes, they're based on the belief that you do not need to be very serious or make the workplace a very formal place. The Seattle fish-sellers had four basic philosophies that lead the way that I sell. These are 'Always be there for the customer', 'Have fun', 'Choose your attitude' and 'Play'. If you follow all these principles, you can sell. It does not matter what the product is.

Interviewer: Tell me about each one of those.

Jo: Well, always being there for the customer means listening and empathizing with them and giving them personal advice. Having fun involves making selling enjoyable and interacting with customers. Choose your attitude is about being positive at work. And playing once involved The Perfume Shop staff choosing spontaneously to dance a huge conga at a company event.

Interviewer: Perfume's a really emotional product, isn't it? Presumably you feel that these principles are particularly appropriate for selling such an emotional product.

Jo: Yes, selling is about having a relationship with the customer that's appropriate and relevant to what you're selling. This relationship is very important in my business because a lot of people don't have the self-confidence to go into a department store and ask about perfumes. And sometimes people really associate perfumes with an occasion like their wedding or with a particular person. It's very emotional.

Interviewer: Can you give me any examples of your philosophy in practice?

Jo: Sure, I can give you a couple of examples of what I regard as my best 'deals', even though I don't know if they actually resulted in sales. One was in a shopping centre when I overheard a girl saying to her friend that she had been using a certain perfume because it was her late grandmother's perfume and she wanted to remind herself of her, but she was worried because her supplies were running out and she did not think it was still available in the shops. I politely intervened and told the girl that the perfume was indeed on sale in The Perfume Shop's store in the town. I just didn't want her to think that she couldn't get it. I've no idea whether she went into the shop and bought it but it was a really nice moment because she was so pleased that I was able to tell her where to get it.

Interviewer: That's a good story. And the other example?

Jo: The other example comes from when I was in one of The Perfume Shop's stores and a man came in looking for a perfume for his wife that I knew had been discontinued. He could not get it anywhere. So I said that I had a bottle at home and I would send it to him, which I did. It's all about having a 24-hours-a-day, seven-days-a-week, 365-days-a-year attitude that you are an ambassador for the company. That gentleman had come into our store. It was just about doing something different. I have not heard if he ever visited that store again. I can only hope that he has shared that experience with lots of people.

Interviewer: I hope so too! Jo, thanks for talking to me.

Jo: You're welcome.